# TORTURE

SOURCES OF

MEDIEVAL HISTORY

*Edited by* Edward Peters

# TORTURE.

HENRY CHARLES LEA

*With original documentary sources in translation.*

*Introduction by*
EDWARD PETERS

University of Pennsylvania Press

Philadelphia

First published 1866, as Part IV of *Superstition and Force*, by
Henry Charles Lea
First *Pennsylvania Paperback* edition 1973
Introduction © 1973 by the University of Pennsylvania Press,
Inc.
Library of Congress Catalog Card No. 73-83292
ISBN: 0-8122-1062-X
Printed in the United States of America. Editorial production
by *Weidner Associates, Inc.,* Cinnaminson, N.J. 08077.
Selection from Cesare Beccaria, *On Crimes and Punishments,*
translated by Henry Paolucci, copyright © 1963 by The Bobbs-
Merrill Company, Inc.; reprinted by permission of the publisher.

# CONTENTS

# INTRODUCTION.

## RES FRAGILIS:
## TORTURE IN EARLY EUROPEAN LAW.

### I.

Rationalist historians of the nineteenth century wrote with a sense of freedom from the institutions of the past and a sense of hope for the future that have since generally disappeared from modern historiography. Having identified the enemies of reason and humanity, having described and denounced them, they—and the society for which they wrote—were at last free of them. Barbarism, superstition, despotism, theology; these terms, in the work of Lecky, White, Lea, and others, stand like gravestones over institutions and beliefs that meticulous scholarship and philosophical hostility had condemned, once and for all, to the buried wreckage of a hopelessly irrational past. When Henry Charles Lea began the final section of his first major historical work, *Superstition and Force*, he looked back at his earlier chapters on compurgation, the judicial duel, and the ordeal and summarily described all of these as "the resources devised by human ingenuity and credulity when called upon to decide questions too intricate for the impatient intellect of a rude and semi-barbarous age." He then linked these with the subject of his last chapters, judicial torture:

> There was another mode, however, of attaining the same object which has received the sanction of the wisest lawgivers during the greater part of the world's history, and our survey of man's devious wanderings in the search of truth would be incomplete without glancing at the subject of the judicial use of torture.

Compurgation, the judicial duel, and the ordeal all belonged, as Lea well knew, to a universe of legal and social ideas that had come under heavy attack and was largely destroyed, at least in the judicial sphere, during the late twelfth and early thirteenth centuries.[1] Judicial torture, however, belonged to a new order of jurisprudence, one whose disappearance from the lawbooks of European and American societies was not complete itself until the nineteenth century, and many of whose traces still constitute the bases of substantive and procedural law in modern societies. Lea wrote with the confident assurance that torture, like the duel and the ordeal, had finally vanished from the world, although he also noted, as have other scholars, the ambiguous place of judicial torture in the rational legal universe of early modern Europe. In the history of western law, torture plays a role that seems to echo at once both a remote and archaic legal universe and, in the decades since Lea's death in 1909, an appallingly contemporary one. The earliest protests against judicial torture in the modern world came from the Italian jurists of the thirteenth century. Two of the most eloquent, immediate, and recent protests come from the French jurist Alec Mellor and the philosopher Jean-Paul Sartre.[2]

A succinct explanation of the appearance of torture in the courts of thirteenth-century Europe was provided in 1892 in an address given by James C. Welling to the Anthropological Society of Washington:

> From this formal species of proof [*duel, ordeal,* and *compurgation*] men pass to a matter-of-fact species of proof, according as their reasoning powers grow stronger and their appliances for the rational discovery of truth become more and more available in the domain of justice. In this passage of the human race from a ceremonial and formal species of negative proof to a rationalistic and substantive species of positive proof, the method of proof by the intervention of torture occupies a place which may be described as a sort of "half-way house" situate between these two typical and distinctive forms of judicial procedure.[3]

Welling belonged to Lea's generation and shared Lea's belief that his world had seen the end of judicial torture—one of the

best intentioned and least securely founded beliefs of that opti-
mistic generation. According to Lea and Welling, judicial torture constitutes a kind of bridge between irrational and
rational legal universes, a significant, if repugnant, step in that
process by means of which rules of evidence, the authority of
judicial enquiry, and the extention of legal reasoning came to
constitute a great humanizing force in the conflict between the
underlying principles of social organization and the momen-
tary, but terrible, exigencies of social fear. Lea and Welling
both knew also that judicial torture had been used long before
the Middle Ages in far more sophisticated systems of jurisprudence, and our own time has witnessed its vigorous resurg-
ence. If judicial torture is a bridge between different legal universes, it is a bridge that has been crossed several times in both
directions.

Torture is one of those signs of increased social rationalism
that praisers of rationalism often neglect. The capacity to
inflict pain wilfully and consciously and, on a civil scale, to
institute systems of terror, is a characteristic feature of most
human societies during most periods of their history, but judicial torture is always a product of an increased reliance upon
reason. Historians of those highly reasonable centuries, the
twelfth and the nineteenth, often fail to see many of the consequences of discarding several of the old irrational bonds to
which society had become accustomed in favor of a greater
reliance upon human energies and the capacity of human analysis. The rejection of compurgation, the duel, and the ordeal
around 1200 meant, to be sure, a new reluctance to depend upon
the intervention of the supernatural in affairs that men felt
able to deal with by their own agency. In the twentieth century
torture has reappeared under a similar guise, that of state
necessity, when it is used to deal with crimes or the threat of
crimes whose enormity and deviousness appear to render due
process ineffective. The temptation to exceed the traditional
limits of the law, or to institute judicial novelties hitherto
repugnant to the law, in order better to protect those institutions and principles that the law itself was designed to protect
usually implies both an acute sense of social danger and a failure of confidence in the efficacy of traditional legal institutions.

Those who approved the use of torture in the thirteenth century were thus, in their own way, humanists; that is, they chose a means of judicial enquiry that relied solely upon human agency to determine complex instances of disputed truth. They were inspired by a new concept of legal personality and responsibility, they developed new judicial procedures to accommodate it, and they grew particularly cautious in designing safeguards for their new procedures.

Henry Charles Lea's study of judicial torture between the sixth and the eighteenth centuries is more than a chapter in remote and archaic legal history. Lea realized that the history of legal procedure is far more than the excessively specialized and recondite subdivision of *Rechtsgeschichte* that scholars often make it appear to be. Like Maitland, he knew that procedure, like all public ritual in traditional societies, is an integral part of social experience that cannot be understood outside of the cultural matrices of the period under consideration. "The history of jurisprudence is the history of civilization," Lea remarked in the later editions of *Superstition and Force,* and Lea's own meticulous scholarship and astute sensitivity to the multiple interactions of life and law between the eighth and the eighteenth centuries made his works not only landmarks in American historical scholarship, but pathfinding contributions to social and cultural history as well.

II.

In Greek and Roman law, torture was contingent upon two conditions: unfree personal status and particularly heinous crimes. Slaves could legally be tortured because they did not possess legal personality and the responsibility of free men. In cases of particularly significant crimes, especially treason, even free men appear to have been generally immune from torture until the end of the first century of the Roman Empire. In spite of the revolting detail in which Suetonius describes the penchant for torture on the part of several first-century emperors, particularly Tiberius, Caligula, and Domitian, judicial torture did not make inroads into criminal procedure, except for cases of treason, until the second and third centuries A.D.[4] The increased and more precisely focussed authority of the state, the wider role of imperial officials in the conduct of civil and criminal cases, and the absorption of Roman jurisprudence and legal education into the administrative bureaucracy of the Empire, all contributed to the new role of judicial torture. A new usage of procedural terms, in which, for example, the old term for the interrogation of witnesses, *quaestio*, became synonymous with torture (hence, the Medieval Latin *quaestio* and Old French *question*, both of which mean torture) as torture became a normal part of the interrogation of both the accused and witnesses, reflects these profound changes in procedural law. By the fourth century, torture had become a standard element in criminal procedure, and the circle of heinous crimes for which even the upper level of free men, the *honestiores*, might be tortured widened perceptibly to include sorcery and other crimes. With the publication of the *Theodosian Code* in 438 and the *Corpus Iuris Civilis* of Justinian in 534, *tormentum*, originally an aggravated sentence of death, was used interchangibly with *tortura* and *quaestio*. The torturers, the *tortor* and *quaesitor*, were legal officials, and the standard definition of *quaestio* became that of the jurist Ulpian as embodied in the *Digest* of Justinian: "*Quaestio* should be understood to mean the torment and suffering of the body in order to elicit the truth."[5]

The new legal universe of the Roman Latin West after the sixth century generally reduced the place torture had attained in Roman law. Although many of the law codes of the Germanic kingdoms of Europe retained some traces of the Roman law of torture, particularly in the cases of slaves, but occasionally, as in Visigothic Spain, in the cases of free men as well, the concept of legal personality in these Germanic laws generally prevented free warriors from being subjected to torture, or, indeed, to any judicial process remotely resembling a modern trial. The ubiquity of the accusatorial procedure, according to which the outcome of a case depended more upon an outright denial of charges or a resort to the judicial duel, compurgation, or the ordeal, considerably restricted the freedom of the judge to ascertain fact, the compulsory power of the public order, and the diminution of personal public status.

xiiINTRODUCTION.

From the seventh through the twelfth centuries, men might
challenge the truth of each other's accusations in a duly constituted court by offering the oath of innocence, sometimes supported by the oaths of others (compurgation), or they might
reject an accusation by submitting, or having someone else
submit on their behalf, to one form or another of the ordeal, or
they might offer to fight a judicial duel. But no court could
countenance the possibility of torturing a free man. Slaves,
serfs, and strangers might still be tortured, but this was precisely because they lacked what free men had: a specific legal
status, a kindred, and an immunity from all but the first accusatorial step in the judicial process.

The history of European law from the seventh through the
twelfth centuries is in large part the history of the transformation of this particularized and limited role of judicial procedure. In the lapidary phrase of Sir Henry Maine, it witnesses
the transformation in law from "status to contract," and it
includes not only a legal revolution, but a new theology and
new concepts of the social bond as well. As Lea points out, the
legal universe of the period 600–1200 was largely irrational;
that is, disabled from inquiring except by the most limited and
rigid procedures into the full dimensions of a legal offense,
courts at the last resort relied upon divine intervention to
determine issues that the personal status of the accuser and the
accused made impossible to settle by any other form. Judicial
procedure is, of course, a form of social control, and the legal
procedures of this period were consonant with the social con-
ceptions of early medieval society. The status of individuals
and the limitations upon judicial procedure, as much as the
concept of immanent justice, shored up the courts of early
medieval Europe.

In the course of the eleventh and twelfth centuries, the
forces that had sustained this legal universe were themselves
transformed. The intellectual and political attacks upon the
ordeal and the judicial duel grew stronger as new ideas of
legal bonds drove out older ideas.[6] The revival of Roman law
studies in the eleventh and twelfth centuries led to new concep-
tions of the role of law in society at the same time as a new
interest in Roman antiquity gave rise to new influences in his-

toriography, literature, and the visual arts. The social dimension of the "Renaissance of the Twelfth Century"—in terms of both social theory and social institutions—has often been slighted in favor of the traditional approach of the history of ideas. Yet it is hardly too much to say that the period between 1050 and 1250 witnessed not as the least influential of its many transformations a legal revolution, the detailed history of which constituted an indispensible commentary upon other profound changes in European society. The appearance of new judicial procedures, the growth and activity of new ecclesiastical and secular courts, the changed character and the distribution of legal education and the concurrent growth of a new legal literature, and the broadened spectrum of careers open to those trained in the law all constituted part of this revolution, and both the social and intellectual changes of this period constitute the backdrop of the reappearance of torture in the courts of the thirteenth century.

### III.

The first documentary evidence of the reappearance of torture in Western Europe is found in the *Liber Juris Civilis* of the city of Verona of 1228, and torture appears in the criminal sections of the laws of a number of other Italian city-republics during the ensuing few decades, in the *Constitutiones Regni Siciliani* of Frederick II in 1231, and, in Castile, with its tradition of continuing torture, in the *Fuero Juzgo* of Ferdinand III in 1241 and the *Siete Partidas* of Alfonso X in 1265. The victim of torture in most of these instances was the notorious criminal; as the laws of Vercelli of 1241 observe, "No man ought to be tortured or executed unless [he is known to be] a common rogue, a thief, or a man of ill repute." The appearance of torture under these circumstances was not, it should be said at the outset, solely the result of the renewed study of Roman law. Rather, as R. C. van Caenegem has suggested,

> in the last analysis it was the needs of criminal practice and new principles for the pursuit of criminals that were responsible for the reappearance of torture in Europe, and not the revival of Roman legal studies. It

seems that the renewal of Roman law and the reception of torture in ecclesiastical practice were the result
of the diffusion of the inquisitorial procedure in
Europe.[7]

Indeed, so much casual historiography has indiscriminately
linked torture both to the revival of Roman legal studies and
the ecclesiastical Inquisition, that it is necessary to clarify the
origins of torture in early thirteeth-century criminal procedure.

Besides the accusatorial process, there were other specialized
judicial procedures in pre-twelfth-century Europe, although
these were often not widely used or were suitable only for particular sets of circumstances. In certain circumstances, as early
as the ninth century, a category of *mala fama*, ill-repute,
existed in the Carolingian courts, and anyone in this category
might be condemned by a judge if he refused to exculpate himself by oath or by ordeal. Also in the ninth century, a notorious offense could be prosecuted by the judge without an
accuser, and by the twelfth century the necessity of an accuser
could be dispensed with in cases involving *infamia*. As a later
lawyer remarked, "In the inquisitorial process, the judge himself does not take the part of the accuser, but *infamia* stands in
the place of the accuser or denouncer." Such phenomena as the
episcopal visitation to the ecclesiastical institutions of a diocese
in canon law and the visitation of royal judicial representatives
to a district in secular law both established the requirement
that the inhabitants of such places were obliged to inform the
proper authorities of crimes committed since the last visitation.
In ecclesiastical and secular terms, this practice was known as
the *denunciatio*, and some writers linked it to several scriptural
and patristic references to social correction in early Christian
communities.[8] Because of the enduring idea that only a charge
brought by an accuser was a complete charge, convictions
under these forerunners of the inquisitorial process tended to
result in lighter penalties, and in some cases authorities
required a full confession from the accused in addition to conviction by *inquisitio* in order that a full penalty might be
imposed. Out of these specialized and tentative beginnings,
there emerged by the twelfth century a consensus that in certain kinds of cases another procedure than the accusatorial

might be used, one which eventually placed considerably greater latitude and power in the hands of the judge than the older procedure, one which dispensed with the traditional accuser and substituted either a denouncer (who might have to furnish proof) or, eventually, a court official, the *promotor*, who formally made charges. Even during these changes, however, some traditional rights of the accused remained relatively undisturbed: he might be informed of the names and the evidence of witnesses and examine them and refute their testimony himself; he was not yet subject to torture; he might have the aid of counsel, and although all his testimony had to be given under oath, another novelty, courts generally conducted such hearings warily.

The most significant aspect of the inquisitorial procedure was the elimination of the necessity of the liable accuser and the increased latitude and power of the courts and of the authorities they represented. Human agency, rather than supernatural, was responsible for investigating the truth or falsehood of an accusation, and the increased judicial liability that had been traditional in ecclesiastical communities now became a presupposition of secular communities as well. The overriding need to protect the public order and to punish crime constituted the background for the adaption of the earlier inquisitorial procedures to new social uses. From the experiences of the notorious heretic, the offending member of a religious community, and the ill-famed villager, a new judicial procedure had been shaped that gave great power to the judicial authorities and imposed a new kind of liability upon the accused.

That liability and that power did not develop everywhere in the twelfth century in quite the same way. As Maitland has pointed out,

> what is peculiar to England is not the dissatisfaction with waged "laws" and supernatural probations, nor the adoption of an "inquisition" or "inquest" as the core of the new procedure, but in the form that the inquest takes, or rather retains. By instituting the Grand Assize and the four Petty Assizes Henry II had placed at the disposal of litigants in certain

actions that "inquest of the country" which ever since
the Norman Conquest had formed part of the governmental machinery of England. His reforms were
effected just in time. But for them, we should indeed
have known the inquest, but it would in all likelihood
have been the inquest of the canon law, the *enquête* of
the new French jurisprudence.[9]

Nor, it must be said, were all of the later repugnant features of
the inquisitorial process immediately clear, either to churchmen
or to French jurists, in the course of the twelfth century. The
inquisitorial procedure offered what to a modern litigant would
seem very familiar and acceptable: avoidance of rigid and
excessively formalized charges; an airing of testimony and a
weighing of evidence, with opportunity for rebuttal, that was
unavailable under the accusatorial process in its eleventh- and
twelfth-century forms; the possibility of a trained judge who
might act equitably in establishing procedure and weighing
intangibles. At its outset in the twelfth century, at least, inquisitorial procedure seemed to reflect precisely that increased reliance upon reason, conscience, and a broadened concept of the
social order that historians have otherwise praised in other
aspects of the life of the period.

What caused the inquisitorial process which, in spite of Maitland's disclaimer for England, might have remained simply a
new procedure giving the court greater investigatory powers,
first, to admit torture, and second, to produce the well-docu-
mented procedural abuses of the thirteenth and fourteenth centuries? The sharpened concept of treason in the twelfth century and the thirteenth-century concept of heresy as a kind of
treason to God certainly constituted opportunities for the laws
of treason in Roman jurisprudence to be invoked once again,
although in England those suspected of treason were probably
not tortured—and even then rather by orders of the monarch
or of Council—until the sixteenth century.[10] Van Caenegem's
suggestion that the reappearance of torture is attributable to
new concepts of criminal law has much to offer. For it was not
the heretic who was the first to be tortured in the Italian laws of
the early thirteenth century, but the notorious criminal. Torture

was first used in the treatment of criminals, particularly, it may be supposed, those accused of concealed crimes in which the identity of the guilty party was not immediately discernible, although strong suspicion of the accused, based upon ill-repute, may well exist. It is but a short step from instituting torture for those strongly suspected of committing a crime to trying those suspected of heresy, an offense much more heinous and more difficult to prove. As Pope Innocent IV observed in 1252 when for the first time he sanctioned the use of torture by the Inquisition, if torture is appropriate for those who break the laws of men, then it is more than fitting for those who break the laws of God.

The twelfth century saw new outbreaks of heresy, and the newly reorganized Church attacked it in areas of society with which ecclesiastical courts were generally unfamiliar.[11] The apparent magnitude of heretical society, the new authority of the Church, and the problems of discovering intellectual crime generated considerable ecclesiastical and lay concern, and the new legal procedure of the inquisitorial process (particularly in cases in which accusers were often hard to find, or unwilling to testify) offered a judicial approach to the problem. The Inquisition, or, technically, the Holy Office, took shape in the third quarter of the twelfth century and the first half of the thirteenth. Its agents were members of the new Orders, at first aiding, then growing independent of, the normal diocesan jurisdiction. In their hands, which were not, at first, necessarily the hands of trained lawyers, the inquisitorial procedure developed its earliest oppressive features, the concealment of the identity of witnesses and the content of evidence, the refusal of counsel, the demands to identify accomplices, the admission of evidence from hitherto unsuitable witnesses, and, in 1252 in the decretal *Ad extirpanda*, the introduction of torture. Henceforth, the inquisitorial process became burdened with perversions of rational procedure that exceeded the accusatorial system and the ordeals at their worst. By the end of the thirteenth century articulate Inquisitors such as Bernard Gui wrote learned and rational handbooks describing and justifying Inquisitorial procedure, and Gui was followed by Nicholas Eymeric and others, whose arguments were echoed in the ecclesiastical literature of the fifteenth and sixteenth centuries and in the literature of those secular courts which adopted both the inquisitorial procedure and its excesses and produced its own learned analyses in the sixteenth and seventeenth centuries.

Yet, in spite of perversion and excess and judicial incompetence, not all manifestations of the inquisitorial procedure, even those which retained torture, developed along lines identical to the ecclesiastical institution. As Walter Ullman has shown, there quickly grew up a cautionary literature concerning the excessive and improper use of torture almost as soon as the institution of torture itself reappeared.[12] Indeed, the lawyers themselves appear to have been among the first and the severest critics of the institution, and, by the sixteenth century, even the trained lawyers of the Inquisition in Rome and Spain became suspicious of the efficacy of torture, long before such suspicions acquired enough weight in the world of secular jurisprudence to begin the process of eliminating torture in the eighteenth and nineteenth centuries. By then, judicial torture and the inquisitorial process had long been used to perform the same grisly service for the monarchies of the sixteenth and seventeenth centuries that they had performed for the Church in the thirteenth and fourteenth—the enforcement of orthodox belief and conduct by a drastic curtailment of traditional judicial liberties and the development of an infallible instrument for detecting concealed and forbidden intellectual forms of dissent, from treason to witchcraft.[13]

The history of judicial torture and of the legal procedures that afforded opportunities for its appearance in thirteenth-century Europe is thus part of a larger chapter in social and intellectual history, as well as a topic of concern to social scientists and jurists who may be more interested in its twentieth-century manifestations than in its Roman and medieval origins. For the thirteenth-century lawyers who first cautioned against its random use, torture was a *res fragilis*, a delicate matter, which, although admissible in certain instances, could easily abort the judicial processes it was originally intended to serve. Those lawyers' warnings should not be taken lightly, nor should their limited approval of its use so obscure the humanitarian vision of twentieth-century investigators that they reject both approval and criticism together. For torture was not, as the decades since the publication of Lea's book have clearly shown, an historical aberration whose death knell was sounded, once and for all, by the irresistible onset of the Age of Reason and the legislative enlightenment of the states of Europe in the late eighteenth and early nineteenth centuries. The means of precise analysis offered by legal history and social science ought not to be expended in describing the history of such institutions as torture solely for the purpose of patronizing what Lea called "the impatient intellect of a rude and semi-barbarous age," but for studying those configurations of social forces that permit, and then encourage, such instruments of public power. Lynn White once remarked that "to know the subliminal mind of a society, one must study the sources of its liturgies of inflicting death."[14] There are many other social liturgies whose sources require the same study, sources that produced both the medieval lawyers' reservations of the *res fragilis* and the enormities of the totalitarian state.[15]

PHILADELPHIA, 1973                                    EDWARD PETERS

# NOTES.

1. The best recent study of these circumstances is John W. Baldwin, "The Intellectual Preparation of the Canon of 1215 against Ordeals," *Speculum* 36 (1961), pp. 613–36; the fullest study is that of Hermann Nottarp, *Gottesurteilstudien*, Bamberger Abhandlungen und Forschungen, Bd. II (Munich, 1956). See also the works cited in the introduction to Henry C. Lea, *The Ordeal* (Philadelphia, 1973).

2. Alec Mellor, *La Torture* (Paris, 1949), the most learned and humane of modern scholarly studies; Jean-Paul Sartre, Introduction to Henri Alleg, *The Question*, trans. John Calder (New York, 1958). Cf. Sartre, p. 17: "If patriotism has to precipitate us into dishonour; if there is no precipice of inhumanity over which nations and men will not throw themselves, then why, in fact, do we go to so much trouble to become, or to remain, men?"

3. *The Law of Torture: A Study in the Evolution of Law* (Washington, 1892), p. 2.

4. See Theodor Mommsen, *Römisches Strafrecht* (rep. Graz, 1955), pp. 401–11. A recent summary is included in Peter Garnsey, *Social Status and Legal Privilege in the Roman Empire* (Oxford, 1970), pp. 141–47; 213–16.

5. *Digest* 47.10.15.41; cited by Garnsey, p. 141.

6. The most recent general study is that of Christopher Brooke, *The Twelfth Century Renaissance* (New York, 1969), with a good bibliography. There are particularly important discussions in R. W. Southern, *The Making of the Middle Ages* (New Haven, 1953) and G. Le Bras, ed., *L'Histoire du droit et des institutions de l'église*, Vol. VII, *L'Age classique, 1140–1378*, by J. Rambaud-Buhaut and Charles Lefebvre (Paris, 1965). See also the sources cited in Lea, *The Ordeal*.

7. "La Preuve dans le droit du moyen âge occidental. Rapport de synthèse," in *La Preuve*, Recueils de la Société Jean Bodin, Vol. XVII (Brussels, 1965), pp. 691–755 at 740. See also the older but valuable work of A. Esmein, *A History of Continental Criminal Procedure*, trans. J. Simpson (Boston, 1913) and Walter Ullmann, "Reflections on Medieval Torture," *Juridical Review* 56 (1944), pp. 123–37.

8. For the development of notoriety, see Jean Philippe Lévy, *La Hiérarchie des preuves dans le droit savant du moyen-âge*, Université de Lyons, Annales, Troisième série, Droit (Paris, 1939), pp. 32–66; see also the studies in the volume *La Preuve* cited in the preceding note.

9. F. Pollock and F. W. Maitland, *The History of English Law*, 2nd. ed., Vol. II (Cambridge, 1968), p. 604.

10. For the history of torture in England, see David Jardine, *A Reading on the Use of Torture in the Criminal Law of England Previously to the Commonwealth* (London, 1837); L. O. Pike, *A History of Crime in England* (London, 1873); Leonard A. Parry, *The History of Torture in England* (London, 1934); R. B. Pugh, *Imprisonment in Medieval England* (Cambridge, 1968); Pollock and Maitland, Vol. II, *passim*.

11. The standard work is Henry C. Lea, *A History of the Inquisition in the Middle Ages* (Philadelphia, 1887), 3 vols. There exist a number of abridged versions, and of these particularly useful for the aspects of legal procedure is Henry Charles Lea, *The Inquisition of the Middle Ages: Its Organization and Operation*, with an Historical Introduction by Walter Ullmann (New York, 1969). On the Church's search for heretics and its attitude toward legal procedure, see Austin P. Evans, "Hunting Subversion in the Middle Ages," *Speculum* 33 (1958), pp. 1–22; Henri Maisonneuve, *Études sur l'origine de l'inquisition*, (Paris, 1960).

12. "Reflections on Medieval Torture," above, n. 7. See also Walter

Ullmann, *The Medieval Idea of Law as Respected by Lucas de Penna* (London, 1946), pp. 159–61.

13. Much of this literature is briefly surveyed in Henry Charles Lea, *Materials Toward a History of Witchcraft*, ed. Arthur Howland (Philadelphia, 1939), Vol. II.

14. "The Legacy of the Middle Ages in the American Wild West," *Speculum* 40 (1965), pp. 191–202 at 199. That such social liturgies exert a continuing and dangerous fascination is obvious to any citizen of a twentieth-century state. See the informative study by Hans von Hentig, "The Pillory: A Medieval Punishment," in his *Studien zur Kriminalgeschichte* (Bern, 1962), pp. 112–28: "There is a metempsychosis of human concepts. Certain punishments which have been abolished as utterly ineffectual, and even damaging, emerge again and get hold of the mind. Being fit dischargers of emotional tensions, they are restored by the return of men of similar emotional instability."

15. The comparative character of legal procedure, particularly as it may apply to the policies of the twentieth-century state in its treatment of criminal and political offenses has not received the attention of many scholars. A particularly original comparative study on these lines, whose footnotes are often as stimulating as the main argument itself, is Mirjan Damaska, "Evidentiary Barriers to Conviction and Two Models of Criminal Procedure: A Comparative Study," *University of Pennsylvania Law Review* 121 (1973), pp. 506–89. Professor Damaska offers considerably less simplified observations on the relation of the inquisitorial procedure to torture than my remarks above.

# BIBLIOGRAPHICAL NOTE.

The greatest work on the history of judicial torture is that of Piero Fiorelli, *La tortura giudiziaria nel diritto comune*, 2 vols. (Milan, 1953–54), an exhaustive and massively documented study that is not likely to be replaced. Among shorter works, that of Alec Mellor, *La Torture* (Paris, 1949) is certainly the most learned and humane and makes an eloquent plea against the revival of judicial torture in the twentieth century. In German, the work of Franz Helbing and Max Bauer, *Die Tortur. Geschichte der Folter im Kriminalverfahren aller Zeiten und Völker* (Berlin, 1926) has extensive documentation. There is a large bibliography of works on recent instances of judicial torture, although many alleged surveys either fail to take historical questions into account or attempt to indict the institution of torture by the use of misplaced psychological investigation or generally uncritical indignation. The work of George Ryley Scott, *The History of Torture Throughout the Ages* (London, 1949) is of this last type and should be used with caution.

A good informal introduction to the social history of crime and punishment is the essay by Christopher Hibbert, *The Roots of Evil* (London, 1963), although the most scholarly general history of criminal procedure is the old work of A. Esmein, *A History of Continental Criminal Procedure,* trans. J. Simpson (Boston, 1913). Two early articles by Walter Ullmann offer additions to Esmein's study: "Reflections on Medieval Torture," *Juridical Review* 56 (1944), pp. 123–37, and "Some Medieval Principles of Criminal Procedure," *Juridical Review* 59 (1947), pp. 1–28. The most useful recent studies on the law of proof in general, with much information upon the ordeal and torture are included in *La Preuve*, Recueils de la Société Jean Bodin, Vol. XVII (Brussels, 1965). Particularly important are the studies of F. L. Ganshof (pp. 71–98), Jean Gaudemet (pp. 99–136), J. Ph. Lévy (pp. 137–68), and R. C. van Caenegem (pp. 691–754).

The most recent study of the principles of political violence is that of E. V. Walter, *Terror and Resistance: A Study of Political Violence* (New York, 1969).

# TORTURE

# CHAPTER I.

THE preceding essays have traced the development of sacramental purgation and of the ordeal as resources devised by human ingenuity and credulity when called upon to decide questions too intricate for the impatient intellect of a rude and semi-barbarous age. There was another mode, however, of attaining the same object which has received the sanction of the wisest lawgivers during the greater part of the world's history, and our survey of man's devious wanderings in the search of truth would be incomplete without glancing at the subject of the judicial use of torture. The ordeal and torture, in fact, are virtually substitutes for each other. It will be seen that they have rarely co-existed, and that, as a general rule, the legislation which depended on the one rejected the other.

In the early stages of society, the judge or the pleader whose faith does not lead him to rely upon an appeal to God naturally seeks to extort from the reluctant witness a statement of what he might desire to conceal, or from the presumed criminal a confession of his guilt. To accomplish this, the readiest means would seem to be the infliction of pain, to escape from which the witness would sacrifice his friends, and the accused would submit to the penalty of his crime. The means of administering graduated and effectual torment would thus be sought for, and the rules for its application would in time be developed into a regular system, forming part of the recognized principles of jurisprudence.

In the earliest civilization, that of Egypt, it would seem as though torture was too opposed to the whole theory of judicial proceedings to be employed, if we are to believe the description which Diodorus Siculus gives of the solemn and mysterious tribunals, where written pleadings alone were allowed, lest the judges should be swayed by the eloquence of the human voice, and where the verdict was announced, in the unbroken silence, by the presiding judge touching the successful suitor with an image of the Goddess of Truth.[1]  Yet a papyrus recently interpreted gives us a judicial record of a trial, in the reign of Rameses IX. of the XXth Dynasty (circa 1200 B. C.), of the robbers of the tomb of the Pharaoh Sebakemsauf, and this shows how the accused, after confession, were tortured for confirmation, first by scourging and then by squeezing the hands and feet, showing that, sometimes at least, this mode of ascertaining the truth was employed.[2]

Among the Semitic races we find torture used as a regular judicial process by the Assyrians,[3] though the Mosaic jurisprudence is free from any indication that the Hebrew law-dispensers regarded it as a legitimate expedient.  Earnest

[1] Diod. Sicul. I. lxxv.—Sir Gardiner Wilkinson (Ancient Egyptians, Vol. II.) figures several of these little images.

[2] See the translation of the Amherst Papyrus by Chabas, Mélanges Égyptologiques, III.ᵉ Serie, T. II. p. 17 (Sept. 1873).  The interpretation of the groups relating to the hands and feet is conjectural, but they unquestionably signify some kind of violence.  M. Chabas qualifies this passage as highly important, being the first evidence that has reached us of the judicial use of torture in Egypt.  The question has been a debated one, but the previous evidence adduced was altogether inconclusive.

[3] Lenormant, Man. de l'Hist. Ancienne de l'Orient, II. 141.

advocates of the torture system, in the eighteenth century, however, did not hesitate to adduce the ordeal of the bitter water of jealousy as a torture which justified the employment in modern times of the rack and strappado.

In the earliest Aryan records, so far as we can judge from the fragments remaining of the Zoroastrian law, torture had no recognized place. Astyages was rather a Mede than a Persian, and therefore no conclusion can be drawn from his readiness to employ it when he sought to extort the truth from unwilling witnesses, as related by Herodotus;[1] but the savage punishments which Darius boasts of inflicting upon the rival pretenders to his throne[2] presuppose a readiness to resort to the most violent means of intimidation, which could scarcely fail to include torture as an extra-judicial means of investigation when milder methods failed.

To the other great branch of the Aryan stock which founded the Indian civilization, torture would likewise seem to have been unknown as a legitimate resource; at least it has left no trace of its existence in the elaborate provisions of the Hindu law as handed down to us for nearly three thousand years. In the Institutes of Manu there are very minute directions as to evidence, the testimony preferred being that of witnesses, whose comparative credibility is very carefully discussed, and when such evidence is not attainable, the parties, as we have seen above, are ordered to be sworn or tried by the ordeal. These principles have been transmitted unchanged to the present day.[3]

In China the juristic principles in force would seem to allow no place for the use of torture (*ante*, p. 251), though doubtless

[1] Herod. I. 116.

[2] Behistun Inscription, col. II. 25-6 (Records of the Past, VII. 98-99). It is worthy of remark that this Medic version of the Inscription is more circumstantial as to these inflictions than the Persian text translated by Rawlinson (Records I. 118-19).

[3] Manu, Bk. VIII.—Institutes of Vishnu, VI. 23, VIII. IX.—Ayeen Akbery, Tit. Beyhar, Vol. II. p. 494 —Halhed's Code of Gentoo Laws, chap. xviii.

it may be occasionally resorted to as an extra-judicial expedient.   In Japan it still retains its place in the criminal codes,
though we may well believe the assertion that practically its
use has been discarded in the progress of modern enlightenment.   As to its former employment, however, the directions
are very explicit.   In the milder form of scourging it might
be used in all preliminary examinations.   Where reasonable
moral certainty existed of guilt in serious and capital crimes,
the severer inflictions, by fire, by various mechanical devices,
by deprivation of food and sleep or by exposure to venomous
reptiles, could be invoked to extort confession, the accused
being notified in advance that it would be used if he persisted
in asserting his innocence, and the official ordering it being
held personally responsible for its undue or improper employment.[1]

## CHAPTER II.

### GREECE AND ROME.

THE absence of torture from the codes of the elder Aryan
races is not to be attributed to any inherent objection to its use,
but rather to the employment of the ordeal, which in all ages
formed part of their jurisprudence, and served as an unfailing
resort in all doubtful cases.   When we turn to the Aryans who
established themselves in Europe and abandoned the ancestral
custom of the ordeal, we find it at once replaced by the use of
torture.   Thus in Greece torture was thoroughly understood and
permanently established.   The oligarchical and aristocratic
tendencies, however, which were so strongly developed in the
Hellenic commonwealths, imposed upon it a limitation characteristic of the pride and self-respect of the governing order.
As a general rule, no freeman could be tortured.   Even freed-

[1] Albany Law Journal, 1879.

men enjoyed an exemption, and it was reserved for the unfortunate class of slaves, and for strangers who formed no part of the body politic. Yet there were exceptions, as among the Rhodians, whose laws authorized the torture of free citizens; and in other states it was occasionally resorted to, in the case of flagrant political offences; while the people, acting in their supreme and irresponsible authority, could at any time decree its application to any one irrespective of privilege. Thus, when Hipparchus was assassinated by Harmodius, Aristogiton was tortured to obtain a revelation of the plot, and several similar proceedings are related by Valerius Maximus as occurring among the Hellenic nations.[1] The inhuman torments inflicted on Philotas, son of Parmenio, when accused of conspiracy against Alexander, show how little real protection existed when the safety of a despot was in question; and illustrations of torture decreed by the people are to be seen in the proceedings relative to the mutilation of the statues of Hermes, and in the proposition, on the trial of Phocion, to put him, the most eminent citizen of Athens, on the rack.

In a population consisting largely of slaves, who were generally of the same race as their masters, often men of education and intelligence and employed in positions of confidence, legal proceedings must frequently have turned upon their evidence, in both civil and criminal cases. Their evidence, however, was inadmissible, except when given under torture, and then, by a singular confusion of logic, it was estimated as the most convincing kind of testimony. Consequently, the torturing of slaves formed an important portion of the administration of Athenian justice. Either party to a suit might offer his slaves to the torturer or demand those of his opponent, and a refusal to produce them was regarded as seriously compromising. When both parties tendered their slaves, the judge decided as to which of them should be received. Even without bringing a suit into court, disputants could have their

[1] Lib. III. cap. iii.

slaves tortured for evidence with which to effect an amicable
settlement.

In formal litigation, the defeated suitor paid whatever
damages his adversary's slaves might have undergone at the
hands of the professional torturer, who, as an expert in such
matters, was empowered to assess the amount of depreciation
that they had sustained.  It affords a curious commentary on
the high estimation in which such testimony was held to
observe that, when a man's slaves had testified against him
on the rack, they were not protected from his subsequent
vengeance, which might be exercised upon them without
restriction.

As the laws of Greece passed away, leaving few traces on
the institutions of other races, save on those of Rome, it will
suffice to add that the principal modes in which torture was
sanctioned by them were the wheel, the ladder or rack, the
comb with sharp teeth, the low vault, in which the unfortunate
patient was thrust and bent double, the burning tiles, the
heavy hogskin whip, and the injection of vinegar into the
nostrils.[1]

In the earlier days of Rome, the general principles governing the administration of torture were the same as in Greece.
Under the Republic, the free citizen was not liable to it, and
the evidence of slaves was not received without it.   With the
progress of despotism, however, the safeguards which surrounded the freeman were broken down, and autocratic emperors had little scruple in sending their subjects to the rack.

Even as early as the second Triumvirate, a prætor named

---

[1] Aristophanes (*Ranæ*, 617) recapitulates most of the processes in vogue.

    *Aiachos.*   καὶ πῶς βασανίζω ;

    *Xanthias.*        πάντα τρόπον, ἐν κλίμακι

          δήσας, κρεμάσας, ὑστριχίδι μαστιγῶν, δέρων,

          στρε²λῶν, ἔτι δ'εἰς τὰς ῥῖνας ὄζος ἐγχέων,

          πλίνθους ἐπιτιθείς, παντα τᾶλλα.

The best summary I have met with of the Athenian laws of torture is in
Eschbach's " Introduction à l'Étude du Droit," § 268.

Q. Gallius, in saluting Octavius, chanced to have a double tablet under his toga. To the timid imagination of the future emperor, the angles of the tablet, outlined under the garment, presented the semblance of a sword, and he fancied Gallius to be the instrument of a conspiracy against his life. Dissembling his fears for the moment, he soon caused the unlucky prætor to be seized while presiding at his own tribunal, and, after torturing him like a slave without extracting a confession, put him to death.[1]

The incident was ominous of the future, when all the powers of the state were concentrated in the august person of the emperor. He was the representative and embodiment of the limitless sovereignty of the people, whose irresponsible authority was transferred to him. The rules and formularies which had regulated the exercise of power, so long as it belonged to the people, were feeble barriers to the passions and fears of Cæsarism. Accordingly, a principle soon became engrafted in Roman jurisprudence that, in all cases of *crimen majestatis*, or high treason, the free citizen could be tortured. In striking at the ruler he had forfeited all rights, and the safety of the state, as embodied in the emperor, was to be preserved at every sacrifice.

The emperors were not long in discovering and exercising their power. When the plot of Sejanus was discovered, the historian relates that Tiberius abandoned himself so entirely to the task of examining by torture the suspected accomplices of the conspiracy, that when an old Rhodian friend, who had come to visit him on a special invitation, was announced to him, the preoccupied tyrant absently ordered him to be placed on the rack, and on discovering the blunder had him quietly put to death, to silence all complaints. The shuddering inhabitants pointed out a spot in Capri where he indulged in these terrible pursuits, and where the miserable victims of his wrath were cast into the sea before his eyes, after having ex-

[1] Sueton. August. xxii.

hausted his ingenuity in exquisite torments.[1]    When the
master of the world took this fearful delight in human agony,
it may readily be imagined that law and custom offered little
protection to the defenceless subject, and Tiberius was not
the only one who relished these inhuman pleasures.    The
half-insane Caligula found that the torture of criminals by
the side of his dinner-table lent a keener zest to his revels,
and even the timid and the beastly Claudius made it a point
to be present on such occasions.[2]

Under the stimulus of such hideous appetites, capricious
and irresponsible cruelty was able to give a wide extension to
the law of treason.    If victims were wanted to gratify the
whims of the monarch or the hate of his creatures, it was easy
to find an offender or to make a crime.    Under Tiberius, a
citizen removed the head from a statue of Augustus, intend-
ing to replace it with another.    Interrogated before the Senate,
he prevaricated, and was promptly put to the torture.    Encouraged by this, the most fanciful interpretation was given to
violations of the respect assumed to be due to the late emperor.    To undress one's self or to beat a slave near his image ;
to carry into a latrine or a house of ill fame a coin or a ring
impressed with his sacred features ; to criticize any act or word
of his became a treasonable offence ; and finally an unlucky
wight was actually put to death for allowing the slaves on his
farm to pay him honors on the anniversary which had been
sacred to Augustus.[3]

So, when it suited the waning strength of paganism to wreak
its vengeance for anticipated defeat upon the rising energy of
Christianity, it was easy to include the new religion in the con-
venient charge of treason, and to expose its votaries to all the
horrors of ingenious cruelty.    If Nero desired to divert from
himself the odium of the conflagration of Rome, he could turn
upon the Christians, and by well-directed tortures obtain con-

[1] Sueton. Tiberii lxii.        [2] Ibid. Caii xxxii.—Claud. xxxiv.
[3] Ibid. Tiber. lviii.

fessions involving the whole sect, thus giving to the populace the diversion of a persecution on a scale until then unknown, besides providing for himself the new sensation of the human torches whose frightful agonies illuminated his unearthly orgies.[1]  Diocletian even formally promulgated in an edict the rule that all professors of the hated religion should be deprived of the privileges of birth and station, and be subject to the application of torture.[2]  The indiscriminate cruelty to which the Christians were thus exposed without defence, at the hands of those inflamed against them by all evil passions, may, perhaps, have been exaggerated by the ecclesiastical historians, but that frightful excesses were perpetrated under sanction of law cannot be doubted by any one who has traced, even in comparatively recent times and among Christian nations, the progress of political and religious persecution.[3]

The torture of freemen accused of crimes against the state or the sacred person of the emperor thus became an admitted principle of Roman law.  In his account of the conspiracy of Piso, under Nero, Tacitus alludes to it as a matter of course, and in describing the unexampled endurance of Epicharis, a freedwoman, who underwent the most fearful torments without compromising those who possessed little claim upon her forbearance, the annalist indignantly compares her fortitude with the cowardice of noble Romans, who be-

[1] Tacit. Annal. xv. xliv.

[2] Lactant. de Mortib. Persecut. cap. xiii.

[3] Tormentorum genera inaudita excogitabantur (Ibid. cap. xv.).—When the Christians were accused of an attempt to burn the imperial palace, Diocletian " ira inflammatus, excarnificari omnes suos protinus præcipit.  Sedebat ipse atque innocentes igne torrebat" (Ibid. cap. xiv.).—Lactantius, or whoever was the real author of the tract, addresses the priest Donatus to whom it is inscribed : " Novies etiam tormentis cruciatibusque variis subjectus, novies adversarium gloriosa confessione vicisti. . . . . Nihil adversus te verbera, nihil ungulæ, nihil ignis, nihil ferrum, nihil varia tormentorum genera valuerunt" (Ibid. cap. xvi.).  Ample details may be found in Eusebius, Hist. Eccles. Lib. v. c. 1, vi. 39, 41, viii. passim, Lib. Martyrum; and in Cyprian, Epist. x. (Ed. Oxon. 1682).

trayed their nearest relatives and dearest friends at the mere
sight of the torture chamber.[1]

Under these limits, the freeman's privilege of exemption
was carefully guarded, at least in theory. A slave while
claiming freedom, or a man claimed as a slave, could not be
exposed to torture;[2] and even if a slave, when about to be
tortured, endeavored to escape by asserting his freedom, it
was necessary to prove his servile condition before proceeding
with the legal torments.[3] In practice, however, these privileges were continually infringed, and numerous edicts of the
emperors were directed to repressing the abuses which constantly occurred. Thus we find Diocletian forbidding the
application of torture to soldiers or their children under accusation, unless they had been dismissed the service igno-
miniously.[4] The same emperor published anew a rescript of
Marcus Aurelius declaring the exemption of patricians and of
the higher imperial officers, with their legitimate descendants
to the fourth generation;[5] and also a dictum of Ulpian
asserting the same privilege in favor of decurions, or local
town councillors, and their children.[6] In 376, Valentinian
was obliged to renew the declaration that decurions were only
liable in cases of *majestas*, and in 399 Arcadius and Hono-
rius found it necessary to declare explicitly that the privilege
was personal and not official, and that it remained to them
after laying down the decurionate.[7] Theodosius the Great, in
385, especially directed that priests should not be subjected
to torture in giving testimony,[8] the significance of which is
shown by the fact that no slave could be admitted to holy
orders.

The necessity of this constant repetition of the law is indicated by a rescript of Valentinian, in 369, which shows that

---

[1] Tacit. Annal. XV. lvi. lvii.          [2] L. 10 § 6, Dig. XLVIII. xviii.
[3] L. 12, Dig. XLVIII. xviii. (Ulpian.).
[4] Const. 8 Cod. IX. xli. (Dioclet. et Maxim.).
[5] Const. 11 Cod. IX. xli.          [6] Ibid. § 1.
[7] Const. 16 Cod. IX. xli.          [8] Const. 8 Cod. I. 3.

freemen were not infrequently tortured in contravention of
law; but that torture could legally be indiscriminately inflicted by any tribunal in cases of treason, and that in other
accusations it could be authorized by the order of the emperor.[1] This power was early assumed and frequently exercised. Though Claudius at the commencement of his reign
had sworn that he would never subject a freeman to the question, yet he allowed Messalina and Narcissus to administer
torture indiscriminately, not only to free citizens, but even to
knights and patricians.[2] So Domitian tortured a man of
prætorian rank on a doubtful charge of intrigue with a vestal
virgin,[3] and various laws were promulgated by several emperors directing the employment of torture irrespective of
rank, in some classes of accusations. Thus, in 217, Caracalla
authorized it in cases of suspected poisoning by women.[4]
Constantine decreed that unnatural lusts should be punished
by the severest torments, without regard to the station of the
offender.[5] Constantius persecuted in like manner sooth-
sayers, sorcerers, magicians, diviners, and augurs, who were
to be tortured for confession, and then to be put to death with
every refinement of suffering.[6] So, Justinian, under certain
circumstances, ordered torture to be used on parties accused
of adultery[7]—a practice, however, which was already common
in the fourth century, if we are to believe the story related by
St. Jerome of a miracle occurring in a case of this nature.[8]
The power thus assumed by the monarch could evidently be
limited only by his discretion in its exercise.

One important safeguard, however, existed, which, if properly maintained, must have greatly lessened the frequency

[1] Const. 4 Cod. IX. viii.

[2] Dion. Cass. Roman. Hist. Lib. IX. (Ed. 1592, p. 776).

[3] Sueton. Domit. cap. viii. To Domitian the historian also ascribes the
invention of a new and infamously indecent kind of torture (Ibid. cap. x.).

[4] Const. 3 Cod. IX. xli.      [5] Const. 31 Cod. IX. ix.

[6] Const. 7 Cod. IX. viii.     [7] Novell. CXVII. cap. xv. § 1.

[8] Hieron. Epist. I. ad Innocent.

of torture as applied to freemen. In bringing an accusation the accuser was obliged to inscribe himself formally, and was exposed to the *lex talionis* in case he failed to prove the justice of the charge.[1] A rescript of Constantine, in 314, decrees that in cases of *majestas*, as the accused was liable to the severity of torture without limitation of rank, so the accuser and his informers were to be tortured when they were unable to make good their accusation.[2] This enlightened legislation was preserved by Justinian, and must have greatly cooled the ardor of the pack of calumniators and informers, who, from the days of Sylla, had been encouraged and petted until they held in their hands the life of almost every citizen.

In all this it must be borne in mind that the freeman of the Roman law was a Roman citizen, and that, prior to the extension of citizenship generally to the subjects of the Empire, there was an enormous class deprived of the protection, such as it was, of the traditional exemption. Thus when, in Jerusalem, the Jews raised a tumult and accused St. Paul, without specifying his offence, the tribune forthwith ordered "that he should be examined by scourging, that he might know wherefore they cried so against him;" and when St. Paul proclaimed himself a Roman, the preparations for his torture were stopped forthwith, and he was examined by regular judicial process.[3] The value of this privilege is fairly exemplified by the envying remark of the tribune, "With a great sum obtained I this freedom."

All these laws relate to the extortion of confessions from the accused. In turning to the treatment of witnesses, we find that even with them torture was not confined to the servile condition. With slaves it was not simply a consequence of slavery, but a mode of confirming and rendering admissible the testimony of those whose character was not sufficiently known to give their evidence credibility without it. Thus a

---

1 Const. 17 Cod. IX ii.—Const. 10 Cod. IX. xlvi.
2 Const. 3 Cod. IX. viii.          3 Acts, XXII. 24 sqq.

legist under Constantine states that gladiators and others of
similar occupation cannot be allowed to bear witness without
torture;[1] and, in the same spirit, a novel of Justinian, in 539,
directs that the rod shall be used to extract the truth from unknown persons who are suspected of bearing false witness or
of being suborned.[2]

It may, therefore, readily be imagined that when the evidence of slaves was required, it was necessarily accompanied
by the application of torture. Indeed, Augustus declared
that while it is not to be expressly desired in trifling matters,
yet in weighty and capital cases the torture of slaves is the
most efficacious mode of ascertaining the truth.[3] When we
consider the position occupied by slavery in the Roman
world, the immense proportion of bondmen who carried on
all manner of mechanical and industrial occupations for the
benefit of their owners, and who, as scribes, teachers, stew-
ards, and in other confidential positions, were privy to almost
every transaction of their masters, we can readily see that
scarce any suit could be decided without involving the testimony of slaves, and thus requiring the application of torture.
It was not even, as among most modern nations, restricted to
criminal cases. Some doubt, indeed, seems at one time to
have existed as to its propriety in civil actions, but Antoninus
Pius decided the question authoritatively in the affirmative,
and this became a settled principle of Roman jurisprudence,
even when the slaves belonged to masters who were not party
to the case at issue.[4]

There was but one limitation to the universal liability of
slaves. They could not be tortured to extract testimony

[1] L. 21 § 2, Dig. XXII. v.      [2] Novell. XC. cap. i. § 1.
[3] Quæstiones neque semper in omni causa et persona desiderari debere
arbitror; et cum capitalia et atrociora maleficia non aliter explorari et in-
vestigari possunt, quam per servorum quæstiones, efficacissimas esse ad re-
quirendam veritatem existimo et habendas censeo.—L. 8, Dig. XLVIII. xviii.
(Paulus).
[4] L. 9, Dig. XLVIII. xviii. (Marcianus).

against their masters, whether in civil or criminal cases;[1] though, if a slave had been purchased by a litigant to get his testimony out of court, the sale was pronounced void, the price was refunded, and the slave could then be tortured.[2] This limitation arose from a careful regard for the safety of the master, and not from any feeling of humanity towards the slave. So great a respect, indeed, was paid to the relationship between the master and his slave that the principle was pushed to its fullest extent. Thus even an employer, who was not the owner of a slave, was protected against the testimony of the latter.[3] When a slave was held in common by several owners, he could not be tortured in opposition to any of them, unless one were accused of murdering his partner.[4] A slave could not be tortured in a prosecution against the father or mother of the owner, or even against the guardian, except in cases concerning the guardianship;[5] though the slave of a husband could be tortured against the wife.[6] Even the tie which bound the freedman to his patron was sufficient to preserve the former from being tortured against the latter;[7] whence we may assume that, in other cases, manumission afforded no protection from the rack and scourge. This question, however, appears doubtful. The exemption of freedmen would seem to be proved by the rescript which provides that inconvenient testimony should not be got rid of by manumitting slaves so as to prevent their being subjected to torture;[8] while, on the other hand, a decision of Diocletian directs that, in

[1] L. 9 § 1, Dig. XLVIII. xviii.—L. 1 § 16, Dig. XLVIII. xvii. (Severus)—L. 1 § 18, Dig. XLVIII. xviii. (Ulpian.).

[2] Pauli Lib. v. Sentt. Tit. xvi. § 7.—The same principle is involved in a rescript of the Antonines.—L. 1 § 14, Dig. XLVIII. xvii. (Severus).

[3] L. 1 § 7, Dig. XLVIII. xvii. The expression "in caput domini" applies as well to civil as to criminal cases.—Pauli Lib. v. Sentt. Tit. xvi. § 5.

[4] L. 3, Dig. XLVIII. xviii.—Const. 13 Cod. IX. xli.

[5] L. 10 § 2, Dig. XLVIII. xviii.—Const. 2 Cod. IX. xli. (Sever. et Antonin. ann. 205).

[6] L. 1 § 11, Dig. XLVIII. xvii.          [7] L. 1 § 9, Dig. XLVIII. xvii.

[8] L. 1 § 13. XLVIII. xvii.—Pauli Lib. v. Sentt. Tit. xvi. § 9.

cases of alleged fraudulent wills, the slaves and even the freed-men of the heir could be tortured to ascertain the truth.[1]

This policy of the law in protecting masters from the evidence of their tortured slaves varied at different periods. From an expression of Tacitus, it would seem not to have been part of the original jurisprudence of the Republic, but to have arisen from a special decree of the Senate. In the early days of the Empire, while the monarch still endeavored to veil his irresponsible power under the forms of law, and showed his reverence for ancient rights by evading them rather than by boldly subverting them, Tiberius, in prosecuting Libo and Silanus, caused their slaves to be transferred to the public prosecutor, and was thus able to gratify his vengeance legally by extorting the required evidence.[2] Subsequent emperors were not reduced to these subterfuges, for the principle became established that in cases of *majestas*, even as the freeman was liable to torture, so his slaves could be tortured to convict him;[3] and as if to show how utterly superfluous was the cunning of Tiberius, the respect towards the master in ordinary affairs was carried to that point that no slave could be tortured against a former owner with regard to matters which had occurred during his ownership.[4] On the other hand, according to Ulpian, Trajan decided that when the confession of a guilty slave under torture implicated his master, the evidence could be used against the master, and this, again, was revoked by subsequent constitutions.[5] Indeed, it became a settled principle of law to reject all incriminations of accomplices.

[1] Const. 10 Cod. IX. xli. (Dioclet. et Maxim.).

[2] Tacit. Annal. II. 30. See also III. 67. Somewhat similar in spirit was his characteristic device for eluding the law which prohibited the execution of virgins (Sueton. Tiber. lxi.).

[3] This principle is embodied in innumerable laws. It is sufficient to refer to Constt. 6 § 2, 7 § 1, 8 § 1, Cod. IX. viii.

[4] L. 18 § 6, Dig. XLVIII. xviii. (Paulus).

[5] L. 1 § 19, Dig. XLVIII. xviii. (Ulpian.).

Having thus broken down the protection of the citizen
against the evidence of his slaves in accusations of treason, it
was not difficult to extend the liability to other special crimes.
Accordingly we find that, in 197, Septimius Severus specified
adultery, fraudulent assessment, and crimes against the state
as cases in which the evidence of slaves against their masters
was admissible.[1]  The provision respecting adultery was repeated by Caracalla in 214, and afterwards by Maximus,[2] and
the same rule was also held to be good in cases of incest.[3]  It
is probable that this increasing tendency alarmed the citizens
of Rome, and that they clamored for a restitution of their im-
munities, for, when Tacitus was elected emperor, in 275, he
endeavored to propitiate public favor by proposing a law to
forbid the testimony of slaves against their masters except in
cases of *majestas*.[4]  No trace of such a law, however, is
found in the imperial jurisprudence, and the collections of
Justinian show that the previous regulations were in full force
in the sixth century.

Yet it is probable that the progress of Christianity produced
some effect in mitigating the severity of legal procedure and
in shielding the unfortunate slave from the cruelties to which
he was exposed.  Under the Republic, while the authority of
the *paterfamilias* was still unabridged, any one could offer his
slaves to the torture when he desired to produce their evidence.  In the earlier times, this was done by the owner himself in the presence of the family, and the testimony thus
extorted was carefully taken down to be duly produced in
court ;  but subsequently the proceeding was conducted by
public officers—the quæstors and triumviri capitales.[5]  How
great was the change effected is seen by the declaration of
Diocletian, in 286, that masters were not permitted to bring

1 Const. 1 Cod. IX. xli. (Sever et Antonin.).
2 Constt. 3, 32 Cod. IX. ix.—L. 17, XLVIII. xviii. (Papin.).
3 L. 5 Dig. XLVIII. xviii. (Marcian.).
4 Fl. Vopisc. Tacit. cap. IX.
5 Du Boys, Hist. du Droit Crim. des Peup. Anciens. pp. 297, 331, 332.

forward their own slaves to be tortured for evidence in cases wherein they were personally interested.[1] This would necessarily reduce the production of slave testimony, save in accusations of *majestas* and other excepted crimes, to cases in which the slaves of third parties were desired as witnesses; and even in these, the frequency of its employment must have been greatly reduced by the rule which bound the party calling for it to deposit in advance the price of the slave, as estimated by the owner, to remunerate the latter for his death, or for his diminished value if he were maimed or crippled for life.[2] When the slave himself was arraigned upon a false accusation and tortured, an old law provided that the master should receive double the loss or damage sustained;[3] and in 383, Valentinian the Younger went so far as to decree that those who accused slaves of capital crimes should inscribe themselves, as in the case of freemen, and should be subjected to the *lex talionis* if they failed to sustain the charge.[4] This was an immense step towards equalizing the legal condition of the bondman and his master. It was apparently in advance of public opinion, for the law is not reproduced in the compilations of Justinian, and probably soon was disregarded.

There were some general limitations imposed on the application of torture, but they were hardly such as to prevent its abuse at the hands of cruel or unscrupulous judges. Antoninus Pius set an example, which modern jurists might well have imitated, when he directed that no one should be tortured after confession to implicate others;[5] and a rescript of the same enlightened emperor fixes at fourteen the minimum limit

[1] Const. 7 Cod. IX. xli. (Dioclet. et Maxim.).

[2] Pauli Lib. v. Sentt. Tit. xvi. § 3.—See also Ll. 6, 13 Dig. XLVIII. xviii.

[3] Const. 6 Cod. IX. xlvi. This provision of the L. Julia appears to have been revived by Diocletian.

[4] Lib. IX. Cod. Theod. i. 14.

[5] L. 16 § 1, Dig. XLVIII. xviii. (Modestin.).

of age liable to torture, except in cases of *majestas*, when, as we have seen, the law spared no one, for in the imperial jurisprudence the safety of the monarch overrode all other considerations.[1]   Women were spared during pregnancy.[2] Moderation was enjoined upon the judges, who were to inflict only such torture as the occasion rendered necessary, and were not to proceed further at the will of the accuser.[3]   No one was to be tortured without the inscription of a formal accuser, who rendered himself liable to the *lex talionis*, unless there were violent suspicions to justify it;[4] and Adrian reminded his magistrates that it should be used for the investigation of truth, and not for the infliction of punishment.[5]   Adrian further directed, in the same spirit, that the torture of slave witnesses should only be resorted to when the accused was so nearly convicted that it alone was required to confirm his guilt.[6] Diocletian ordered that proceedings should never be commenced with torture, but that it might be employed when requisite to complete the proof, if other evidence afforded rational belief in the guilt of the accused.[7]

What was the exact value set upon evidence procured by torture it would be difficult at this day to determine.   We have seen above that Augustus pronounced it the best form of proof, but other legislators and jurists thought differently. Modestinus affirms that it is only to be believed when there is no other mode of ascertaining the truth.[8]   Adrian cautions his judges not to trust to the torture of a single slave, but to examine all cases by the light of reason and argument.[9]   According to Ulpian, the imperial constitutions provided that it

---

1 L. 10 Dig. XLVIII. xviii. (Arcad.).

2 L. 3 Dig. XLVIII. xix. (Ulpian.).

3 L. 10 § 3, Dig. XLVIII. xviii.

4 L. 22 Dig. XLVIII. xviii.

5 L. 21 Dig. XLVIII. xviii.

6 L. 1 § 1, Dig. XLVIII. xviii. (Ulpian.).

7 Const. 8 Cod, IX. xli. (Dioclet. et Maxim.).

8 L. 7, Dig. XX. v.          9 L. 1 § 4, Dig. XLVIII. xviii. (Ulpian.).

was not always to be received nor always rejected ; in his own opinion it was unsafe, dangerous, and deceptive, for some men were so resolute that they would bear the extremity of torment without yielding, while others were so timid that through fear they would at once inculpate the innocent.[1] From the manner in which Cicero alternately praises and discredits it, we can safely assume that lawyers were in the habit of treating it, not on any general principle, but according as it might affect their client in any particular case; and Quintilian remarks that it was frequently objected to on the ground that under it one man's constancy makes falsehood easy to him, while another's weakness renders falsehood necessary.[2] That these views were shared by the public would appear from the often quoted maxim of Publius Syrus—" Etiam innocentes cogit mentiri dolor"—and from Valerius Maximus, who devotes his chapter *De Quæstionibus* to three cases in which it was erroneously either trusted or distrusted. A slave of M. Agrius was accused of the murder of Alexander, a slave of C. Fannius. Agrius tortured him, and, on his confessing the crime, handed him over to Fannius, who put him to death. Shortly afterwards, the missing slave returned home. This same Alexander was made of sterner stuff, for when he was subsequently suspected of being privy to the murder of C. Flavius, a Roman knight, he was tortured six times and persistently denied his guilt, though he subsequently confessed it and was duly crucified.[3] A somewhat similar case gave Apollonius of Tyana an opportunity of displaying his supernatural power. Meeting in Alexandria twelve convicts on their way to execution as robbers, he pronounced one of them to be innocent, and asked the executioners to reserve him to the last, and, moreover, delayed them by his conversation. After eight had been

<hr/>

[1] L. I § 23, Dig. XLVIII. xviii.—Res est fragilis et periculosa et quæ veritatem fallat.

[2] Altera sæpe etiam causam falsa dicendi, quod aliis patientia facile mendacium faciat, aliis infirmitas necessarium.—M. F. Quintil. Inst. Orat. v. iv.

[3] Val. Maximi Lib. VIII. c. iv.

beheaded, a messenger came in hot haste to announce that
Phanion, the one selected by Apollonius, was innocent, though
he had accused himself to avoid the torture.[1]  A curious instance, moreover, of the little real weight attached to such
evidence is furnished by the case of Fulvius Flaccus, in which
the whole question turned upon the evidence of his slave
Philip.  This man was actually tortured eight times, and refused through it all to criminate his master, who was nevertheless condemned.[2]  The same conclusion is to be drawn
from the story told by St. Jerome of a woman of Vercelli repeatedly tortured on an accusation of adultery, and finally
condemned to death in spite of her constancy in asserting her
innocence, the only evidence against her being that of her
presumed accomplice, extorted under torment.[3]  Quintus
Curtius probably reflects the popular feeling on the subject, in
his pathetic narrative of the torture of Philotas on a charge of
conspiracy against Alexander.  After enduring in silence the
extremity of hideous torment, he promised to confess if it
were stopped, and when the torturers were removed he addressed his brother-in-law Craterus, who was conducting the
investigation : "Tell me what you wish me to say."  Curtius
adds that no one knew whether or not to believe his final confession, for torture is as apt to bring forth lies as truth.[4]

From the instances given by Valerius Maximus, it may be
inferred that there was no limit set upon the application of
torture.  The extent to which it might be carried appears to
have rested with the discretion of the tribunals, for, with the
exception of the general injunctions of moderation alluded to
above, no instructions for its administration are to be found
in the Roman laws which have been preserved to us, unless
it be the rule that when several persons were accused as

[1] Philostrati vit. Apollon. VII. xxiv.

[2] Valer. Maxim. Lib. VIII. c. iv.

[3] Hieron. Epist. I. ad Innocentium.

[4] Q. Curt. Ruf. Hist. VI. xi.  Anceps conjectura est quoniam et vera con-
fessis et falsa dicentibus idem doloris finis ostenditur.

accomplices, the judges were directed to commence with the youngest and weakest.[1]

Since the time of Sigonius, much antiquarian research has been directed to investigating the various forms of torture employed by the Romans.  They illustrate no principles, however, and it is sufficient to enumerate the rack, the scourge, fire in its various forms, and hooks for tearing the flesh, as the modes generally authorized by law.  The Christian historians, in their narratives of the persecutions to which their religion was exposed, give us a more extended idea of the resources of the Roman torture chamber.  Thus Prudentius, in his description of the martyrdom of St. Vincent, alludes to a number of varieties, among which we recognize some that became widely used in after times, showing that little was left for modern ingenuity to invent.[2]

I have dealt thus at length on the details of the Roman law of torture because, as will be seen hereafter, it was the basis of all modern legislation on the subject, and has left its impress on the far less humane administration of criminal justice in Europe almost to our own day.  Yet at first it seemed destined to disappear with the downfall of the Roman power.

---

## CHAPTER III.

### THE BARBARIANS.

In turning from the nicely poised and elaborate provisions of the Imperial laws to the crude jurisprudence of the Barbarian hordes who gradually inherited the crumbling remains of the Empire of the West, we enter into social and political conditions so different that we are naturally led to expect a cor-

---

[1] Pauli Lib. v. Sentt. Tit. xiv. § 2.—L. 18 Dig. XLVIII. xviii.
[2] Aurel. Prudent. de Vincent. Hymn. v.

responding contrast in every detail of legislation. For the
cringing suppliant of the audience chamber, abjectly pros-
trating himself before a monarch who combines in his own
person every legislative and executive function, we have the
freeman of the German forests, who sits in council with his
chief, who frames the laws which both are bound to respect,
and who pays to that chief only the amount of obedience
which superior vigor and intellect may be able to enforce.
The structure of such a society is fairly illustrated by the incident which Gregory of Tours selects to prove the kingly
qualities of Clovis. During his conquest of Gaul, and before
his conversion, his wild followers pillaged the churches with
little ceremony. A bishop, whose cathedral had suffered
largely, sent to the king to request that a certain vase of unusual size and beauty might be restored to him. Clovis could
only promise that if the messenger would accompany him to
Soissons, where the spoils were to be divided, and if the vase
should chance to fall to his share, it should be restored. When
the time came for allotting the plunder, he addressed his men,
requesting as a special favor that the vase might be given to
him before the division, but a sturdy soldier, brandishing his
axe, dashed it against the coveted article, exclaiming, "Thou
shalt take nothing but what the lot assigns to thee." For a
year, Clovis dissembled his resentment at this rebuff, but at
length, when opportunity offered, he was prompt to gratify it.
While reviewing and inspecting his troops, he took occasion
to reproach bitterly the uncourtly Frank with the condition of
his weapons, which he pronounced unserviceable. The battle-
axe excited his especial displeasure. He threw it angrily to
the ground, and as the owner stooped to pick it up, Clovis
drove his own into the soldier's head, with the remark, "It
was thus you served the vase at Soissons."[1]

This personal independence of the freeman is one of the dis-
tinguishing characteristics of all the primitive Teutonic institu-

[1] Greg. Turon. Hist. Franc. Lib. II. c. xxvii.

tions. Corporal punishments for him were unknown to the laws. The principal resource for the repression of crime was by giving free scope to the vengeance of the injured party, and by providing fixed rates of composition by which he could be bought off. As the criminal could defend himself with the sword against the *faida* or feud of his adversary, or could compound for his guilt with money, the suggestion of torturing him to extort a confession would seem an absurd violation of all his rights. Crimes were regarded solely as injuries to individuals, and the idea that society at large was interested in their discovery, punishment, and prevention, was entirely too abstract to have any influence on the legislation of so barbarous an age.

Accordingly, the codes of the Feini, the Ripuarians, the Alamanni, the Angli and Werini, the Frisians, the Saxons, and the Lombards contain no allusion to the employment of torture under any circumstances; and such few directions for its use as occur in the laws of the Salien Franks, of the Burgundians, and of the Baioarians, do not conflict with the general principle.

The personal inviolability which shielded the freeman cast no protection over the slave. He was merely a piece of property, and if he were suspected of a crime, the readiest and speediest way to convict him was naturally adopted. His denial could not be received as satisfactory, and the machinery of sacramental purgation or the judicial duel was not for him. If he were charged with a theft at home, his master would undoubtedly tie him up and flog him until he confessed, and if the offence were committed against a third party, the same process would necessarily be adopted by the court. Barbarian logic could arrive at no other mode of discovering and repressing crime among the friendless and unprotected, whose position seemed to absolve them from all moral responsibility.

The little that we know of the institutions of the ancient Gauls presents us with an illustration of the same principle developed in a somewhat different direction. Cæsar states that,

when a man of rank died, his relatives assembled and investigated the circumstances of his death. If suspicion alighted
upon his wives, they were tortured like slaves, and if found
guilty they were executed with all the refinements of torment.[1]

In accordance with this tendency of legislation, therefore,
we find that among the Barbarians the legal regulations for
the torture of slaves are intended to protect the interests of
the owner alone. When a slave was accused of crime the
master, indeed, could not refuse to hand him over to the torturer, unless he were willing to pay for him the full *wergild*
of a freeman, and if the slave confessed under the torture, the
master had no claim for compensation arising either from the
punishment or crippling of his bondman.[2] When, however,
the slave could not be forced to confess and was acquitted,
the owner had a claim for damages, though no compensation
was made to the unfortunate sufferer himself. The original
law of the Burgundians, promulgated in 471, is the earliest of
the Teutonic codes extant, and in that we find that the accuser
who failed to extract a confession was obliged to give to the
owner another slave, or to pay his value.[3] The Baioarian law
is equally careful of the rights of ownership, but seems in addition to attach some criminality to the excess of torture by
the further provision that, if the slave die under the torment
without confession, the prosecutor shall pay to the owner two
slaves of like value, and if unable to do so, that he shall himself be delivered up as a slave.[4] The Salic law, on the other

[1] De Bell. Gall. vi. xix.

[2] These provisions are specified only in the Salic Law (First Text of
Pardessus, Tit. xl. §§ 6, 7, 8, 9, 10.—L. Emend. Tit. xlii. §§ 8, 9, 10,
11, 12, 13), but they were doubtless embodied in the practice of the other
tribes.

[3] L. Burgund. Tit. vii.—The other allusions to torture in this code, Tit.
xxxix. §§ 1, 2, and Tit. lxxvii. §§ 1, 2, also refer only to slaves, *coloni*,
and *originarii*. Persons suspected of being fugitive slaves were always
tortured to ascertain the fact, which is in direct contradiction to the principles of the Roman law.

[4] L. Baioar. Tit. viii. c. xviii. §§ 1, 2, 3.

hand, only guards the interests of the owner by limiting the torture to 120 blows with a rod of the thickness of the little finger. If this does not extort a confession, and the accuser is still unsatisfied, he can deposit with the owner the value of the slave, and then proceed to torture him at his own risk and pleasure.[1]

It will be observed that all these regulations provide merely for extracting confessions from accused slaves, and not testimony from witnesses. Indeed, the system of evidence adopted by all the Barbarian laws for freemen was of so different a character, that no thought seems to have been entertained of procuring proof by the torture of witnesses. The only allusion, indeed, to such a possibility shows how utterly repugnant it was to the Barbarian modes of thought. In some MSS. of the Salic law there occurs the incidental remark that when a slave accused is under the torture, if his confession implicates his master, the charge is not to be believed.[2]

Such was the primitive legislation of the Barbarians, but though in principle it was long retained, in practice it was speedily disregarded by those whom irresponsible power elevated above the law. The Roman populations of the conquered territories were universally allowed to live under their old institutions; in fact, law everywhere was personal and not territorial, every race and tribe, however intermingled on the

---

[1] L. Salic. First Text, Tit. XL. §§ 1, 2, 3, 4.—L. Emend. Tit. XLII. §§ 1, 2, 3, 4, 5.—In a treaty between Childebert and Clotair, about the year 593, there is, however, a clause which would appear to indicate that in doubtful cases slaves were subjected, not to torture, but to the ordeal of chance. " Si servus in furto fuerit inculpatus, requiratur a domino ut ad viginti noctes ipsum in mallum præsentet. Et si dubietas est, ad sortem ponatur" (Pact. pro Tenore pacis cap. v.—Baluz.). This was probably only a temporary international regulation to prevent frontier quarrels and reprisals. That it had no permanent force of law is evident from the retention of the procedures of torture in all the texts of the Salic law, including the revision by Charlemagne.

[2] First Text, Tit. XL. § 4.—MS. Monaster. Tit. XL. § 3.—L. Emend. Tit. XLII. § 6.

same soil, being subjected to its own system of jurisprudence.
The summary process of extracting confessions and testimony
which the Roman practice thus daily brought under the notice
of the Barbarians could not but be attractive to their violent
and untutored passions. Their political system was too loose
and undefined to maintain the freedom of the Sicambrian
forests in the wealthy plains of Gaul, and the monarch, who,
beyond the Rhine, had scarce been more than a military chief,
speedily became a despot, whose power over those immediately
around him was limited only by the fear of assassination, and
over his more distant subjects by the facility of revolution.

When all thus was violence, and the law of the strongest
was scarcely tempered by written codes, it is easy to imagine
that the personal inviolability of the freeman speedily ceased
to guarantee protection. Even amid the wild tribes which
remained free from the corruptions of civilization the idea of
torturing for confession the friendless and unprotected was
not unfamiliar, and in the Elder Edda we find King Geirröd
using the torment of fire for eight days on Odin, who visits
him in disguise for the purpose of testing his hospitality.[1]
Among the Gallic Franks, therefore, it need not surprise us
to see irresponsible power readily grasping at such means to
gratify hate or ambition. In the long and deadly struggle
between Fredegonda and Brunhilda, for example, the fierce
passions of the adversaries led them to employ without scruple
the most cruel tortures in the endeavor to fathom each other's
plots.[2] A single case may be worth recounting to show how
completely torture had become a matter of course as the first
resource in the investigation of doubtful questions. When
Leudastes, about the year 580, desired to ruin the pious Bishop
Gregory of Tours, he accused him to Chilperic I. of slander-

[1] Grimnismal, Thorpe's Sæmund's Edda, I. 20.
[2] Greg. Turon. Hist. Franc. Lib. VII. c. xx.; Lib. VIII. cap. xxxi. Also,
Lib. v. cap. xxxvii.—Aimoin. Lib. III. c. xxx. xlii. li. lxiv. lxvii.—Flodoard.
Hist. Remens. Lib. ii. c. ii.—Greg. Turon. Miraculorum Lib. I. cap. 73.

ing the fair fame of Queen Fredegonda, and suggested that full proof for condemnation could be had by torturing Plato and Gallienus, friends of the bishop. He evidently felt that nothing further was required to substantiate the charge, nor does Gregory himself, in narrating the affair, seem to think that there was anything irregular in the proposition. Gallienus and Plato were seized, but from some cause were discharged unhurt. Then a certain Riculfus, an accomplice of Leudastes, was reproached for his wickedness by a man named Modestus, whereupon he accused Modestus to Fredegonda, who promptly caused the unhappy wretch to be severely tortured without extracting any information from him, and he was imprisoned until released by the miraculous aid of St. Medard. Finally, Gregory cleared himself canonically of the imputation, and the tables were turned. Leudastes sought safety in flight. Riculfus was not so fortunate. Gregory begged his life, but could not save him from being tortured for confession. For six hours the wretched man was hung up with his hands tied behind his back, after which, stretched upon the rack, he was beaten with clubs, rods, and thongs, by as many as could get at him, until, as Gregory naïvely remarks, no piece of iron could have borne it. At last, when nearly dead, his resolution gave way, and he confessed the whole plot by which it had been proposed to get rid of Chilperic and Fredegonda, and to place Clovis· on the throne.[1] Now, Plato, Gallienus, and Modestus were probably of Gallo-Roman origin, but Riculfus was evidently of Teutonic stock; moreover, he was a priest, and Plato an archdeacon, and the whole transaction shows that Roman law and Frankish law were of little avail against the unbridled passions of the Merovingian.

[1] Gregor. Turon. Hist. Franc. Lib. v. c. xlix.

## CHAPTER IV.

### THE GOTHS AND SPAIN.

OF all the Barbarian tribes, none showed themselves so amenable to the influences of Roman civilization as the Goths. Their comparatively settled habits, their early conversion to Christianity, and their position as allies of the empire long before they became its conquerors, rendered them far less savage under Alaric than were the Franks in the time of Clovis. The permanent occupation of Septimania and Catalonia by the Wisigoths, also, took place at a period when Rome was not as yet utterly sunk, and when the power of her name still possessed something of its ancient influence, which could not but modify the institutions of the new-comers as they strove to adapt their primitive customs to the altered circumstances under which they found themselves. It is not to be wondered at, therefore, if their laws reflect a condition of higher civilization than those of kindred races, and if the Roman jurisprudence has left in them traces of the appreciation of that wonderful work of the human intellect which the Goths were sufficiently enlightened to entertain.

The Ostrogoths, allowing for the short duration of their nationality, were even more exposed to the influences of Rome. Their leader, Theodoric, had been educated in Constantinople, and was fully as much a Roman as many of the Barbarian soldiers who had risen to high station under the emperors, or even to the throne itself. All his efforts were directed to harmonizing the institutions of his different subjects, and he was too sagacious not to see the manifest superiority of the Roman polity.

His kingdom was too evanescent to consolidate and perfect

its institutions or to accumulate any extended body of jurisprudence.   What little exists, however, manifests a compromise between the spirit of the Barbarian tribes of the period
and that of the conquered mistress of the world.   The Edict
of Theodoric does not allude to the torture of freemen, and
it is probable that the free Ostrogoth could not legally be subjected to it.   With respect to slaves, its provisions seem mainly
borrowed from the Roman law.   No slave could be tortured
against a third party for evidence unless the informer or accuser
was prepared to indemnify the owner at his own valuation of
the slave.   No slave could be tortured against his master, but
the purchase of a slave to render his testimony illegal was
pronounced null and void ; the purchase money was returned,
and the slave was tortured.   The immunity of freedmen is
likewise shown by the cancelling of any manumission conferred for the purpose of preventing torture for evidence.[1]
Theodoric, however, allowed his Roman subjects to be governed by their ancient laws, and he apparently had no repugnance to the use of torture when it could legally be inflicted.
Thus he seems particularly anxious to ferret out and punish
sorcerers, and in writing to the Prefect and Count of Rome
he urges them to apprehend certain suspected parties, and try
them by the regular legal process, which, as we have seen, by
the edicts of Constantius and his successors, was particularly
severe in enjoining torture in such cases, both as a means of
investigation and of punishment.[2]

On the other hand, the Wisigoths founded a permanent
state, and as they were the only race whose use of torture was
uninterrupted from the period of their settlement until modern
times, and as their legislation on the subject was to a great extent a model for that of other nations, it may be worth while
to examine it somewhat closely.

---

[1] Edict. Theodor. cap. c. ci. cii.
[2] Cassiodor. Variar. iv. xxii. xxiii.

The earliest code of the Wisigoths is supposed to have been compiled by Eurik, in the middle of the fifth century, but it was subsequently much modified by recensions and additions. It was remoulded by Chindaswind and Recaswind about the middle of the seventh century, and it has reached us only in this latest condition, while the MSS. vary so much in assigning the authorship of the various laws that but little reliance can be placed upon the assumed dates of most of them. Chindaswind, moreover, in issuing his revised code, prohibited for the future the use of the Roman law, which had previously been in force among the subject populations, under codes specially prepared for them by order of Alaric II. Thus the Wisigothic laws, as we have them, are not laws of race, like the other Barbarian codes, but territorial laws carefully digested for a whole nation by men conversant alike with the Roman and with their own ancestral jurisprudence.

It is therefore not surprising to find in them the use of torture legalized somewhat after the fashion of the imperial constitutions, and yet with some humane modifications and restrictions.   Slaves were liable to torture under accusation, but the accuser had first to make oath that he was actuated by neither fraud nor malice in preferring the charge ; and he was further obliged to give security that he would deliver to the owner another slave of equal value if the accused were acquitted.   If an innocent slave were crippled in the torture, the accuser was bound to give two of like value to the owner, and the sufferer received his freedom.   If the accused died under the torture, the judge who had manifested so little feeling and discretion in permitting it was also fined in a slave of like value, making three enuring to the owner, and careful measures were prescribed to insure that a proper valuation was made. If the accuser was unable to meet the responsibility thus incurred, he was himself forfeited as a slave.   Moreover, the owner was always at liberty to save his slave from the torture by proving his innocence otherwise if possible; and if he succeeded, the accuser forfeited to him a slave of equal value, and was obliged to pay all the costs of the proceedings.[1]

Freedmen were even better protected. They could only be tortured for crimes of which the penalties exceeded a certain amount, varying with the nature of the freedom enjoyed by the accused. If no confession were extorted, and the accused were crippled in the torture, the judge and the accuser were both heavily fined for his benefit, and if he died, the fines were paid to his family.[2]

There could have been little torturing of slaves as witnesses, for in general their evidence was not admissible, even under torture, against any freeman, including their masters. The slaves of the royal palace, however, could give testimony as though they were freemen,[3] and, as in the Roman law, there were certain excepted crimes, such as treason, adultery, homicide, sorcery, and coining, in accusations of which slaves could be tortured against their masters, nor could they be preserved by manumission against this liability.[4]

As regards freemen, the provisions of different portions of the code do not seem precisely in harmony, but all of them throw considerable difficulties in the way of procedures by torture. An early law directs that, in cases of theft or fraud, no one shall be subjected to torture unless the accuser bring forward the informer, or inscribe himself with three sureties to undergo the *lex talionis* in case the accused prove innocent. Moreover, if no confession were extorted, the informer was to be produced. If the accuser could not do this, he was bound to name him to the judge, who was then to seize him, unless he were protected by some one too powerful for the judicial authority to control. In this event it was the duty of the judge to summon the authorities to his aid, and in default of so doing he was liable for all the damages arising from the

[1] L. Wisigoth. Lib. VI. Tit. i. l. 5.        [2] Ibid.

[3] Ibid. II. iv. 4.

[4] Ibid. VI. i. 4; VII. vi. 1; VIII. iv. 10, 11.

case. The informer, when thus brought within control of the
court, was, if a freeman, declared infamous, and obliged to
pay ninefold the value of the matter in dispute; if a slave,
sixfold, and to receive a hundred lashes. If the freeman were
too poor to pay the fine, he was adjudged as a slave in common to the accuser and the accused.[1]

A later law, issued by Chindaswind, is even more careful
in its very curious provisions. No accuser could force to the
torture a man higher in station or rank than himself. The
only cases in which it could be inflicted on nobles were those
of treason, homicide, and adultery, while for freemen of
humbler position the crime must be rated at a fine of 500
solidi at least. In these cases, an open trial was first prescribed. If this were fruitless, the accuser who desired to
push the matter bound himself in case of failure to deliver
himself up as a slave to the accused, who could maltreat him
at pleasure, short of taking his life, or compound with him at
his own valuation of his sufferings. The torture then might
last for three days; the accuser himself was the torturer, subject to the supervision of the judge, and might inflict torment
to any extent that his ingenuity could suggest, short of pro-
ducing permanent injury or death. If death resulted, the
accuser was delivered to the relatives of the deceased to be
likewise put to death; the judge who had permitted it through
collusion or corruption was exposed to the same fate, but if he
could swear that he had not been bribed by the accuser, he
was allowed to escape with a fine of 500 solidi. A very remarkable regulation, moreover, provided against false confessions extorted by torment. The accuser was obliged to
draw up his accusation in all its details, and submit it secretly
to the judge. Any confession under torture which did not
agree substantially with this was set aside, and neither convicted the accused nor released the accuser from the penalties
to which he was liable.[2]

---

[1] L. Wisigoth. VI. i. I.          [2] Ibid. VI. i. 2.

Under such a system, strictly enforced, few persons would be found hardy enough to incur the dangers of subjecting an adversary to the rack. As with the Franks, however, so among the Wisigoths, the laws were not powerful enough to secure their own observance. The authority of the kings grew gradually weaker and less able to repress the assumptions of ambitious prelates and unruly grandees, and it is easy to imagine that in the continual struggle all parties sought to maintain and strengthen their position by an habitual disregard of law. At the Thirteenth Council of Toledo, in 683, King Erwig, in his opening address, alludes to the frequent abuse of torture in contravention of the law, and promises a reform. The council, in turn, deplores the constantly recurring cases of wrong and suffering wrought "regiæ subtilitatis astu vel profanæ potestatis instinctu," and proceeds to decree that in future no freeman, noble, or priest shall be tortured unless regularly accused or indicted, and properly tried in public ; and this decree duly received the royal confirmation.[1]

As the Goths emerge again into the light of history after the Saracenic conquest, we find these ancient laws still in force among the descendants of the refugees who had gathered around Don Pelayo. The use of the Latin tongue gradually faded out among them, and about the twelfth or thirteenth century the Wisigothic code was translated into the popular language, and this Romance version, known as the *Fuero Juzgo*, long continued the source of law in the Peninsula. In this, the provisions of the early Gothic monarchs respecting torture are textually preserved, with two trifling exceptions, which may reasonably be regarded as scarcely more than mere errors of copyists.[2] Torture was thus maintained in Spain as

---

[1] Concil. Toletan. XIII. ann. 683, can. ii.

[2] See the Fuero Juzgo, Lib. I. Tit. iii. l. 4; Tit. iv. l. 4.—Lib. III. Tit. iv. ll. 10, 11.—Lib. VI. Tit. i. ll. 2, 4, 5.—Lib. VII. Tit. i. l. 1; Tit. vi. l. 1. The only points in which these vary from the ancient laws are that, in Lib. VI. Tit. i. l. 2, adultery is not included among the crimes for suspicion of which nobles can be tortured, and that the accuser is not directed to con-

an unbroken ancestral custom, and the earliest reference which I have met with of it in mediæval jurisprudence occurs in 1228, when Don Jayme el Conquistador of Aragon forbade his representatives from commencing proceedings by its employment without special orders.[1] When Alfonso the Wise, about the middle of the thirteenth century, attempted to revise the jurisprudence of his dominions, in the code known as *Las Siete Partidas*, which he promulgated, he only simplified and modified the proceedings, and did not remove the practice. Although he proclaimed that the person of man is the noblest thing of earth—"La persona del home es la mas noble cosa del mundo"[2]—he held that stripes and other torture inflicted judicially were no dishonor even to Spanish sensitiveness.[3] Asserting that torture was frequently requisite for the discovery of hidden crimes,[4] he found himself confronted by the Church, which taught, as we shall see hereafter, that confessions extorted under torture were invalid. To this doctrine he gave his full assent,[5] and then, to reconcile these apparently incompatible necessities, he adopted an expedient partially suggested not long before by Frederic II., which subsequently became almost universal throughout Europe, whereby the prohibition of conviction on extorted confessions

duct the torture. In Lib. VII. Tit. i. l. 1, also, the informer who fails to convict is condemned only in a single fine, and not ninefold; he is, however, as in the original, declared infamous, as a *ladro;* if a slave, the penalty is the same as with the Wisigoths.

[1] Jacobi Regis constitutio adversus Judæos, etc. c. xiii. (Marca Hispanica, p. 1416).

[2] Partidas, P. VII. Tit. i. l. 26.          [3] Ibid. P. VII. Tit. ix. l. 16.

[4] Ca por los tormentos saben los judgadores muchas veces la verdad de los malos fechos encubiertos, que non se podrian saber dotra guisa.—Ibid. P. VII. Tit. xxx. l. 1.

[5] Por premia de tormentos ó de feridas, ó por miedo de muerte ó de deshonra que quieren facer á los homes, conoscen á las vegadas algunas cosas que de su grado non las conoscerien : e por ende decimos que la conoscencia que fuere fecha en algunas destas maneras que non debe valer nin empesce al que la face.—Ibid. P. III. Tit. xiii. l. 5.

was eluded. After confession under torture, the prisoner was remanded to his prison. On being subsequently brought before the judge he was again interrogated, when, if he persisted in his confession, he was condemned. If he recanted, he was again tortured ; and, if the crime was grave, the process could be repeated a third time ; but, throughout all, he could not be convicted unless he made a free confession apart from the torture. Even after conviction, moreover, if the judge found reason to believe that the confession was the result of fear of the torture, or of rage at being tortured, or of insanity, the prisoner was entitled to an acquittal.[1] The humane interference of the Church thus resulted only in a redoublement of cruelty ; and the system once introduced, speedily tended to break down the limits imposed on it. In a little more than half a century after the death of Alfonso, judges were in the habit of not contenting themselves with three inflictions, but continued the torture as long as the prisoner confessed on the rack and retracted his confession subsequently.[2]

Alfonso's admiration of the Roman law led him to borrow much from it rather than from the Gothic code, though both are represented in the provisions which he established. Thus, except in accusations of treason, no one of noble blood could be tortured, nor a doctor of laws or other learning, nor a member of the king's council, or that of any city or town, except for official forgery, nor a pregnant woman, nor a child under fourteen years of age.[3] So, when several accomplices were on trial, the torturer was directed to commence with the

---

[1] Partidas, P. VII. Tit. xxx. l. 4.—Porque la conoscencia que es fecha en el tormento, si non fuere confirmada despues sin premia, non es valedera.

[2] Alvari Pelagii de Planctu Ecclesiæ, Lib. II. Art. xli.

[3] Partidas, P. VII. Tit. xxx. l. 2. Except the favor shown to the learned professions, " por honra de la esciencia," which afterwards became general throughout Europe, these provisions may all be found in the Roman law —Const. 4 Cod. IX. viii.; L. 3, Dig. XLVIII. xix.; L. 10, Dig. XLVIII. xviii.; Const. 11 Cod. IX. xli.

youngest and worst trained, as the truth might probably be more readily extracted from him.[1]  The provision, also, that when a master, or mistress, or one of their children was found dead at home, all the household slaves were liable to torture in the search for the murderer, bears a strong resemblance to the cruel law of the Romans, which condemned them to death in case the murderer remained undiscovered.[2]

The regulations concerning the torture of slaves are founded, with little variation, on the Roman laws.  Thus, the evidence of a slave was only admissible under torture, and no slave could be tortured to prove the guilt of a present or former owner, nor could a freedman, in a case concerning his patron, subject to the usual exceptions which we have already seen.  The excepted crimes enumerated by Alfonso are seven, viz. : adultery, embezzlement of the royal revenues by tax collectors, high treason, murder of a husband or wife by the other, murder of a joint owner of a slave by his partner, murder of a testator by a legatee, and coining.  With the slave, as with the free-man, all testimony under torture required subsequent confirmation.[3]

There is one noteworthy innovation, however, in the Partidas which was subsequently introduced widely into the torture codes of Europe, and which, in theory at least, greatly extended their sphere of action.  This was the liability of freemen as witnesses.  When a man's evidence was vacillating and contradictory, so as to afford reasonable suspicion that he was committing perjury, all criminal judges were empowered to subject him to torture, so as to ascertain the truth, provided always that he was of low condition, and did not belong to the excepted classes.[4]

With all this, there are indications that Alfonso designed

---

[1] Partidas, P. VII. Tit. xxx. 1. 5.—Imitated from L. 18, Dig. XLVIII. xviii.

[2] Partidas, P. VII. Tit. xxx. 1. 7.   Cf. Tacit. Annal. XIV. xliii.-xlv.

[3] Partidas, P. VII. Tit. xxx. 1. 16.

[4] Ibid. P. III. Tit. xvi. 1. 43.—P. VII. Tit. xxx. 1. 8.

rather to restrict than to extend the use of torture, and, if his general instructions could have been enforced, there must have been little occasion for its employment under his code. In one passage he directs that when the evidence is insufficient to prove a charge, the accused, if of good character, must be acquitted ; and in another he orders its application only when common report is adverse to a prisoner, and he is shown to be a man of bad repute.[1] Besides, an accuser who failed to prove his charge was always liable to the *lex talionis*, unless he were prosecuting for an offence committed on his own person, or for the murder of a relative not more distant than a brother or sister's child.[2] The judge, moreover, was strictly enjoined not to exceed the strict rules of the law, nor to carry the torture to a point imperilling life or limb. If he deviated from these limits, or acted through malice or favoritism, he was liable to a similar infliction on his own person, or to a penalty greater than if he were a private individual.[3] The liability of witnesses was further circumscribed by the fact that in cases involving corporal punishment, no one could be forced to bear testimony who was related to either of the parties as far as the fourth degree of consanguinity, in either the direct or collateral lines, nor even when nearly connected by marriage, as in the case of fathers-in-law, step-children, etc.[4] Orders to inflict torture, moreover, were one of the few procedures which could be appealed from in advance.[5] Several of these limitations became generally adopted through Europe. We shall see, however, that they afforded little real protection to the accused, and it is more than probable that they received as little respect in Spain as elsewhere.

There were many varieties of torture in use at the period, but Alfonso informs us that only two were commonly employed,

[1] Partidas, P. VII. Tit. i. l. 26, " Home mal enfamado."—P. VII. Tit. xxx. l. 3, " Et si fuere home de mala fame ò vil."

[2] Ibid. P. VII. Tit. i. l. 26.

[3] Ibid. P. VII. Tit. xxx. l. 4 ; Tit. ix. l. 16.

[4] Ibid. P. VII. Tit. xxx. l. 9.  [5] Ibid. P. III. Tit. xxiii. l. 13.

the scourge and the strappado, which consisted in hanging the prisoner by the arms while his back and legs were loaded with heavy weights.[1] The former of these, however, seems to be the only one alluded to throughout the code.

As a whole, the Partidas were too elaborate and too much in advance of the wants of the age to be immediately success-ful as a work of legislation, and they were not confirmed by the Córtes until 1348. In the Ordenamiento de Alcalà of Alfonso XI., issued in that year, they are referred to as sup-plying all omissions in subsequent codes.[2]

It is probable that in his system of torture Alfonso the Wise merely regulated and put into shape the customs preva-lent in his territories, for the changes in it which occurred during the succeeding three or four centuries are merely such as can be readily explained by the increasing influence of the revived Roman jurisprudence, and the introduction of the doctrines of the Inquisition with respect to criminal proced-ures. In the final shape which the administration of torture assumed in Castile, as described by Villadiego, an eminent legist writing about the year 1600, it was only employed when the proof was strong, and yet not sufficient for conviction. No allusion is made to the torture of witnesses, and Villadiego condemns the cruelty of some judges who divide the torture into three days in order to render it more effective, since, after a certain prolongation of torment, the limbs begin to lose their sensibility, which is recovered after an interval, and on the second and third days they are more sensitive than at first. This he pronounces rather a repetition than a continuation of torture, and repetition was illegal unless rendered necessary by the introduction of new testimony.[3] As in the thirteenth century, nobles, doctors of law, pregnant women, and child-ren under fourteen were not liable, except in cases of high

---

[1] Partidas, P. vıɪ. Tit. xxx. l. 1.

[2] Ordenamiento de Alcalà, Tit. xxviii. l. 1.

[3] Simancas, however, states that a single repetition of the torture was allowable.—De Cathol. Instit. Tit. LXV. No. 76.

treason and some other heinous offences. The clergy also were now exempted, unless previously condemned as infamous, and advocates engaged in pleading enjoyed a similar privilege. With the growth of the Inquisition, however, heresy had now advanced to the dignity of a crime which extinguished all prerogatives, for it was held to be a far more serious offence to be false to Divine than to human majesty.[1] The Partidas allow torture in the investigation of comparatively trivial offences, but Villadiego states that it should be employed only in the case of serious crimes, entailing bodily punishment more severe than the torture itself, and torture was worse than the loss of the hands. Thus, when only banishment, fines, or imprisonment were involved, it could not be used. The penalties incurred by judges for its excessive or improper application were almost identical with those prescribed by Alfonso, and the limitation that it should not be allowed to endanger life or limb was only to be exceeded in the case of treason, when the utmost severity was permissible.[2] In 1489 Ferdinand and Isabella had directed that no criminal case should be heard by less than three alcaldes or judges sitting together, and torture could not be employed without a formal decision signed unanimously by all three. In 1534 Charles V. called attention to the neglect of this rule, whereby the accused was deprived of the right of appeal, and he ordered that it should be strictly observed in future—regulations which duly maintained their place on the statute book as long as the use of torture was continued.[3]

Many varieties were in use, but the most common were the strappado and pouring water down the throat ; but when the accused was so weak as to render these dangerous, fire was applied to the soles of the feet ; and the use of the scourge

[1] De Cathol. Instit. Tit. LXV. No. 44–48. Cf. Novísima Recopilacion, Lib. VI. Tit, ii. leis 4 y 5 (Ed. 1775).

[2] Villadiego, Gloss. ad Fuero Juzgo, Lib. VI. Tit. i. l. 2, Gloss. *c, d, e, f, g.*

[3] Novísima Recopilacion, Lib. II. vii. leis 1 y 13.

was not unusual. As in the ancient laws, the owner of slaves was entitled to compensation when his bondmen were unjustly tortured. If there was no justification for it, he was reimbursed in double the estimated value; if the judge exceeded the proper measure of torment, he made it good to the owner with another slave.[1]

Whatever limitations may theoretically have been assigned to the application of torture, however, it is probable that they received little respect in practice. Simancas, Bishop of Badajos, who was a little anterior to Villadiego, speaks of it as a generally received axiom that scarcely any criminal accusation could be satisfactorily tried without torture.[2] This is confirmed by the account recently discovered by Bergenroth of the secret history of the execution of Don Carlos, for, whether it be authentic or not, it shows how thoroughly the use of torture had interpenetrated the judicial system of Spain. It states that when Philip II. determined to try his wretched son for the crime of encouraging the rebellious movements in the Netherlands, and the prince denied the offence, torture was applied until he fainted, and, on recovering his senses, consented to confess in order to escape the repetition which was about to be applied. It is hardly to be believed that even a Spanish imagination could invent the dark and terrible details of this dismal story; and even if it be not true, its author must have felt that such an incident was too probable to destroy its vraisemblance.

At the same time, Castilian justice kept itself free from one of the worst abuses which, as we shall see hereafter, grew out of the use of torture, in the secret inquisitorial process which established itself almost everywhere. A law of Alfonso XI. issued in 1325 peremptorily ordered that the accused should not be denied the right to know the contents of the inquest made with respect to him, and that the names of the witnesses

---

[1] Villadiego, *op. cit.* Lib. VI. Tit. i. l. 5, Gloss. *b, c.*
[2] Simancæ de Cathol. Instit. Tit. LXV. No. 8.

CARLOVINGIAN AND FEUDAL LAW.

should be communicated to him so that he could defend himself freely and have all the means to which he was entitled of establishing his innocence. Ferdinand and Isabella, moreover, in 1480, decreed that all who desired counsel should be allowed the privilege, those who were poor being furnished at the public expense, and no torture could be inflicted before this was complied with. These laws, which offer so creditable a contrast to the legislation of other lands, remained in force and were embodied in the Recopilacion.[1]

## CHAPTER V.

### CARLOVINGIAN AND FEUDAL LAW.

In turning to the other barbarian races which inherited the fragments of the Roman empire, we find that the introduction of torture as a recognized and legal mode of investigation was long delayed. Under the Merovingians, as we have seen, its employment, though not infrequent, was exceptional and without warrant of law. When the slow reconstruction of society at length began, the first faint trace of torture is to be found in a provision respecting the crimes of sorcery and magic. These were looked upon with peculiar detestation, as offences against both God and man. It is no wonder then if the safeguards which the freeman enjoyed under the ordinary modes of judicial procedure were disregarded in the cases of those who violated every law, human and divine. The legislation of Charlemagne, indeed, was by no means merciful in its general character. His mission was to civilize, if possible, the

---

[1] Novísima Recopilacion, Lib. II. Tit. vi. lei 6; Lib. VIII. Tit. i. lei 4. Aragon is said to have been an exception as regards the use of torture (Gomez Var. Resolut. T. III. c. 13—*ap*. Gerstlacher. de Quæst. per Torment. p. 68). In Navarre there is no trace of the use of torture prior to the fifteenth century.—G. B. de Lagrèze, La Navarre Française, II. 342.

savage and turbulent races composing his empire, and he was not overnice in the methods selected to accomplish the task. Still, he did not venture, even if he desired, to prescribe torture as a means of investigation, except in the case of suspected sorcerers, for whom, moreover, it is ordered indirectly rather than openly.[1] Yet, by this time, the personal inviolability of the freeman was gone. The infliction of stripes and of hideous mutilations is frequently directed in the Capitularies, and even torture and banishment for life are prescribed as a punishment for insulting bishops and priests in church.[2]

This apparent inconsistency is only a repetition of what we have seen in the Persian and Indian institutions, where torture was superfluous in the presence of other forms of proof, and in Greece and Rome where it makes its appearance in the absence of those forms. Though there was no theoretical objection to torture as a process of investigation, yet there was no necessity for its employment as a means of evidence. That the idea of thus using it in matters of great moment was not unfamiliar to the men of that age is evident when we find it officially stated that the accomplices of Bernard, King of Italy, in his rebellion against Louis le Débonnaire, in 817, on their capture confessed the whole plot without being put to the torture.[3] Such instances, however, were purely exceptional. In ordinary matters, there was a complete system of attack and defence which supplemented all deficiencies of testimony in doubtful cases. Sacramental purgation, the wager of battle, and the various forms of vulgar ordeals were not only primæval customs suited to the feelings and modes of thought of the race, but they were also much more in harmony with the

[1] Capit. Carol. Mag. II. ann. 805, § xxv. (Baluz.). No other interpretation can well be given of the direction " diligentissime examinatione constringantur si forte confiteantur malorum quæ gesserunt. Sed tali moderatione fiat eadem districtio ne vitam perdant."

[2] Capitul. Lib. VI. cap. cxxix.

[3] Non solum se tradunt sed ultro etiam non admoti quæstionibus omnem technam hujus rebellionis detegunt.—Goldast. Constit. Imp. I. 151.

credulous faith inculcated by the Church, and the Church had by this time entered on the career of temporal supremacy which gave it so potent a voice in fashioning the institutions of European society. For all these, the ministrations of the ecclesiastic were requisite, and in many of them his unseen agency might prove decisive. On the other hand, the humane precepts which forbade the churchman from intervening in any manner in judgments involving blood precluded his interference with the torture chamber; and in fact, while torture was yet frequent under the Merovingians, the canons of various councils prohibited the presence of any ecclesiastic in places where it was administered.[1] Every consideration, therefore, would lead the Church in the ninth century to prefer the milder forms of investigation, and to use its all-powerful influence in maintaining the popular belief in them. The time had not yet come when, as we shall see hereafter, the Church, as the spiritual head of feudal Christendom, would find the ordeal unnecessary and torture the most practicable instrumentality to preserve the purity of faith and the steadfastness of implicit obedience.

In the ninth century, moreover, torture was incompatible with the forms of judicial procedure handed down as relics of the time when every freeman bore his share in the public business of his sept. Criminal proceedings as yet were open and public. The secret inquisitions which afterwards became so favorite a system with lawyers did not then exist. The *mallum*, or court, was perhaps no longer held in the open air,[2]

---

[1] Non licet presbytero nec diacono ad trepalium ubi rei torquentur stare. —Concil. Autissiodor. ann. 578, can. xxxiii.

Ad locum examinationis reorum nullus clericorum accedat.—Concil. Matiscon. II. ann. 585, can. xix.

[2] Under Charlemagne and Louis le Débonnaire seems to have commenced the usage of holding the court under shelter. Thus Charlemagne, "Ut in locis ubi mallus publicus haberi solet, tectum tale constituatur quod in hiberno et in æstate observandus esse possit" (Capit. Carol. Mag. II. ann. 809, § xiii.). See also Capit. I. eod. ann. § xxv. Louis le Débon-

nor were the freemen of the district constrained as of old to be present,[1] but it was still free to every one. The accuser and his witnesses were confronted with the accused, and the criminal must be present when his sentence was pronounced.[2] The purgatorial oath was administered at the altar of the parish church; the ordeal was a public spectacle; and the judicial duel drew thousands of witnesses as eager for the sight of blood as the Roman plebs. These were all ancestral customs, inspiring implicit reverence, and forming part of the public life of the community. To substitute for them the gloomy dungeon through whose walls no echo of the victim's screams could filter, where impassible judges coldly compared the incoherent confession wrung out by insufferable torment with the anonymous accusation or the depositions of secret witnesses, required a total change in the constitution of society.

The change was long in coming. Feudalism arose and consolidated its forces on the ruins of the Carlovingian empire without altering the principles upon which the earlier procedures of criminal jurisdiction had been based. As the

---

naire prohibits the holding of courts in churches, and adds, " Volumus utique ut domus a comite in locum ubi mallum teneri debet construatur ut propter calorem solis et pluviam publica utilitas non remaneat" (Capit. Ludov. Pii. I. ann. 819, § xiv.).

[1] In 769, we find Charlemagne commanding the presence of all freemen in the general judicial assembly held twice a year, "Ut ad mallum venire nemo tardet, unum circa æstatem et alterum circa autumnum." At others of less importance, they were only bound to attend when summoned, " Ad alia vero, si necessitas fuerit, vel denunciatio regis urgeat, vocatus venire nemo tardet" (Capit. Carol. Mag. ann. 769, § xii.).

In 809, he desired that none should be forced to attend unless he had business, " Ut nullus ad placitum venire cogatur, nisi qui caussam habet ad quærendam" (Capit. I. ann. 809, § xiii.).

In 819, Louis ordered that the freemen should attend at least three courts a year, " et nullus eos amplius placita observare compellat, nisi forte quilibet aut accusatus fuerit, aut alium accusaverit, aut ad testimonium perhibendum vocatus fuerit" (Capit. Ludov. Pii. V. ann. 819, § xiv.).

[2] Placuit ut adversus absentes non judicetur. Quod si factus fuerit prolata sententia non valebit.—Capit. Lib. V. § cccxi.

local dignitaries seized upon their fiefs and made them hered-
itary, so they arrogated to themselves the dispensation of
justice which had formerly belonged to the central power, but
their courts were still open to all. Trials were conducted in
public upon well-known rules of local law and custom ; the
fullest opportunities were given for the defence ; and a denial
of justice authorized the vassal to renounce the jurisdiction of
his feudal lord and seek a superior court.[1]

Still, as under the Merovingians, torture, though unrecog-
nized by law, was occasionally employed as an extraordinary
element of judicial investigation, as well as a means of punishment to gratify the vengeance of the irresponsible and cruel
tyrants who ruled with absolute sway over their petty lord-
ships. A few such instances occur in the documents and
chronicles of the period, but the terms in which they are
alluded to show that they were regarded as irregular.

Thus, it is related of Wenceslas, Duke of Bohemia, in the
early part of the tenth century, that he destroyed the gibbets
and fearful instruments of torture wherewith the cruelty of
his judges had been exercised, and that he never allowed
them to be restored.[2] An individual case of torture which
occurred in 1017 has chanced to be preserved to us by its
ending in a miracle, and being the occasion of the canoniza-
tion of a saint. A pious pilgrim, reputed to belong to the
royal blood of Scotland, while wandering on the marches
between the Bavarians and the Moravians, was seized by the
inhabitants on suspicion of being a spy, and, to extort a confession, was exposed to a succession of torments which ended

---

[1] This right of appeal was not relished by the seigneurs, who apparently
foresaw that it might eventually become the instrument of their destruction.
It was long in establishing itself, and was resisted energetically. Thus the
Kings of England who were Dukes of Aquitaine, sometimes discouraged
the appeals of their French subjects to the courts of the King of France by
hanging the notaries who undertook to draw up the requisite papers.—
Meyer, Instit. Judiciaires, I. 461.

[2] Annalist. Saxo ann. 928.

in hanging him on a withered tree until he died.   The falsity
of the accusation and the sanctity of the victim were manifested by the uninterrupted growth of his hair and nails and
the constant flowing of blood from a wound, while the dead
tree suddenly put forth leaves and flowers.   Margrave Henry
of Bavaria had him reverently buried, and he was duly en-
rolled in the catalogue of saints.[1]   A letter of Gerard, Bishop
of Cambrai, in 1025, relating how certain suspected heretics
could not be forced by torment to confession, shows that
ecclesiastics already were prepared, in spite of the received
dogmas of the Church, to have recourse to such means when
no others could be found to protect the purity of the faith.[2]
In the celebrated case, also, of the robbery of the church of
Laon, about the year 1100, the suspected thief, after conviction by the cold water ordeal, was tortured by command of
the bishop in order to make him surrender the sacred vessels
which he had concealed.   Basting with hot lard was tried unsuccessfully ; he was then hanged by the neck and let down
at intervals for nearly a whole day, and when life was almost
extinct his resolution gave way and he agreed to discover the
place where the valuables were hidden.[3]   When Charles the
Good of Flanders was murdered in 1127, one of the assassins
fled to Terouane, where he was discovered and forced by
scourging to disclose the names of his accomplices.[4]   About
1130 at Petersberg, in Saxony, we are told of a shepherd
tortured by his lord to extract money, and saved from suffering by an earnest prayer to St. Peter.[5]   When Richard I. of

[1] Dithmari Chron. Lib. VII. ad. fin.

[2] Multa dissimulatione renitebant, adeo ut nullis suppliciis possent cogi
ad confessionem.—Synod. Atrebatens. ann. 1025 (Hartzheim III. 68).

[3] Hermannus de S. Mariæ Lauden. Mirac.   Cf. Guibert. Noviogent. de
Vita Sua. cap. xvi.

[4] "Cumque captum eduxissit Isaac, virgis et vinculis coactum et flagel-
latum constringit, et ita extorsit ab eo ut reos in comitis traditione proderet."
—Galberti Vit. Caroli Boni cap. ix. n. 66.

[5] Chron. Montis Sereni (Mencken. Script. Rer. Germ. II. 172).

England was endeavoring to return through Germany from the crusade, it was by the torture of his page that the identity of the royal traveller was discovered, and he was delivered to his enemy the Duke of Austria.[1]

These are evidently rather sporadic and exceptional cases than indications of any systematic introduction of the practice. A more significant allusion, however, is found in the reproof administered, about 1125, by Hildebert, Bishop of le Mans, to one of his priests, who had been concerned in the torture of a suspected thief, for the purpose of extracting a confession. Hildebert argues that the infliction of torture for confession is a matter for judicial decision and not of Church discipline, and therefore not fit for a clerk to be engaged in.[2] This would seem to show that it occasionally was a recognized means of proof in the lay tribunals of the period, though as yet not favored by the Church. If so, no record of its introduction or evidence of its customary use has been preserved to us, though there is abundant evidence of its employment as a punishment and for the extortion of money.

As a punishment legally inflicted, we find it prescribed, in 1168, by Frederic Barbarossa in cases of petty thefts,[3] and in the next century by Frederic II. as a penalty for high treason.[4] Special cases, too, may be instanced, where its infliction on a large scale shows that the minds of men were not unfamiliar with its use. Thus when, in 1125, the inhabitants of Erfurt were guilty of some outrages on the imperial authority, and the town was besieged and captured by the Emperor Lothair, the chronicler relates that large numbers of the citizens were either killed, blinded, or tortured in various ways by the vindictive conqueror,[5] and in 1129 he treated the citizens of Halle in the same manner.[6]

---

[1] Radulf. de Coggeshale Chron. Anglic. ann. 1192.

[2] Hildebert. Cenoman. Epist. xxx.

[3] Feudor. Lib. II. Tit. xxvii. § 8.

[4] Fred. II. Lib. Rescript. II. §§ 1, 6. (Goldast. Constit. Imp. II. 54).

[5] Erphurdianus Variloquus, ann. 1125.

[6] Annal. Bosovienses, ann. 1129.

Even towards the close of the thirteenth century, we find
Rodolph of Hapsburg interfering in favor of a prisoner whom
one of his nobles was afflicting with cruel torments. The
Emperor, however, does not venture to command, but merely
entreats that the tortures be suspended until he shall have an
interview with the aggressor.[1]

So summary and effective a mode of forcing the weak and
unprotected to ransom themselves was not likely to be over-
looked in those ages of violence, and though the extra-judicial
use of torture is foreign to our purpose, yet, as showing how men
educated themselves in its employment, it may be worth while
to allude briefly to this aspect of the subject. Thus, Duke
Swantopluck of Bohemia, in a marauding expedition into
Hungary in 1108, caused to be racked or put to death all
prisoners who could not purchase escape by heavy ransoms.[2]
At the same period, Germany is described to us by an eye-
witness as covered with feudal chieftains who lived a life of
luxury by torturing the miserable wretches that could scarce
obtain bread and water for their own existence.[3] In Spain,
the same means were understood and employed by the savage
nobles of that barbarous period.[4] In England, the fearful
anarchy which prevailed under King Stephen encouraged a
similar condition of affairs. The baronial castles which then
multiplied so rapidly became mere dens of robbers who ran-
sacked the country for all who had the unfortunate reputation
of wealth. From these they extracted the last penny by
tortures; and the chronicler expatiates on the multiplicity and
horrid ingenuity of the torments devised—suspension by the
feet over slow fires; hanging by the thumbs; knotted ropes
twisted around the head; crucet-houses, or chests filled with

[1] Cod. Epist. Rudolphi I. p. 216–7 (Lipsiæ, 1806).

[2] Cosmæ Pragens. Lib. III. ann. 1108.

[3] Annalist. Saxo ann. 1123. See also, about the same date, the Chron.
S. Trudon. Lib. XII. (D'Achery II. 704); and the Epist. Friderici Episc.
Leodiens. in Martene, Ampliss. Collect. I. 654.

[4] Gerardi Hist. Compostellan. Lib. II. cap. 80.

sharp stones, in which the victim was crushed; sachentages, or frames with a sharp iron collar preventing the wearer from sitting, lying, or sleeping; dungeons filled with toads and adders; slow starvation, &c. &c.[1] Even in the more settled times of the close of the reign of Henry II. a case is recorded of a heavy fine inflicted on a man for illegally capturing and torturing a woman;[2] under Richard I. an epistle of Clement III. refers to a knight who had confessed that he had tortured a priest and forced him to redeem himself with a large sum of money;[3] and in 1210 King John seized all the Jews in England and tortured them until they ransomed themselves heavily.[4]

In all this, however, there is no evidence of the revival of torture as a means of legal investigation. The community was satisfied with the old barbaric forms of trial, and the Church, still true to its humanizing instincts, lost no opportunity of placing the seal of its disapprobation on the whole theory of extorting confessions. At an early period, it had even been a matter of dispute whether a Christian magistrate, after baptism, was at liberty to inflict torment and pronounce sentence of death. The Synod of Rome in 384 had declared that no Christian could exercise secular power without sin, because he was obliged to contravene the teachings of the Church by ordering the application of torture in judicial pleadings;[5] and if Innocent I., in 405, had decided that such proceedings were lawful, it was only on the ground that the Church had no right to resist the laws or to oppose the powers ordained of God.[6] About the same time St. Augustin had exposed the cruel absurdity of torture with a cogent terseness that has rarely been excelled, and had stamped it with the

[1] Anglo Saxon Chronicle, ann. 1137.
[2] Pike, History of Crime in England, I. 427.
[3] Jaffé Regesta p. 884.
[4] Matt. Paris. Hist. Ang. ann. 1210.
[5] Synod. Roman. ann. 384, can. 10.
[6] Innocent PP. I. Epist. III. cap. iii.

infamy which it deserved.[1]  The great name of Gregory I.
was on record in the sixth century, denouncing as worthless a
confession extorted by incarceration and hunger.[2]  When
Nicholas I., who did so much to build up ecclesiastical power
and influence, addressed, in 866, his well-known epistle to the
Bulgarians to aid and direct them in their conversion to ortho-
doxy, he recites that he is told that, in cases of suspected
theft, their courts endeavor to extort confession by stripes, and
by pricking with a pointed iron.  This he pronounces to be
contrary to all law, human and divine, for confessions to be
valid should be spontaneous ; and he argues at some length on
the uncertainty of the system of torture, and the injustice to
which it leads, concluding with a peremptory prohibition of
its continuance.[3]

In the first half of the same century, the manufacturers of
the False Decretals had attributed to Alexander I. an epistle
designed to protect the Church from pillage and oppression,
in which that pontiff is made to threaten with infamy and
excommunication those who extort confessions or other writ-
ings from ecclesiastics by force or fear, and to lay down the
general rule that confessions must be voluntary and not compulsory.[4]  On the authority of this, Ivo of Chartres, at the
commencement of the twelfth century, declares that men in
holy orders cannot be forced to confess ;[5] and half a century
later, Gratian lays down the more general as well as more
explicit rule that no confession is to be extorted by the instrumentality of torture.[6]  This position was consistently maintained until the revival of the Roman law familiarized the

---

[1] De Civ. Dei Lib. xix. cap. vi.

[2] Gregor. PP. I. Lib. viii. Epist. xxx.

[3] Nicolai PP. I. Epist. xcvii. ⸹ 86.

[4] Pseudo-Alexand. decret. "Omnibus orthodoxis."

[5] Ministrorum confessio non sit extorta sed spontanea.—Ivon. Panorm.
iv. cxvii.

[6] Quod vero confessio cruciatibus extorquenda non est.—C. i Decreti
Caus. xv. q. vi.

minds of men with the procedures of the imperial jurisprudence, when the policy of the Church altered, and it yielded
to the temptation of obtaining so useful a means of reaching
and proving the otherwise impalpable crime of heresy.

--------

## CHAPTER VI.

### REAPPEARANCE OF TORTURE.

THE latter half of the twelfth century saw the study of the
civil law prosecuted with intense ardor, and, in the beginning
of the thirteenth, Innocent III. struck a fatal blow at the
barbaric systems of the ordeal and sacramental compurgation
by forbidding the rites of the Church to the one and altering
the form of oath customary to the other. The unreasoning
faith which had reposed confidence in the boiling caldron, or
the burning ploughshare, or the trained champion as the
special vehicle of Divine judgment, was fading before the
Aristotelian logic of the schools, and dialectical skill could
not but note the absurdity of acquitting a culprit because he
could beg or buy two, or five, or eleven men to swear to their
belief in his oath or denial.

Yet with all these influences at work, the ancestral customs
maintained their ground long and stubbornly. It is not until
the latter half of the thirteenth century that the first faint
traces of legalized torture are to be found in France, at whose
University of Paris for more than a hundred years the study
of the Pandects had become the absorbing topic, and where
the constantly increasing power of the crown found its most
valuable instruments in the civil lawyers, and its surest weapon
against feudalism in the extension of the royal jurisdiction.
In Germany, the progress was even slower. The decline of
the central authority, after the death of Frederic Barbarossa,
rendered any general change impossible, and made the abso-
lutist principles of the imperial jurisprudence especially dis-

tasteful to the crowd of feudal sovereigns, whose privileges were best supported by perpetuating organized anarchy. The early codes, therefore, the Sachsenspiegel, the Schwabenspiegel, the Kayser-Recht, and the Richstich Landrecht, which embodied the judicial proceedings of the Teutonic nations from the thirteenth to the fifteenth centuries, seem to know no other mode of deciding doubtful questions than sacramental purgation and the various forms of ordeal. During the latter portion of this period, it is true, torture begins to appear, but it is an innovation.[1]

The first indications of the modern use of torture show distinctly that its origin is derived from the civil law. In the Latin Kingdoms of the East, the Teutonic races were brought into contact with the remains of the old civilization, impressive even in its decrepitude. It was natural that, in governing the motley collection of Greeks, Syrians, and Franks, for whom they had to legislate, they should adopt some of the institutions which they found in force amid their new possessions, and it is only surprising that torture did not form a more prominent feature in their code. The earliest extant text of the *Assises de Jerusalem* is not older than the thirteenth century,

---

[1] Cæsarius of Heisterbach, writing in 1221, gives a story of an occurrence happening in 1184 which, if not embellished by some later transcriber, would seem to indicate that the judicial use of torture was known at an earlier period than is stated in the text. A young girl, in the disguise of a man, was despatched with letters to Lucius III. by the partisans of Wolmar in his struggle with Rudolph for the bishopric of Trèves. Near Augsburg she was joined by a robber, who, hearing his pursuers approaching, gave her his bag to hold while he retired on some pretext to a thicket. Captured with the stolen property she was condemned, but she told her story to a priest in confession, the wood was surrounded and the robber captured. He was tortured until he confessed the crime. Then he retracted, and the question between the two was settled, at the suggestion of the priest, by the ordeal of hot iron, when the robber's hand was burnt, and the girl's uninjured. The tale is a long one, very romantic in its details, and may very probably have been ornamented by successive scribes.—
—Cæsar. Heisterb. Dial. Mirac. Dist. i. c. xl.

and the blundering and hesitating way in which it recognizes, in a single instance, the use of torture shows how novel was the idea of such procedure to the feudal barons, and how little they understood the principles governing its application. When a murderer was caught in the act by two witnesses, he could be promptly hanged on their testimony, if they were strangers to the victim. If, however, they were relatives, their testimony was held suspect, and the confession of the accused was requisite to his conviction. To obtain this, he was subjected to torture for three days; if he confessed, he was hanged; if obdurate, he was imprisoned for a year and a day, with the privilege of clearing himself during that period by the ordeal of the red-hot iron. If he declined this, and if during his confinement no additional evidence was procured, he was acquitted, and could not be again appealed for the murder.[1]

This shows the transition state of the question. The criminal is caught with the red hand and the evidence of guilt is complete, save that the witnesses may be interested; confession thus becomes requisite, yet the failure to extort it by prolonged torment does not clear the accused; the ordeal is resorted to in order to supplement the torture, and solve the doubts which the latter could not remove; and finally, the criminal is absolved, though he dare not trust the judgment of God, and though the uncertainties in which torture had left the case are not removed.

Italy was the centre from which radiated the influences of the Roman law throughout Western Europe, and, as might be expected, it is to Italy that we must look for the earliest incorporation of torture in the procedures of modern criminal jurisprudence. The Veronese laws in force in 1228 already show a mixture of proceedings suggestive, like the Assises de Jerusalem, of the impending change. In doubtful cases, the podestà was empowered to ascertain the truth of testimony by

---

[1] Assises de Jerusalem, Baisse Court, cap. cclix.

either inquest, torture, or the duel.[1] This shows that the
employment of torture was by this time recognized to some
extent, though as the code is a very full one and this is the
only allusion to it, it evidently had not yet grown into one of
the regular legal processes. So in the legislation of Frederic
II. for his Neapolitan provinces, promulgated in 1231, the
mode in which it is prescribed shows that it was as yet but
sparingly employed. As Frederic was one of the earliest
secular legislators who discountenanced and restricted the
various forms of the ordeal, it was natural that, with his
education and temperament, he should seek to replace them
with the system of the Roman codes which he so much
admired.

When a secret murder or other heinous crime was committed, and the most stringent investigation could not convict
the perpetrators, if the weight of suspicion fell on persons of
humble station and little consequence, they could be tortured
for confession. If no torment could wring from them an
acknowledgment of guilt, or if, as often happened ("prout
accidere novimus in plerisque"), their resolution gave way
under insufferable torment and they subsequently recanted,
then the punishment, in the shape of a fine, was inflicted on
the district where the crime had occurred.[2] From this it is
evident that torture was not exactly a novelty, but that as yet
it was only ventured upon with the lowest and most unprotected class of society, and that confession during its infliction
was not regarded as sufficient for conviction, unless subsequently ratified.

During the remainder of the century, the statutes of many
of the Italian cities show the gradual introduction of torture
to replace the barbarian processes which were not indigenous,[3] and which the traditional hate of the Italian States for

---

[1] Lib. Juris Civilis Veronæ cap. 75 (p. 61).

[2] Constit. Sicular. Lib. I. Tit. xxvii.

[3] Du Boys, Droit Criminel des Peup. Mod. II. 405.

the Tedeschi was not likely to render popular.  That by the middle of the century, indeed, the practical applications of torture had been profoundly studied and were thoroughly understood in all their most inhuman ramifications is sufficiently evident from the accounts which we possess of the fearful cruelties habitually practised by petty despots such as Eccelino da Romano.[1]

The manner in which the use of torture thus in time was superimposed upon the existing customs of Europe is clearly shown in the law of Lubeck.  The mercantile law of the Middle Ages disregarded, as we have seen, all the irregular forms of evidence, such as the ordeal, the judicial duel, &c., and it naturally was not favorable to torture.  As the chief of the Hanse-towns Lubeck, therefore, in its legislation preserved the principles of the mercantile law, but in time these came to be expounded by a race of lawyers imbued with the ideas of the imperial jurisprudence, and little was left of the primitive simplicity of the original code.  Thus the latter, when treating of adultery, simply provides that the accused must clear himself by oath, or be held guilty of the charge ; but a commentary on it, written in 1664, assumes that as the crime is a peculiarly secret one recourse must be at once had to torture where there is colorable ground for suspicion.[2]

About this time we also find, in the increasing rigor and gradual systematizing of the Inquisition, an evidence of the growing disposition to resort to torture, and a powerful element in extending and facilitating its introduction.  The Church had been actively engaged in discountenancing and

---

[1] Monach. Paduan. Chron. Lib. II. ann. 1252-3 (Urstisii Script. Rer. German. p. 594).—Quotidie diversis generibus tormentorum indifferenter tam majores quam minores a carnificibus necabuntur.  Voces terribiles clamantum in tormentis die noctuque audiebantur de altis palatiis. . . . Quotidie sine labore, sine conscientiæ remorsione magna tormenta et inexogitata corporibus hominum infligebat, etc.

[2] Mevii Comment. in Jus Lubecense, Lib. IV. Tit. vi. Art. 4 (Francofurt. 1664).

extirpating the ordeal, and it now threw the immense weight
of its authority in favor of the new process of extorting confessions. When Frederic II., from 1220 to 1239, published
his three constitutions directed against heresy, cruel and un-
sparing as they were, they contained no indication that torture
was even contemplated as a mode of investigation. In con-
formity with the provisions of the Lateran Council of 1215,
parties suspected on insufficient evidence were directed to
prove their innocence by some fitting mode of purgation, and
the same instructions were given by Gregory IX. in 1235.[1]
In 1252, however, when Innocent IV. issued his elaborate
directions for the guidance of the Inquisition in Tuscany and
Lombardy, he ordered the civil magistrates to extort from all
heretics by torture not merely a confession of their own guilt,
but an accusation of all who might be their accomplices; and
this derives additional significance from his reference to similar proceedings as customary in trials of thieves and robbers.[2]
It shows the progress made during the quarter of the century
and the high appreciation entertained by the Church for the
convenience of the new system.

At first the canons of the Church, which prohibited ecclesiastics from being concerned in such matters, or even from
being present, under pain of "irregularity," rendered it
necessary for inquisitors to call in the secular executioners;
but this interfered with promptness and secrecy, and the difficulty was removed with characteristic indirection. A series
of papal bulls from 1256 to 1266 authorized inquisitors and

[1] Concil. Lateran. IV. can. iii.—Goldast. Constit. Imp. I. 293-5.—Harduin. Concil. VII. 164. See above, p. 89.

[2] Teneatur præterea potestas seu rector omnes hæreticos quos captos habu-
erit, cogere citra membri diminutionem et mortis periculum, tanquam vere
latrones et homicidas animarum et fures sacramentorum Dei et fidei Chris-
tianæ, errores suos expresse fateri et accusare alios hæreticos quos sciunt, et
bona eorum, et credentes et receptatores et defensores eorum, sicut cogun-
tur fures et latrones rerum temporalium accusare suos complices et fateri
maleficia quæ fecerunt.—Innocent IV. Bull. Ad extirpanda § 26.

their assistants to grant mutual absolution and dispensation for irregularities,[1] and thus they were able to take the business of inflicting torture into their own hands—an opportunity of which they availed themselves fully.

As yet, however, this did not extend beyond Italy. There is extant a tract, written not long after this time, containing very minute instructions as to the established mode of dealing with the Waldensian sectaries known as the "Poor Men of Lyons." It gives directions to break down their strength and overcome their fortitude by solitary confinement, starvation, and terror, but it abstains from recommending the infliction of absolute and direct torture, while its details are so full that the omission is fair negative evidence that such measures were not then customary.[2]

The whole system of the Inquisition, however, was such as to render the resort to torture inevitable. Its proceedings were secret; the prisoner was carefully kept in ignorance of the exact charges against him, and of the evidence upon which they were based. He was presumed to be guilty, and his judges bent all their energies to force him to confess. To accomplish this, no means were too base or too cruel. According to the tract just quoted, pretended sympathizers were to be let into his dungeon, whose affected friendship might entrap him into an unwary admission; officials armed with fictitious evidence were directed to frighten him with assertions of the testimony obtained against him from supposititious witnesses; and no resources of fraud or guile were to be spared in overcoming the caution and resolution of the poor wretch whose mind, as we have seen, had been carefully weakened by solitude, suffering, hunger, and terror. From this to the rack and estrapade the step was easily taken, and was not

[1] Alex. P. P. IV. Bull. *Ut negotium*, 7 Julii, 1256 (MSS. Doat, XXXI. 196).—Ripoll. Bullar. Ord. Prædic. I. 430.—Mag. Bullar. Roman. I. 132.
[2] Trac. de Hæres. Paup. de Lugd. (Martene Thesaur. V. 1787). In the tract, Frederic II., who died in 1250, is spoken of as " quondam imperator."

long delayed. In 1301, we find even Philippe le Bel protesting against the cruelty of Fulk, the Dominican Inquisitor, and interfering to protect his subjects from the refinements of torture to which, on simple suspicion of heresy, unfortunate victims were habitually exposed.[1] Yet when, a few years later, the same monarch resolved upon the destruction of the Templars, he made the Inquisition the facile instrument to which he resorted, as a matter of course, to extort from De Molay and his knights, with endless repetition of torments, the confessions from which he hoped to recruit his exhausted treasury with their broad lands and accumulated riches.[2]

The history of the Inquisition, however, is too large a subject to be treated here in detail, and it can only be alluded to for the purpose of indicating its influence upon secular law. That influence was immense. The legists who were endeavoring to eradicate the feudal customs could not expect the community to share their admiration of the Roman law, and naturally grasped with eagerness the advantage offered them in adducing the example of ecclesiastical institutions. In founding their new system they could thus hardly avoid copying that which presented itself under all the authority of an infallible Church, and which had been found to work so successfully in unveiling the most secret of hidden crimes, those of faith and belief.[3] When, therefore, men were taught

[1] Clamor validus et insinuatio luctuosa fidelium subditorum . . . processus suos in inquisitionis negotio a captionibus, quæstionibus et excogitatis tormentis incipiens personas quas pro libito asserit hæretica labe notatas, abnegasse Christum . . . . vi vel metu tormentorum fateri compellit.—Lit. Philip. Pulchri (Vaissette, Hist. Gén. de Languedoc, T. IV. Preuves p. 118).

[2] The fearful details of torture collected by Raynouard (Mon. Hist. rel. à la Condamnation des Chev. du Temple) show that the Inquisition by this time was fully experienced in such work.

[3] Simancæ de Christ. Instit. Tit. LXV. No. 19.—To the Inquisition is likewise attributable another of the monstrous iniquities of criminal justice—the denial to the accused of the assistance of counsel. Under the customary law of the feudal courts, the avocat or " avantparlier" was freely admitted,

that in these cases the ordinary forms and safeguards of the law were not to stand in the way of the public good, a principle was enunciated capable of illimitable development.

About the time when Innocent IV. was prescribing torture in Italy, we find the first evidence of its authoritative use in France as an ordinary legal procedure. In December, 1254, an assembly of the nobles of the realm at Paris adopted an ordonnance regulating many points in the administration of justice. Among these occurs an order that persons of good reputation, even though poor, shall not be put to the torture on the evidence of one witness, lest, on the one hand, they may be forced to convict themselves falsely, or, on the other, to buy themselves off from the infliction.[1]

This would seem to indicate that the system of judicial torture was so completely established that its evils and abuses had begun to render themselves apparent and to require restrictive legislation. Yet the contemporaneous remains of jurisprudence show no trace of the custom, and some of them are of a nature to render their silence a negative proof of no little weight. To this period, for instance, belongs the earliest extant coutumier of Normandy, published by Ludewig, and it contains no allusion to torture. The same may be said of the *For de Béarn*,

but such privilege was incompatible with the arbitrary process of which the sole object was to condemn for a crime scarce susceptible of proof. The decretal against heretics issued in 1235 by Gregory IX. forbids all judges, advocates, and notaries from helping the suspected heretic under pain of perpetual deprivation of function—" Item, judices, advocati, et notarii nulli eorum officium suum impendant ; alioquin eodem officio perpetuo sint privati" (Harduin. Concil. VII. 164) ; and the same rule was enjoined " ne " Inquisitionis negotium per advocatorum strepitum retardetur" by the Council of Valence (can. xi.) in 1248 and that of Alby (can. xxiii.) in 1254 (Harduin. VII. 426, 461).

[1] Personas autem honestas vel bonæ famæ, etiam si sint pauperes, ad dictum testis unici, tormentis seu quæstionibus inhibemus, ne ob metum falsum confiteri, vel suam vexationem redimere compellantur.—Fontanon, Edicts et Ordonn. I. 701.—A somewhat different reading is given by Isambert, Anciennes Loix Françaises I. 270.

granted in 1288, and recently printed by MM. Mazure and
Hatoulet, which is very full in its details of judicial procedure.
The collection of the laws of St. Louis, known as the *Établis-
sements*, is likewise free from any instructions or directions as
to its application, though it could scarcely have been omitted
had it formed part of the admitted jurisprudence of the age.
It may be argued, indeed, that these codes and laws assume
the existence of torture, and therefore make no reference to it,
but such an argument would not hold good with respect to
the books of practice which shrewd and experienced lawyers
commenced at that time to draw up for the guidance of courts
in the unsettled period of conflict between the ancient feudal
customs and the invading civil law.   For instance, no text-
book can well be more minute than the *Livres de Justice et de
Plet*, written about the year 1260, by a lawyer of the school
of Orleans, then celebrated as the headquarters of the study of
the imperial jurisprudence.   He manifests upon almost every
page his familiar acquaintance with the civil and canon law,
and he could not possibly have avoided some reference to torture if it had been even an occasional resource in the tribunals
in which he pleaded, and yet he does not in any way allude
to it.

The same conclusion is derivable from the *Coutumes du
Beauvoisis*, written about 1270 by Philippe de Beaumanoir.
In his position as royal bailli, Beaumanoir had obtained the
fullest possible familiarity with all the practical secular jurisprudence of his day, and his tendencies were naturally in
favor of the new system with which St. Louis was endeavoring to break down the feudal customs.   Yet, while he details
at much length every step in all the cases, civil and criminal,
that could be brought into Court, he makes no allusion to
torture as a means of obtaining evidence.   In one passage, it
is true, he seems to indicate that a prisoner could be forced,
while in prison, to criminate himself, but the terms employed
prove clearly that this was not intended to include the

administration of torment.[1] In another place, moreover, when
treating of robberies, he directs that all suspected parties
should be long and closely confined, but that, if they cannot
be convicted by external evidence, they must at last be discharged.[2] All this is clearly incompatible with the theory of
torture.

The *Conseil* of Pierre de Fontaines, which was probably
written about the year 1260, affords the same negative evidence in its full instructions for all the legal proceedings then
in use. In these three works, notwithstanding the reforms
attempted by St. Louis, the legist seems to imagine no other
solution than the wager of battle for the settlement of doubtful
cases, wherein testimony is insufficient. The form of trial is
still public, in the feudal or royal courts, and every opportunity is given both for the attack and the defence. The
work of de Fontaines, moreover, happens to furnish another
proof that he wrote at the commencement of a transition
period, during which the use of torture was introduced. In
the oldest MSS. of his work, which are considered to date
from 1260 to 1280, there is a passage to the effect that a
man convicted of crime may appeal, if he has not confessed,
or, when he has confessed, if it has been in consequence of
some understanding (*covent*). In later MSS., transcribed in
the early part of the fourteenth century, the word "covent"

[1] Cil qui est pris et mis en prison, soit por meffet ou por dete, tant comme
il est en prison il n'est tenus à respondre à riens c'on li demande fors es cas
tant solement por quoi il fu pris. Et s'on li fet respondre autre coze contre
se volenté, et sor ce qu'il allige qu'il ne veut pas respondre tant comme il
soit en prison; tout ce qui est fait contre li est de nule valeur, car il pot
tout rapeler quand il est hors de prison.—Beaumanoir, cap. LII. § xix.

[2] Quant tel larrecin sunt fet, le justice doit penre toz les souspeçonneus
et fere moult de demandes, por savoir s'il porra fere cler ce qui est orbe.
Et bien les doit en longe prison tenir et destroite, et toz cex qu'il ara
souspechonneus par malvese renommée. El si'l ne pot en nule maniere
savoir le verité du fet, il les doit delivrer, se nus ne vient avant qui partie
se voille fere d'aus acuser droitement du larrecin.—Ibid. cap. XXXI. § vi.

is replaced by "tourmenz,"[1] thus showing not only the introduction of torture during the interval, but also that a conviction obtained by it was not final.

The Ordonnance of 1254, indeed, as far as it relates to torture, is asserted by modern criticism to have been applicable only to Languedoc.[2] If so, its importance is reduced to a minimum, for in the document as registered in the council of Béziers in 1255, the section respecting torture is omitted,[3] and this would seem to show that even in the south, where the traditions of the Roman law were continuous, torture was still regarded as an innovation not to be legally sanctioned. Still it was gradually winning its way against popular repugnance, for we have in 1260 a charter from Alphonse de Poitiers to the town of Auzon (Auvergne), in which he grants exemption from torture in all trials irrespective of the gravity of the crime.[4]

While giving due weight, however, to all this, we must not lose sight of the fact that the laws and regulations prescribed in royal ordonnances and legal text-books were practically applicable only to a portion of the population. All non-nobles, who had not succeeded in extorting special privileges by charter from their feudal superiors, were exposed to the caprices of barbarous and irresponsible power. It was a maxim of feudal law that God alone could intervene between the lord and his villein—"Mès par notre usage n'a-il, entre toi et ton vilein, juge fors Deu"[5]—the villein being by no

[1] Si li hons n'est connoissans de son mesfet, ou s'il l'a coneu et ce a esté par covent, s'en li fait jugement, apeler en puet.—Conseil, ch. xxii. art. 28 (Édition Marnier, Paris, 1846).

[2] Tanon, Registre Criminel de la justice de S. Martin-des-Champs, Introd. p. lxxxvi. (Paris, 1877); Vaissette, Ed. Privat, VIII. 1348.—L'Oiseleur (Les Crimes et les Peines, Paris, 1863, p. 113) says that it was enacted for the baillages of Beauvais and Cahors, but we have seen from Beaumanoir that torture was not used in the Beauvoisis.

[3] Baluz. Concil. Gall. Narbon. p. 75.

[4] Chassaing, Spicilegium Brivatense, p. 92.

[5] Conseil ch. xxi. art. 8.

means necessarily a serf; and another rule prohibited absolutely the villein from appealing from the judgment of his lord.[1] Outside of law, and unauthorized by coutumiers and ordonnances, there must, under such institutions, have been habitually vast numbers of cases in which the impatient temper of the lord would seek a solution of doubtful matters, in the potent cogency of the rack or scourge, rather than waste time or dignity in endeavoring to cross-question the truth out of a quick-witted criminal.

Still, as an admitted legal procedure, the introduction of torture was very gradual. The *Olim*, or register of cases decided by the Parlement of Paris, extends, with some intervals, from 1255 to 1318, and the paucity of affairs recorded in which torture was used shows that it could not have been habitually resorted to during this period. The first instance, indeed, only occurs in 1283, when the Bishop of Amiens complains of the bailli of that town for having tried and tortured three clerks in defiance of the benefit of clergy which entitled them to exemption from secular jurisdiction. The bailli pleaded ignorance of their ecclesiastical character, and his plea was admitted as sufficient.[2] The next instance of the use of torture is found in 1299, when the royal bailli of Senlis cites the mayor and jurats of that town before the Parlement, because in a case of theft they had applied the question to a suspected criminal; and although theft was within their competence, the bailli argued that torture was an incident of "haute justice" which the town did not possess. The decision was in favor of the municipality.[3] The next year (1300) we find a clerk, wearing habit and tonsure, complaining that the royal officials of the town of Villeneuve in Rouergue had tortured him in divers ways, with ropes and heavy weights, heated eggs and fire, so that he was crippled,

---

[1] Fontaines, Conseil, art. 14. Et encor ne puisse li vileins fausser le jugement son seignor.

[2] Actes du Parlement de Paris, I. 382 (Paris, 1863).

[3] Olim. T. II. p. 451.

and had been forced to expend three hundred livres Tournois in medicines and physicians. This, with other proper damages, he prays may be made good to him by the perpetrators, and the arrêt of the Parlement orders their persons and property to be seized, and their possessions valued, in order that the amount may be properly assessed among them.[1] Philippe le Bel, notwithstanding his mortal quarrel with the papacy—or perhaps in consequence of it—was ever careful of the rights and privileges of the clergy, among which the immunity from secular jurisdiction and consequently from torture was prominent. The case evidently turned upon that point.

The fourth case does not present itself until 1306. Two Jews, under accusation of larceny by their brethren, complain that they had been illegally tortured by the bailli of Bourges, and though one of them under the infliction had confessed to complicity, the confession is retracted and damages of three thousand livres Tournois are demanded. On the other hand, the bailli maintains that his proceedings are legal, and asks to have the complainants punished in accordance with the confession. The Parlement adopts a middle course; it acquits the Jews and awards no damages, showing that the torture was legal and a retracted confession valueless.[2]

The fifth case, which occurs in 1307, is interesting as having for its reporter no less a personage than Guillaume de Nogaret, the captor of Boniface VIII. A certain Guillot de Ferrières, on a charge of robbery, had been tried by the judge of Villelongue and Nicolas Bourges, royal chatelain of Mont-Ogier. The latter had tortured him repeatedly and cruelly, so that he was permanently crippled, and his uncle, Étienne de Ferrières, Chatelain of Montauban, claims damages. The decision condemns Nicolas Bourges in a mulct of one thousand livres Tournois, half to Guillot for his sufferings and half to Étienne for his expenses, besides a fine to the

[1] Olim. III. 49-50.      [2] Ibid. III. 185-6.

crown.[1] It is evident that judges were not allowed to inflict unlimited torment at their pleasure.

The sixth case, occurring in 1310, may be passed over, as the torture was not judicial, but merely a brutal outrage by a knight on a noble damsel who resisted his importunities: though it may be mentioned that of the fine inflicted on him, fifteen hundred livres Tournois enured to the crown and only one hundred to the victim.[2]

The seventh case took place in 1312, when Michael de Poolay, accused of stealing a sum of money from Nicolas Loquetier, of Rouen, was subjected to a long imprisonment and torture at Château-Neuf de Lincourt, and was then brought to the Châtelet at Paris, where he was again examined without confession or conviction. Meanwhile, the real criminal confessed the theft, and Nicolas applies to the Parlement for the liberation of Michael, which is duly granted.[3]

A long interval then occurs, and we do not hear of torture again until 1318, when Guillaume Nivard, a money-changer of Paris, was accused of coining, and was tortured by the Prevôt of the Châtelet. He contends that it was illegal, while the Prevôt asserts that his jurisdiction empowered him to administer it. The Parlement investigates the case, and acquits the prisoner, but awards him no damages.[4]

The essentially commonplace and trivial character of these cases has its interest in showing that the practice of appealing to the Parlement was not confined to weighty matters, and therefore that the few instances in which torture was involved in such appeals afford a fair index of the rarity of its use during this period. These cases, too, have seemed to me worth reciting, as they illustrate the principles upon which its application was based in the new jurisprudence, and the tentative and uncertain character of the progress by which the primitive customs of the European races were gradually becoming supplanted by the resuscitated Roman law.

[1] Olim. III. 221–2.
[2] Ibid. III. 505–6.
[3] Ibid. III. 751–2.
[4] Ibid. III. 1299.

A few instances, moreover, are on record in which torture was used in affairs of state. Thus in 1304 we find Charles of Valois torturing a Flemish beguine who was accused of an attempt to poison him. The mode adopted was the application of fire to the soles of the victim's feet, and though she was said to have confessed, still he liberated her after a short imprisonment.[1] In the frightful scandal, also, of the daughters-in-law of Philippe le Bel, which occurred in 1314, though torture does not seem to have been used in examining the principals, either the princesses or their paramours, it was freely employed upon the numerous persons who were accused as accessories.[2] In 1315, during the long trial of Enguerrand de Marigny, sacrificed after the death of Philippe le Bel to the hatred of Charles of Valois, torture was freely used to obtain evidence from his dependents;[3] and in the same year Raoul de Presles, accused of the death of the late king, was exposed to torture without obtaining a confession, and was finally liberated.[4]

This undermining of the ancient customs had not been allowed to continue uninterrupted by protest and resistance. In the closing days of the reign of Philippe le Bel the feudal powers of France awoke to the danger with which they were menaced by the extension of the royal prerogative during the preceding half-century. A league was formed which seemed to threaten the existence of the institutions so carefully nurtured by St. Louis and his successors. It was too late, however, and though the storm broke on the new and untried royalty of Louis Hutin, the crown lawyers were already too powerful for the united seigneurie of the kingdom. When the various provinces presented their complaints and their demands for the restoration of the old order of things, they were met with a little skilful evasion, a few artful promises, some con-

---

[1] Guill. de Nangis Continuat. ann. 1304.
[2] Ibid. ann. 1314.                    [3] Ibid. ann. 1315.
[4] Grandes Chroniques, T. V. p. 221 (Ed. Paris, 1837).

cessions which were readily withdrawn, and negatives care-fully couched in language which seemed to imply assent.

Among the complaints we find the introduction of torture enumerated as an innovation upon the established rights of the subject, but the lawyers who drew up the replies of the king took care to infringe as little as they could upon a system which their legal training led them to regard as an immense improvement in procedure, especially as it enabled them to supersede the wager of battle, which they justly regarded as the most significant emblem of feudal independence.

The movement of the nobles resulted in obtaining from the king a series of charters for the several provinces, by which he defined, as vaguely, indeed, as he could, the extent of royal jurisdiction claimed, and in which he promised to relieve them from certain grievances. In some of these charters, as in those granted to Britanny, to Burgundy, and to Amiens and Verman-dois, there is no allusion made to torture.[1] In the two latter, the right to the wager of battle is conceded, which may ex-plain why the nobles of those provinces were careless to pro-tect themselves from a process which they could so easily avoid by an appeal to the sword. In the charter of Languedoc, all that Louis would consent to grant was a special exemption to those who had enjoyed the dignity of capitoul, consul, or de-curion of Toulouse and to their children, and even this trifling concession did not hold good in cases of *lèse-majesté* or other matters particularly provided for by law; the whole clause, indeed, is borrowed from the Roman law, which may have reconciled Louis's legal advisers to it, more especially as, for the first time in French jurisprudence, it recognized the crime of *lèse-majesté*, which marked the triumph of the civil over the feudal law.[2] Normandy only obtained a vague promise that no freeman should be subjected to torture unless he were the object of violent presumptions in a capital offence, and

---

[1] Isambert, Anciennes Loix Françaises, III. 131, 60, 65.
[2] Ordonnance, 1ier Avril, 1315, art. xix. (Ibid. III. 58).

that the torture should be so regulated as not to imperil life
or limb; and though the Normans were dissatisfied with this
charter, and succeeded in getting a second one some months
later, they gained nothing on this point.[1]

The official documents concerning Champagne have been
preserved to us more in detail. The nobles of that province
complained that the royal prevôts and serjeants entered upon
their lands to arrest their men and private persons, whom they
then tortured in defiance of their customs and privileges ("contre leurs coustumes et libertez"). To this Louis promised to
put an end. The nobles further alleged that, in contravention
of the ancient usages and customs of Champagne ("contre les
us et coustumes enciens de Champagne"), the royal officers
presumed to torture nobles on suspicion of crime, even though
not caught in the act, and without confession. To this Louis
vaguely replied that for the future no nobles should be tortured, except under such presumptions as might render it
proper, in law and reason, to prevent crime from remaining
unpunished; and that no one should be convicted unless confession was persevered in for a sufficient time after torture.[2]
This, of course, was anything but satisfactory, and the Cham-
penois were not disposed to accept it; but all that they could
obtain after another remonstrance was a simple repetition of
the promise that no nobles should be tortured except under
capital accusations.[3] The struggle apparently continued, for,
in 1319, we find Philippe le Long, in a charter granted to
Périgord and Quercy, promising that the proceedings preliminary to torture should be had in the presence of both parties,
doubtless to silence complaints as to the secret character which
criminal investigations were assuming.[4]

[1] Cart. Norman I. Mar. 1315, cap. xi. Cart. II. Jul. 1315, cap. xv.
(Ibid. 51, 109).

[2] Ordonn. Mai 1315, art. v. xiv. (Bourdot de Richebourg, III. 233-4).

[3] Ordonn. Mars 1315, art. ix. (Ibid. p. 235). This ordonnance is in-
correctly dated. It was issued towards the end of May, subsequently to
the above.

[4] Ordonn. Jul. 1319, art. xxii. (Isambert, III. 227).

The use of torture was thus permanently established in the judicial machinery of France as one of the incidents in the great revolution which destroyed the feudal power. Even yet, however, it was not universal, especially where communes had the ability to preserve their franchises. Count Beugnot has published, as an appendix to the *Olim*, a collection known as the *Tout Lieu de St. Disier*, consisting of 314 decisions of doubtful cases referred by the magistrates of St. Dizier to the city of Ypres for solution, as they were bound to do by their charter. This especially directed that all cases not therein provided for should be decided according to the customs of Ypres, and consequently, for two hundred and fifty years, whenever the eschevins of the little town in Champagne felt in doubt they referred the matter to the lordly burghers of Flanders as to a court of last resort. In the *Tout Lieu* the cases date mostly from the middle third of the fourteenth century, and were selected as a series of established precedents. The fact that, throughout the whole series, torture is not alluded to in a single instance shows that it was a form of procedure unknown to the court of the eschevins of St. Dizier, and even to the superior jurisdiction of the bailli of their suzerain, the Seigneur of Dampierre. Many of these cases seem peculiarly adapted to the new inquisitorial system. Thus, in 1335, a man was attacked and wounded in the street at night. A crowd collected at his cries, and he named the assailant. No rule was more firmly established than the necessity of two impartial witnesses to justify condemnation, and the authorities of St. Dizier, not knowing what course to take, applied as usual for instructions to the magistrates of Ypres. The latter defined the law to be that the court should visit the wounded man on his sick-bed and adjure him by his salvation to tell the truth. If on this he named any one and subsequently died, the accused should be pronounced guilty; if, on the other hand, he recovered, then the accused should be treated according to his reputation : that is, if of good fame, he should

be acquitted; if of evil repute, he should be banished.[1]   No
case more inviting under the theory of torture could well be
imagined, and yet neither the honest burghers of St. Dizier
nor the powerful magnates of Ypres seem to have entertained
the idea of its application.   So, again, when the former inquire what proof is sufficient when a man accuses another of
stealing, the answer is that no evidence will convict, unless
the goods alleged to be stolen are found in the possession of
the accused.[2]   The wealthy city of Lille equally rejected the
process of torture.   The laws in force there, about the year
1350, prescribe that in cases of homicide conviction ought to
be based upon absolute evidence, but where this is unattainable then the judges are allowed to decide on mere opinion
and belief, for uncertain matters cannot be rendered certain.[3]
In such a scheme of legislation, the extortion of a confession
as a condition precedent to condemnation can evidently find
no place.

Attempts to introduce torture in Aquitaine were apparently
made, but they seem to have been resisted.   In the Coutumier of Bordeaux, during the fourteenth century there is a
significant declaration that the sages of old did not wish to
deprive men of their liberties and privileges.   Torture, therefore, was prohibited in the case of all citizens except those of
evil repute and declared to be infamous.   The nearest approach to it that was permitted was tying the hands behind
the back, without using pulleys to lift the accused from the
ground.[4]

[1] Tout Lieu de Saint Disier, cap. cclxxii. (Olim, T. II. Append. p. 856).
[2] Ibid. cap. cclxxiii.
[3] Roisin, Franchises, Lois et Coutumes de Lille, p. 119.   Thus, "on
puet et doit demander de veir et de oir," but when this is impossible, "on
doit et puet bien demander et enquerre de croire et cuidier.   Et sour croire
et sour cuidier avoec un veritet aparent de veir et d'oir, et avoec l'omechide
aparant, on puet bien jugier, lonc l'usage anchyen, car d'oscure fait oscure
veritet."
[4] Rabanis, Revue Hist. de Droit, 1861, p. 515.—No volgoren los savis
antiquament qu'om pergossa sa franquessa ni sa libertat.

By this time, however, places where torture was not used were exceptional. An allusion to it in 1335 in the register of the court of the Priory of St. Martin-des-Champs shows that already it was. not confined to the royal jurisdiction, but that it was recognized as an incident to the possession of haute justice.[1] By a document of 1359, it appears that it was the custom to torture all malefactors brought to the Châtelet of Paris,[2] and though privileged persons constantly endeavored to exempt themselves from it, as the consuls of Villeneuve in 1371,[3] and the Seigneur d'Argenton in 1385,[4] other privileged persons as constantly sought to obtain the power of inflicting it, as shown in the charter of Milhaud, granted in 1369, wherein the consuls of that town are honored with the special grace that no torture shall be administered except in their presence, if they desire to attend.[5] At the end of the century, indeed, the right to administer torture in cases wherein the accused denied the charge was regularly established among the privileges of haute justiciers.[6]

By this time criminal procedures were fully recognized as divisible into two classes—the *procès ordinaire* and the *procès extraordinaire*. The former of these was carried on by the form of inquest, the latter by inquisition, in which torture was habitually employed. There were no definite rules to determine the class to which any given case might be referred, and though at the beginning of the fourteenth century the

[1] Registre Criminel de la Justice de St. Martin-des-Champs, p. 50.

[2] Du Cange s. v. *Quæstionarius*.

[3] Letters granting exemption from torture to the consuls of Villeneuve for any crimes committed by them were issued in 1371 (Isambert, V. 352). These favors generally excepted the case of high treason.

[4] He pleaded his rank as baron as an exemption from the torture, but was overruled. Dumoulin, however, admits that persons of noble blood are not to be as readily exposed to it as those of lower station.—Desmaze, Les Pénalités Anciennes, d'après des Textes inédits, p. 39 (Paris, 1866).

[5] Du Cange s. v. *Quæstio* No. 3.

[6] Pour denier mettre à question et tourment.—Jean Desmarres, Décisions, Art. 295 (Du Boys, Droit Criminel II. 48).

*procès ordinaire*, as its name infers, was the usual mode of trying criminals, gradually the choice between the two was left to the discretion of the judge, and this discretion leaned so constantly in favor of the *procès extraordinaire* that by the close of the century it had become the rule rather than the exception.[1]

This is very clearly shown by the records of the Châtelet of Paris from 1389 to 1392,[2] which enable us to form a tolerably distinct idea of the part assigned to torture in the criminal procedure of this period. It had virtually become the main reliance of the tribunal, for the cases in which it was not employed appear to be simply exceptional. Noble blood afforded no exemption, for gentlemen were placed on the rack for petty crimes as freely as roturiers.[3] No avenue of escape was open to the miserable culprit. If he denied the alleged offence, he was tortured at once for a confession, and no settled rules seem to have existed as to the amount of evidence requisite to justify it. Thus, in one case, a man on the *tresteau* relating the misdeeds of his evil life chanced to mention the name of another as a professional thief. The latter was immediately arrested, and though there was no specific crime charged against him, he was tortured repeatedly until sufficient confession was extracted from him to justify his execution.[4] If, on the other hand, the prisoner persistently denied his guilt there was no limit to the repetition of the torture, and yet, even when no confession could be thus extracted, the failure did not always serve to exempt him

[1] L. Tanon, Registre Criminel de la Justice de S. Martin-des-Champs, Introd. p. lxxxv. (Paris, 1877).

[2] Registre Criminel du Châtelet de Paris. Publié pour la première fois par la Société des Bibliophiles Français. 2 tom. 8vo. Paris, 1864.

[3] Ibid. I. 9, 14.

[4] Ibid. I. 143. See also the similar case of Raoulin du Pré (p. 149), who recanted on the scaffold and protested his innocence " sur la mort qu'il attendoit à avoir et recevoir presentement," but who nevertheless was executed. Also that of Perrin du Quesnoy (p. 164).

from punishment.[1] If he retracted the confession extorted from him, he was tortured again and again until he ceased to assert his innocence, for it was a positive necessity for conviction that the confession under torture should be confirmed by the prisoner without constraint—"sans aucune force, paour ou contrainte de gehayne"—when sentence came to be passed upon him outside of the torture-chamber.

If, again, the luckless prisoner confessed the crime of which he stood accused, he was further promptly tortured to find out what other offences he might at some previous time have committed. This, which we will see hereafter, continued to be to the end one of the worst abuses of the torture system, was already a practice at least half a century old,[2] and it had become so habitual that it is scarcely worth while to cite particular examples, though the case of Gervaise Caussois may be briefly referred to on account of its quaintness. Arrested for stealing some iron tools, he promptly confessed the crime. Among the reasons on record for proceeding to

---

[1] See the case of Berthaut Lestalon (Ibid. p. 501) accused of sundry petty thefts and tortured unsuccessfully. The court decided that in view of the little value of the articles stolen and of their having been recovered by the owners, the prisoner should be tortured again, when, if he confessed, he should be hanged, and if he still denied, he should have his right ear cropped and be banished from Paris. This logical verdict was carried out. No confession was obtained, and he was punished accordingly. Somewhat similar was the case of Jehan de Warlus (Ibid. p. 157), who was punished after being tortured five times without confession; also that of Jaquet de Dun (Ibid. p. 494).

[2] In the Registre Criminel de St. Martin-des-Champs the cases are recorded with too much conciseness to give details as to the process, only the charge and the sentence being stated. It frequently happens, however, that a man convicted of some petty larceny is stated to have confessed more serious previous crimes, which necessarily implies their confession being extorted. See, for instance, the case of Jehannin Maci, arrested in 1338 for having in his possession two brass pots, the stealing of which he not only confessed but also "plusures murtres et larrecins avoir fais" for which he was duly drawn on a hurdle and hanged (*op. cit.* pp. 120–1). The case of Phelipote de Monine (p. 178) is also suggestive.

torture him in order to elicit an account of his other presumed misdemeanors, is included the excellent one, "attendu qu'il est scabieux." Under the torment the poor wretch accused himself of some other petty thefts, but even this did not satisfy his examiners, for the next day he was again brought before them and bound to the *tresteau*, when he confessed a few more trifling larcenies. Having apparently thus obtained enough evidence to satisfy their consciences, his judges mercifully hanged him without further infliction.[1] In fact, the whole matter apparently was left very much to the discretion of the court, which seems to have been bound by no troublesome limitations to its curiosity in investigating the past career of the miserable beings brought before it.

How that discretion was habitually exercised may be judged from the case of a certain Fleurant de Saint-Leu, who was brought up for examination Jan. 4, 1390, on the charge of stealing a silver buckle. Denying the accusation, he was twice tortured with increasing severity, until he confessed the alleged crime, but asserted it to be a first offence. On Jan. 8th the court decided that as the petty theft was insufficient to merit death, he should be tortured repeatedly to ascertain whether he had not been guilty of something else worthy of capital punishment. On that day he was therefore thrice exposed to the question, in an ascending scale of severity, but without success. On the 13th he was again twice tortured, when the only admission that rewarded the examiners was that three years before he had married a prostitute at Senlis. This uncommon obduracy seems to have staggered the court, for he was then kept in his dungeon until April 9th, when his case was carefully considered, and though nothing had been extorted from him since his first confession, he was condemned, and was hanged the same day—thus proving how purely gratuitous were the fearful sufferings to which he had been

---

[1] Registre Criminel du Châtelet de Paris, I. 36.

exposed in order to gratify the curiosity or satisfy the consciences of his remorseless judges.[1]

Few criminals, however, gave so much trouble as Fleurant. The "petit et grand tresteaux," on which the torture was customarily administered, were a sword which cut many a Gordian knot, and, by rendering the justice of the Châtelet sharp and speedy, saved the court a world of trouble. It was by no means unusual for the accused to be arraigned, tortured, condemned, and executed all on the same day,[2] and not a few of the confessions read as though they were fictions composed by the accused in order to escape by death from the interminable suffering to which they were exposed. The sameness frequently visible in a long catalogue of crimes seems to indicate this, but it is especially notable in some singular cases of parties accused of poisoning wells throughout the north of France, when there was an evident necessity for the authorities to satisfy the excited populace by procuring them some victims, and the unfortunate wretches who were arrested on suspicion were tortured until they were ready to accuse themselves of anything.[3] In one case, indeed, the prisoner stated that he had known a person

[1] Ibid. I. 201–209.—Somewhat similar was the case of Marguerite de la Pinele (Ibid. p. 322), accused of stealing a ring, which she confessed under torture. As she did not, however, give a satisfactory account of some money found upon her, though her story was partially confirmed by other evidence, she was again twice tortured. This was apparently done to gratify the curiosity of her judges, for, though no further confession was extracted from her, she was duly buried alive.

Crimes for which a man was hanged or decapitated were punished in a woman by burying or burning. Jews were executed by being hanged by the heels between two large dogs suspended by the hind legs—a frightful death, the fear of which sometimes produced conversion and baptism on the gallows (Ibid. II. 43).

[2] Ibid. I. pp. 1, 268, 289; II. 66, etc.

[3] Ibid. I. 419–475.—The same result is evident in a very curious case in which an old sorceress and a young "fille de vie" were accused of bewitching a bride and groom, the latter of whom had been madly loved by the girl (Ibid. I. p. 327).

tortured at the Châtelet with such severity that he died in the
hands of his torturers, and for himself he declared, after one
or two inflictions, that he would confess whatever would relieve
him from a repetition of what he had endured.[1]

Yet, with all this reckless disregard of the plainest principles
of justice, the torture process had not yet entirely obliterated
the memory of the old customary law. The prisoner was not,
as we shall see practised hereafter, kept in ignorance of the
charges against him and of the adverse testimony. The accusation was always made known to him, and when witnesses
were examined, the record is careful to specify that it was
done in his presence.[2] The court deliberated in private, but
the prisoner was brought before it to receive condemnation
either to torture or to death. Facilities were likewise afforded
him to procure evidence in his favor, when the swift justice of
the Châtelet might allow him leisure for such defence, for his
friends were allowed to see him in prison during the intervals
of his trial.[3]

Thus, in the capital, the royal power, aided by the civil
lawyers, was fast encroaching upon all the liberties of the
subject, but in the provinces a more stubborn resistance was
maintained. It was some little time after the period under
consideration that the ancient Coutumier of Britanny was
compiled, and in it we find the use of torture, though fully
established as a judicial expedient, yet subjected to much
greater restrictions. A prisoner, accused of a capital crime
and denying the charge, was liable to torture only if positive
evidence was unattainable, and then only if he had been under
accusation within the previous five years. Moreover, if he
endured its application three times without confession, he
was discharged acquitted as one in whose favor God would
work a miracle[4]—thus showing how torture was assimilated

[1] Ibid. I. 516.
[2] Ibid. I. 151, 163, 164, 173–77, 211, 269, 285, 306, 350, etc.
[3] See, for instance, the case of Pierre Fournet (Ibid. I. 516).
[4] Très Ancienne Cout. de Bretagne, cap. CI. (Bourdot de Richebourg

in the popular mind to the ordeal which it had supplanted. Such escape indeed might well be regarded as a miracle, for the reckless barbarity of the age had little scruple in pushing the administration of the question to the utmost rigor. About this same time, the Council of Reims, in 1408, drew up a series of instructions for the bishops of the province in visiting their dioceses; and among the abuses enumerated for investigation was whether the judges were in the habit of torturing prisoners to death on feast days.[1] It was not the cruelty, but the sacrilege to which the Church took exception.

Even in Germany, the citadel of feudalism, the progress of the new ideas and the influence of the Roman law had spread to such an extent that in the Golden Bull of Charles IV., in 1356, there is a provision allowing the torture of slaves to incriminate their masters in cases of sedition against any prince of the empire;[2] and the form of expression employed shows that this was an innovation. Liége, which at that period formed part of the empire, furnishes us with a case in 1376 which shows not only that torture then was an habitual resource in procedure, but also that it was applied as illogically there as we have seen it in Paris. The young wife of a burgher named Gilles Surlet was found one morning strangled in bed. The husband, as though conscious of innocence, at once presented himself to the authorities asserting with fearful oaths his ignorance of the crime. A servant girl of the household was then arrested, and she, without torture, immediately confessed that she had committed the murder; but the judges, not satisfied with this, submitted her to the question, when she denied her guilt with the most

IV. 224–5)—"Et s'il se peut passer sans faire confession en la gehenne, ou les jons, il se sauveroit, et il apparestroit bien que Dieu montreroit miracles pour luy."

[1] Concil. Remens. ann. 1408, cap. 49 (Martene Ampliss. Collect. VII. 420).

[2] Bull. Aur. cap. xxiv. § 9 (Goldast. I. 365).

provoking constancy. Suspicion then grew against the husband, and he was duly tortured without extorting a confession, though at the same time he declared that the girl was innocent; and on being taken back to his cell he strangled himself during the night. The chronicler does not record what was the fate of the girl, but the body of Gilles was treated as that of a murderer—it was dragged to the place of execution and broken on the wheel, while the superstitious did not fail to note that on this dreary transit it was accompanied by a black hog, which refused to be driven away until the gallows was reached.[1]

In Corsica, at the same period, we find the use of torture fully established, though subject to careful restrictions. In ordinary cases, it could only be employed by authority of the governor, to whom the judge desiring to use it transmitted all the facts of the case; the governor then issued an order, at his pleasure, prescribing the mode and degree to which it might be applied.[2] In cases of treason, however, these limitations were not observed, and the accused was liable to its infliction as far and as often as might be found requisite to effect a purpose.[3]

The Italian communities seem to have still at this period preserved some limitations on the application of torture. In Milan, in 1338, it could be only employed in capital cases where there was evidence or public repute; it could only be ordered by the lord of the city, his vicar, the podestà, and the criminal judges, and even these were heavily fined if they used it illegally or elsewhere than in the accustomed torture-chamber; the abuse of torturing witnesses had already been introduced, but the judge was warned that this could be done only when the witness swore to having been personally present and then varied in his testimony or gave false evidence. Torture, moreover, could only be inflicted once unless new

---

[1] Chron. Cornel. Zantfleit, ann. 1376 (Martene Ampl. Coll. V. 308-9).

[2] Statut. Criminali cap. xiv. (Gregorj, Statuti di Corsica, p. 101).

[3] Ibid. cap lx. (p. 163).

evidence supervened.[1] In the statutes of Mirandola, revised in 1386, it could not be employed in cases which did not involve corporal punishment or a fine of at least twenty-five lire ; nor even then unless the podestà submitted all the evidence to the accused and gave him a sufficient and definite term in which to purge himself.[2] In Piacenza, about the same period, torture was guarded with even more careful restrictions. There is no indication that witnesses were exposed to it. Every effort to obtain testimony was to be exhausted, and the accused was to be afforded full opportunities for defence before he could be subjected to it, and then there must be sufficient indications of guilt, mere rumor being inadequate to justify it. More-over, except in cases of high treason, theft, highway robbery, assassination, and arson, a single judge could not order it, but the case had to be submitted to all the judges and the podestà, who determined by a majority in secret ballot whether it should be employed. If any of these formalities were omitted, the confession extorted was invalid, and the judge was mulcted in a fine of a hundred lire.[3]

The peculiar character of Venetian civilization made tor-ture almost a necessity. The atmosphere of suspicion and secrecy which surrounded every movement of that republican despotism, the mystery in which it delighted to shroud itself, and the pitiless nature of its legislation conspired to render torture an indispensable resource. How freely it was admin-istered, especially in political affairs, is well illustrated in the statutes of the State Inquisition, where the merest suspicion is sufficient to authorize its application. Thus, if a senatorial secretary were observed to be more lavish in his expenditures than his salary would appear to justify, he was at once sus-pected of being in the pay of some foreign minister, and

[1] Statuta Criminalia Mediolani e tenebris in lucem edita, cap. 3, 24–28 (Bergomi, 1694).

[2] Statuti della Terra del Comune della Mirandola, Modena, 1885, p. 91.

[3] Statuta et Decreta antiqua Civitatis Placentiæ, Lib. v. Rubr. 96 (Placen-tiæ, 1560, fol. 63b).

spies were ordered on his track. If he were then simply found to be absent from his house at undue hours, he was immediately to be seized and put to the torture. So, if any one of the innumerable secret spies employed by the inquisitors were insulted by being called a spy, the offender was arrested and tortured to ascertain how he had guessed the character of the emissary.[1] Human life and human suffering were of little account in the eyes of the cold and subtle spirits who moulded the policy of the mistress of the Adriatic.

The rude mountaineers of the Valtelline preserved to a later date their respect for the ancient guarantees of the law. In their statutes as revised in 1548 torture is indeed permitted, but only in case of persons accused of crimes involving the penalty of blood. In accusations of less heinous offences and in matters concerning money, it was strictly forbidden; and even in cases where it was allowed it could not be employed without the assent of the central authority of the territory. When proceedings were had by inquisition, moreover, all the evidence was submitted to the accused, and a sufficient delay was accorded to him in which to frame a defence before he could be ordered to the torture. Thus were avoided the worst abuses to which the system had been made subservient long before that time in all the surrounding regions.[2]

Other races adopted the new system with almost equal hesitation. Thus in Hungary the first formal embodiment of torture in the law occurs in 1514, and though the terms employed show that it had been previously used to some extent, yet the restrictions laid down manifest an extreme jealousy of its abuse. Mere suspicion was not sufficient. To justify its application, a degree of proof was requisite which was almost competent for condemnation, and the nature of this evidence is well exemplified in the direction that if a judge himself

---

[1] Statuts de l'Inquisition d'Etat, I⁰ Supp. §§ 20, 21 (Daru).

[2] Li Statuti de Valtellina Riformati nella Città di Coira nell' anno del S. MDXLVIII. Stat. Crimin. cap. 8, 9, 10 (Poschiavo, 1549).

witnessed a murder, he could not order the homicide to be tortured unless there was other testimony sufficient, for he could not be both witness and judge, and his knowledge of the crime belonged to his private and not to his judicial capacity.[1] With such refinements, there would seem to be little danger of the extension of the custom.

In Poland, torture does not make its appearance until the fifteenth century, and then it was introduced gradually, with strict instructions to the tribunals to use the most careful discretion in its administration.[2] Until, at least, the seventeenth century, there remained in force laws of Casimir the Great promulgated in the fourteenth, prohibiting any prosecution not brought by a proper accuser, in whose presence alone could the matter be heard, thus showing that the inquisitorial process found no foothold in the Polish courts.[3] In Russia, the first formal allusion to it is to be found in the Ulagenié Zakonof, a code promulgated in 1497, by Ivan III., which merely orders that persons accused of robbery, if of evil repute, may be tortured to supply deficiencies of evidence; but as the duel was still freely allowed to the accused, the use of torture must have been merely incidental.[4] From another source, dating about 1530, we learn that it was customary to extort confessions from witches by pouring upon them from a height a small stream of cold water; and in cases of contumacious and stubborn criminals, the finger-nails were wrenched off with little wooden wedges.[5] Still, torture makes

---

[1] Synod. Reg. ann. 1514, Prooem. (Batthyani Legg. Eccles. Hung. I. 574). According to some authorities, this was a general rule—" Judex quamvis viderit committi delictum non tamen potest sine aliis probationibus reum torquere, ut per Specul. etc."—Jo. Emerici a Rosbach Process. Criminal. Tit. v. cap. v. No. 13 (Francof. 1645).

[2] Du Boys, Droit Criminel, I. 650.

[3] Jo. Herb. de Fulstin. Statut. Reg. Polon. (Samoscii, 1597, p. 7).

[4] Esneaux, Hist. de Russie, III. 236.

[5] Pauli Jovii Moschovia.—This is a brief account of Russia, compiled about the year 1530, by Paulus Jovius, from his conversations with Dmitri,

but little show in the subsequent codes, such as the Sudebtnick, issued in 1550, and the Sobornoié Ulagenié, promulgated in 1648.[1] In fact, these regions were still too barbarous for so civilized a process.

In addition to these national jurisdictions there was a wide field open to the use of torture in the spiritual courts established everywhere, for it was not confined to the secular tribunals and to the Inquisition. The latter had so fully familiarized

ambassador to Clement VII. from Vasili V., first Emperor of Russia. Olaus Magnus, in the pride of his Northern blood, looks upon the statement in the text as a slander on the rugged Russ—"hoc scilicet pro terribili tormento in ea durissima gente reputari, quæ flammis et eculeis adhibitis, vix, ut acta revelet, tantillulum commovetur"—and he broadly hints that the wily ambassador amused himself by hoaxing the soft Italian : "Sed revera vel ludibriose bonus præsul a versuto Muscovitici principis nuntio Demetrio dicto, tempore Clementis VII. informatus est Romæ" (Gent. Septent. Hist. Brev. Lib. XI. c. xxvi.). The worthy archbishop doubtless spoke of his own knowledge with respect to the use of the rack and fire in Russia, but the contempt he displays for the torture of a stream of water is ill-founded. In our prisons the punishment of the shower-bath is found to bring the most refractory characters to obedience in an incredibly short time, and its unjustifiable severity in a civilized age like this may be estimated from the fact that it has occasionally resulted in the death of the patient. Thus, at the New York State Prison at Auburn, in December, 1858, a strong, healthy man, named Samuel Moore, was kept in the shower-bath from a half to three-quarters of an hour, and died almost immediately after being taken out. A less inhumane mode of administering the punishment is to wrap the patient in a blanket, lay him on his back, and, from a height of about six feet, pour upon his forehead a stream from an ordinary watering-pot without the rose. According to experts, this will make the stoutest criminal beg for his life in a few seconds.

During the later period of our recent war, when the prevalence of exaggerated bounties for recruits led to an organized system of desertion, the magnitude of the evil seemed to justify the adoption of almost any means to arrest a practice which threatened rapidly to exhaust the resources of the country. Accordingly, the shower-bath was occasionally put into requisition by the military authorities to extort confession from suspected deserters, when legal evidence was not attainable, and it was found exceedingly efficacious.

[1] Du Boys, op. cit. I. 618.

the minds of churchmen with it that it came to be employed generally in the episcopal tribunals which, through their exclusive jurisdiction over clerks and over all matters that could be connected with spiritual offences, had considerable criminal business.   We may assume, however, that in this respect they were limited by the laws of the land and were debarred from its use in countries where it was not allowed in secular matters. In 1310 it required the most urgent pressure from Clement V. to induce Edward II. to violate the common law by permitting the papal emissaries to torture the English Templars, and the King sought to conceal the illegality of the act by an order to the gaolers which bore that the inquisitors and episcopal ordinaries should be allowed to deal with the bodies of the prisoners "in accordance with ecclesiastical law,"[1] showing how completely in the minds of men torture was identified with the spiritual courts.   When the canons of the council of Vienne were promulgated in 1317 and the inquisitor Bernard Gui remonstrated with John XXII. against a clause intended to diminish the abuse of torture by inquisitors, he argued that it was a reflection on the Inquisition, because the episcopal courts were subject to no such restrictions on its use.[2]   The Church carried this blessing with it wherever it went.   When in 1593 St. Toribio, Archbishop of Lima, sought to reform the abuses of the episcopal courts throughout his vast province, he issued an *arancel* or tariff of fees for all their officials. In this we find that the executioner was not to charge more than a peso for torturing a prisoner, while the notary was entitled to two reales for drawing up a sentence of torture, and one real for each folio of his record of its administration and the confession of the accused.[3]

---

[1] Quod iidem prælati et inquisitores de ipsis Templariis et eorum corporibus, quotiens voluerint, ordinent et faciant id quod eis, secundum legem ecclesiasticam, videbitur faciendum.—Rymer, Fœdera, III. 203.

[2] C. 1 § 1 Clement. v. 3.—Bern. Guidonis Gravamina (MSS. Doat, XXX.).

[3] Haroldus, Lima limata Conciliis etc. Romæ, 1672, pp. 75, 76.

# CHAPTER VII.

THE INQUISITORIAL PROCESS.

DURING this period, while Central and Western Europe had advanced with such rapid strides of enlightenment, the inquisitorial process, based upon torture, had become the groundwork of all criminal procedure, and every detail was gradually elaborated with the most painstaking perverseness.

Allusion has already been made to the influence of the Inquisition in introducing the use of torture. Its influence did not cease there, for with torture there gradually arose the denial to the accused of all fair opportunity of defending himself, accompanied by the system of secret procedure which formed so important a portion of the inquisitorial practice. In the old feudal courts, the prosecutor and the defendant appeared in person. Each produced his witnesses; the case was argued on both sides, and unless the wager of battle or the ordeal intervened, a verdict was given in accordance with the law after duly weighing the evidence, while both parties were at liberty to employ counsel and to appeal to the suzerain. When St. Louis endeavored to abolish the duel and to substitute a system of inquests, which were necessarily to some extent *ex parte*, he did not desire to withdraw from the accused the legitimate means of defence, and in the Ordonnance of 1254 he expressly instructs his officers not to imprison the defendant without absolute necessity, while all the proceedings of the inquest are to be communicated freely to him.[1] All this changed with time and the authoritative adoption of torture. The theory of the Inquisition, that the suspected man was to

---

[1] Statut. S. Ludov. ann. 1254, §§ 20, 21 (Isambert, I. 270).

be hunted down and entrapped like a wild beast, that his guilt was to be assumed, and that the efforts of his judges were to be directed solely to obtaining against him sufficient evidence to warrant the extortion of a confession without allowing him the means of defence—this theory became the admitted basis of criminal jurisprudence.   The secrecy of these inquisitorial proceedings, moreover, deprived the accused of one of the greatest safeguards accorded to him under the Roman law of torture.   That law, as we have seen, required the formality of inscription, by which the accuser who failed to prove his charge was liable to the *lex talionis*, and in crimes which involved torture in the investigation he was duly tortured. This was imitated by the Wisigoths, and its principle was admitted and enforced by the Church before the introduction of the Inquisition had changed its policy;[1] but modern Europe, in borrowing from Rome the use of torture, combined it with the inquisitorial process, and thus in civilized Christendom it speedily came to be used more recklessly and cruelly than ever it had been in pagan antiquity.

In 1498, an assembly of notables at Blois drew up an elaborate ordonnance for the reformation of justice in France.   In this, the secrecy of the inquisitorial process is dwelt upon with peculiar insistence as of the first importance in all criminal cases.   The whole investigation was in the hands of the government official, who examined every witness by himself, and secretly, the prisoner having no knowledge of what was done, and no opportunity of arranging a defence.   After all the testimony procurable in this one-sided manner had been obtained, it was discussed by the judges, in council with other persons named for the purpose, who decided whether the accused should be tortured.   He could be tortured but once, unless fresh evidence subsequently was collected against him,

---

[1] Thus Gratian, in the middle of the twelfth century—" Qui calumniam illatam non probat poenam debet incurrere quam si probasset reus utique sustineret."—Decreti P. II. caus. v. quæst. 6, c. 2.

and his confession was read over to him the next day, in order that he might affirm or deny it. A secret deliberation was then held by the same council, which decided as to his fate.[1]

This cruel system was still further perfected by Francis I., who, in an ordonnance of 1539, expressly abolished the inconvenient privilege assured to the accused by St. Louis, which was apparently still occasionally claimed, and directed that in no case should he be informed of the accusation against him, or of the facts on which it was based, nor be heard in his defence. Upon examination of the *ex parte* testimony, without listening to the prisoner, the judges ordered torture proportioned to the gravity of the accusation, and it was applied at once, unless the prisoner appealed, in which case his appeal was forthwith to be decided by the superior court of the locality.[2] The whole process was apparently based upon the conviction that it was better that a hundred innocent persons should suffer than that one culprit should escape, and

---

[1] Ordonnance, Mars 1498, §§ 110–116 (Isambert, XI. 365.—Fontanon, I. 710). It would seem that the only torture contemplated by this ordonnance was that of water, as the clerk is directed to record "la quantité de l'eau qu'on aura baillée audit prisonnier." This was administered by gagging the patient, and pouring water down his throat until he was enormously distended. It was sometimes diversified by making him eject the water violently, by forcible blows on the stomach (Fortescue de Laudibus Legg. Angliæ, cap. xxii.). Sometimes a piece of cloth was used to conduct the water down his throat. To this, allusion is made in the "Appel de Villon":—

> " Se fusse des hoirs Hue Capel
> Qui fut extraict de boucherie,
> On ne m'eust, parmy ce drapel,
> Faict boyre à celle escorcherie."

[2] Ordonn. de Villers Cotterets, Août 1539, §§ 162–164 (Isambert, XIII. 633–4). "Ostant et abolissant tous styles, usances ou coutumes par lesquels les accusés avoient accoutumés d'être ouïs en jugement pour sçavoir s'ils devoient être accusés, et à cette fin avoir communication des faits et articles concernant les crimes et délits dont ils étoient accusés."

it would not be easy to devise a course of procedure better fitted to render the use of torture universal. There was some protection indeed, theoretically at least, in the provision which held the judge responsible when an innocent prisoner was tortured without sufficient preliminary proof to justify it; but this salutary regulation, from the very nature of things, could not often be enforced, and it was so contrary to the general spirit of the age that it soon became obsolete. Thus, in Brittany, perhaps the most independent of the French provinces, the Coutumier, as revised in 1539, retains such a provision,[1] but it disappears in the revision of 1580.

But even this was not all. Torture, as thus employed to convict the accused, became known as the *question préparatoire;* and, in defiance of the old rule that it could be applied but once, a second application, known as the *question définitive* or *préalable,* became customary, by which, after condemnation, the prisoner was again subjected to the extremity of torment in order to discover whether he had any accomplices, and, if so, to identify them. In this detestable practice we find another instance of the unfortunate influence of the Inquisition in modifying the Roman law. The latter expressly and wisely provided that no one who had confessed should be examined as to the guilt of another;[2] and in the ninth century the authors of the False Decretals had emphatically adopted the principle, which thus became embodied in ecclesiastical law,[3] until the ardor of the Inquisition in hunting down here-

---

[1] Anc. Cout. de Bretagne, Tit. I. art. xli.—D'Argentré's labored commentary on this article is a lamentable exhibition of the utter confusion which existed as to the nature of preliminary proof justifying torture. Comment. pp. 139, sqq.

[2] Nemo igitur de proprio crimine confitentem super conscientia scrutetur aliena.—Const. 17 Cod. IX. ii. (Honor. 423).

[3] Nemini de se confesso credi potest super crimen alienum, quoniam ejus atque omnis rei professio periculosa est, et admitti adversus quemlibet non debet.—Pseudo-Julii Epist. II. cap. xviii.—Gratian. Decret. P. II. caus. v. quæst. 3, can. 5.

tics caused it to regard the conviction of the accused as a barren triumph unless he could be forced to incriminate his possible associates. It thus finally became a rule of the Inquisition, promulgated by papal authority, that all who confessed or were convicted should be tortured at the discretion of the inquisitor to reveal the names of their accomplices.[1]

Torture was also generically divided into the *question ordinaire* and *extraordinaire*—a rough classification to proportion the severity of the infliction to the gravity of the crime or the urgency of the case. Thus, in the most usual kind of torment, the strappado, popularly known as the *Moine de Caen*, the ordinary form was to tie the prisoner's hands behind his back with a piece of iron between them; a cord was then fastened to his wrists by which, with the aid of a pulley, he was hoisted from the ground with a weight of one hundred and twenty-five pounds attached to his feet. In the extraordinary torture, the weight was increased to two hundred and fifty pounds, and when the victim was raised to a sufficient height he was dropped and arrested with a jerk that dislocated his joints, the operation being thrice repeated.[2]

Thus, in 1549, we see the system in full operation in the case of Jacques de Coucy, who, in 1544, had surrendered Boulogne to the English. This was deemed an act of treachery, but he was pardoned in 1547; yet, notwithstanding his pardon, he was subsequently tried, convicted, condemned to decapitation and quartering, and also to the *question extraordinaire* to obtain a denunciation of his accomplices.[3]

---

[1] Inhærendo decretis alias per felicis recordationis Paulum papam quartum Sanctissimus dominus noster Pius papa quintus decrevit omnes et quoscunque reos convictos et confessos de heresi pro ulteriori veritate habenda et super complicibus fore torquendos arbitrio dominorum judicum.—Locati Opus Judiciale Inquisitorum, Romæ, 1570, p. 477.

[2] Chéruel, Dict. Hist. des Institutions, etc. de la France, p. 1220 (Paris, 1855).

[3] Isambert, XIV. 88. Beccaria comments on the absurdity of such proceedings, as though a man who had accused himself would make any difficulty in accusing others.—" Quasi●che l'uomo che accusa sè stesso, non

When Louis XIV., under the inspiration of Colbert, re-moulded the jurisprudence of France, various reforms were introduced into the criminal law, and changes both for better and worse were made in the administration of torture. The Ordonnance of 1670 was drawn up by a committee of the ablest and most enlightened jurists of the day, and it is a melancholy exhibition of human wisdom when regarded as the production of such men as Lamoignon, Talon, and Pus-sort. The cruel mockery of the *question préalable* was re-tained; and in the principal proceedings all the chances were thrown against the prisoner. All preliminary testimony was still *ex parte*. The accused was heard, but he was still ex-amined in secret. Lamoignon vainly endeavored to obtain for him the advantage of counsel, but Colbert obstinately refused this concession, and the utmost privilege allowed the defence was the permission accorded to the judge, at his dis-cretion, to confront the accused with the adverse witnesses. In the *question préliminaire*, torture was reserved for capital cases, when the proof was strong and yet not enough for conviction. During its application it could be stopped and resumed at the pleasure of the judge, but if the accused were once unbound and removed from the rack, it could not be

accusi più facilmente gli altri. E egli giusto il tormentare gli uomini per l'altrui delitto?"—Dei Delitte e delle Pene, § XII. A curious illustration of its useless cruelty when applied to prisoners of another stamp is afforded by the record of a trial which occurred at Rouen in 1647. A certain Jehan Lemarinier, condemned to death for murder, was subjected to the *question définitive*. Cords twisted around the fingers, scourging with rods, the strappado with fifty pounds attached to each foot, the thumb-screw were applied in succession and together, without eliciting anything but fervent protestations of innocence. The officials at last wearied out remanded the convict to prison, when he sent for them and quietly detailed all the particulars of his crime, committed by himself alone, requesting especially that they should record his confession as having been spontaneous, for the relief of his conscience, and not extorted by torment.—Desmaze, Les Pénalités Anciennes, p. 159, Paris, 1866.

repeated, even though additional evidence were subsequently obtained.[1]

It was well to prescribe limitations, slender as these were ; but in practice it was found impossible to enforce them, and they afforded little real protection to the accused when judges, bent upon procuring conviction, chose to evade them.   A contemporary whose judicial position gave him every opportunity of knowing the truth, remarks :  "They have discovered a jugglery of words and pretend that though it may not be permissible to *repeat* the torture, still they have a right to *continue* it, though there may have been an interval of three whole days. Then, if the sufferer, through good luck or by a miracle, survives this reduplication of agony, they have discovered the notable resource of *nouveaux indices survenus*, to subject him to it again without end.   In this way they elude the intention of the law, which sets some bounds to these cruelties and requires the discharge of the accused who has endured the question without confession, or without confirming his confession after torture."[2]   Nor were these the only modes by which the scanty privileges allowed the prisoner were curtailed in practice.   In 1681, a royal Declaration sets forth that, in the jurisdiction of Grenoble, judges were in the habit of refusing to listen to the accused, and of condemning him unheard, an abuse which was prohibited for the future.   Yet other courts subsequently assumed that this prohibition was only applicable to the Parlement of Grenoble, and in 1703 another Declaration was necessary to enforce the rule throughout the kingdom.[3]

The Ordonnance of 1670, moreover, gave formal expression to another abuse which was equally brutal and illogical— the employment of torture *avec réserve des preuves*.   When the judge resolved on this, the silence of the accused under

[1] Ordonnance Criminel d'Août 1670, Tit. xiv. xix. (Isambert, XIX. 398, 412).

[2] Nicolas, Dissertation Morale et Juridique sur la Torture, p. 111 (Amsterd. 1682).

[3] Déclaration du 13 Avril 1703 (Ordonnances d'Alsace, I. 340).

torment did not acquit him, though the whole theory of the question lay in the necessity of confession. He simply escaped the death penalty, and could be condemned to any other punishment which the discretion of the judge might impose, thus presenting the anomaly of a man neither guilty nor innocent, relieved from the punishment assigned by the law to the crime for which he had been arraigned, and condemned to some other penalty without having been convicted of any offence. This punishing for suspicion was no new thing. Before torture came fully into vogue, in the early part of the fourteenth century, a certain Estevenes li Barbiers of Abbeville was banished under pain of death for suspicion of breach of the peace, and was subsequently tried, acquitted, and allowed to return.[1] About the same period a barber of Anet and his sons were arrested by the monks of St. Martin-des-Champs on suspicion of killing a guard who was keeping watch over some hay. The evidence against them was insufficient, and they were taken to the gallows as a kind of moral torture not infrequently used in those days. Still refusing to confess, they were banished forever under pain of hanging, because, as the record ingenuously states, the crime was not fully proved against them.[2] So in the records of the Parlement of Paris there is a sentence rendered in 1402 against Jehan Dubos, a procureur of the Parlement, and Ysabelet his wife, for suspicion of the poisoning of another procureur, Jehan le Charron, the first husband of Ysabelet, and Dubos was accordingly hanged, while his wife was burnt.[3] Jean Bodin, one of the clearest intellects of the sixteenth century, lays it down as a rule that the penalty should be proportioned to the proof; he ridicules as obsolete the principle that when the evidence is not sufficient for conviction the accused should be discharged, and mentions stripes, fines, imprisonment, the

---

[1] Coutumier de Picardie, Éd. Marnier, p. 88.

[2] Registre Criminel de la Justice de S. Martin-des-Champs. Paris, 1877, p. 229.

[3] Desmaze, Pénalités Anciennes, p. 204.

galleys, and degradation as proper substitutes for death when
there is no evidence and only violent presumption. He gives
in illustration of this a case personally known to him of a noble
of Le Mans, who was condemned to nine years of the galleys
for violent suspicion of murder.[1] The application to the tor-
ture-process of this determination not to allow a man to escape
unless his innocence was proved led to the illogical system of
the *réserve des preuves*.

The theory on which the doctors of the law proceeded was
that if there were evidence sufficient for conviction and the
judge yet tortured the criminal in surplusage without obtaining
a confession, the accused could not be condemned to the full
punishment of his offence, because the use of torture in itself
weakened the external proofs, and therefore the culprit must
be sentenced to some lighter punishment—a refinement worthy
of the inconsequential dialectics of the schools.[2] The cruel
absurdities which the system produced in practice are well
illustrated by a case occurring in Naples in the sixteenth century. Marc Antonio Maresca of Sorrento was tried by the
Admiralty Court for the murder of a peasant of Miani, in the
market-place. The evidence was strong against him, but there
were no eye-witnesses, and he endured the torture without confession. The court asserted that it had reserved the evidence,
and condemned him to the galleys for seven years. He appealed to the High Court of the royal council, and the case
was referred to a distinguished jurisconsult, Tomaso Gram-
matico, a member of the council. The latter reported that
he must be considered as innocent, after having passed through
torture without confession, and denied the right of the court to
reserve the evidence. Then, with an exhibition of the peculiar
logic characteristic of the criminal jurisprudence of the time,
he concluded that Maresca might be relegated to the islands
for five years, although it was a recognized principle of Nea-

---

[1] Bodini de Magor. Dæmonoman. Basil. 1581, pp. 325, 334, 390.
[2] Scialojæ Praxis torquendi Reos c. i. No. 12 (Neap. 1653).

politan law that torture could be inflicted only in accusations of crimes of which the penalty was greater than relegation. The only thing necessary to complete this tissue of legal wisdom was afforded by the council, which set aside the judgment of the Admiralty Court, rejected the report of their colleague, and condemned the prisoner to the galleys for three years.[1] Somewhat less complicated in its folly, but more inexcusable from its date, was the sentence of the court of Orléans in 1740, by which a man named Barberousse, from whom no confession had been extorted, was condemned to the galleys for life, because, as the sentence declared, he was *strongly suspected* of premeditated murder.[2] A more pardonable, but not more reasonable, example occurred at Halle in 1729, where a woman accused of infanticide refused to confess, and as she labored under a physical defect which rendered the application of torture dangerous to life, the authorities, after due consideration and consultation of physicians, spared her the torture and banished her without conviction.[3]

The same tendency to elude all restrictions on the use of torture was manifested in the Netherlands, where the procedure was scarcely known until the 16th century, and where it was only administered systematically by the ordonnance on criminal justice of Philip II. in 1570. When once employed it rapidly extended until it became almost universal, both in the provinces which threw off the yoke of Spain and in those which remained faithful. The limits which Philip had imposed on it were soon transcended. He had forbidden its employment in all cases "où il n'y a plaine, demye preuve, ou bien où la preuve est certaine et indubitable," thus restricting it to those where there was very strong presumption without absolute certainty. In transcription and translation, however, the wording of the

[1] Thomæ Grammatici Decisiones Neapolitanæ, pp. 1275-6 (Venetiis, 1582). Cf. Scialojæ *op. cit.* c. i. No. 22.

[2] L'Oiseleur, Les Crimes et les Peines, pp. 206-7.

[3] Braune Dissert. de Tortura Valetudinar. Halæ Cattor. 1740, p. 28.

ordonnance became changed to "plaine ou demye preuve, ou
bien où la preuve est incertaine ou douteuse," thus allowing
it in all cases where the judge might have a doubt not of the
guilt but of the innocence of the accused; and by the time
these errors were discovered by a zealous legal antiquarian, the
customs of the tribunals had become so fixed that the attempt
to reform them was vain.[1]  Even the introduction of torture
could not wholly eradicate the notion on which the ordeal
system was based, that a man under accusation must virtually
prove his innocence.

In Germany, torture had been reduced to a system, in 1532,
by the Emperor Charles V., whose *Caroline Constitutions*
contain a more complete code on the subject than had
previously existed, except in the records of the Inquisition.
Inconsistent and illogical, it quotes Ulpian to prove the deceptive nature of the evidence thence derivable; it pronounces
torture to be "res dira, corporibus hominum admodum noxia
et quandoque lethalis, cui et mors ipsa prope proponenda;"[2]
in some of its provisions it manifests extreme care and tender-
ness to guard against abuses, and yet practically it is merciless
to the last degree.  Confession made during torture was not
to be believed, nor could a conviction be based upon it; yet
what the accused might confess after being removed from torture was to be received as the deposition of a dying man, and
was full evidence.[3]  In practice, however, this held good only
when adverse to the accused, for he was brought before his
judge after an interval of a day or two, when, if he confirmed
the confession, he was condemned, while if he retracted it he
was at once thrust again upon the rack.  In confession under
torture, moreover, he was to be closely cross-questioned, and
if any inconsistency was observable in his self-condemnation
the torture was at once to be redoubled in severity.[4]  The

---

[1] Meyer, Institutions Judiciaires, IV. 285, 293.
[2] Legg. Capital. Caroli V. c. lx. lviii.
[3] Ibid. c. xx. lviii.                    [4] Ibid. c. lv. lvi. lvii.

legislator thus makes the victim expiate the sins of his own
vicious system ; the victim's sufferings increase with the de-
ficiency of the evidence against him, and the legislator con-
soles himself with the remark that the victim has only himself
to thank for it, " de se tantum non de alio quæratur." To
complete the inconsistency of the code, it provided that confession was not requisite for conviction ; irrefragable external
evidence was sufficient ; and yet even when such evidence was
had, the judge was empowered to torture in mere surplusage.[1]
Yet there was a great show of tender consideration for the
accused. When the weight of conflicting evidence inclined
to the side of the prisoner, torture was not to be applied.[2]
Two adverse witnesses, or one unexceptionable one, were a condition precedent, and the legislator shows that he was in advance of his age by ruling out all evidence resting on the
assertions of magicians and sorcerers.[3] To guard against
abuse, the impossible effort was made to define strictly the exact quality and amount of evidence requisite to justify torture,
and the most elaborate and minute directions were given with
respect to all the various classes of crime, such as homicide,
child-murder, robbery, theft, receiving stolen goods, poisoning, arson, treason, sorcery, and the like ;[4] while the judge
administering torture to an innocent man on insufficient
grounds was liable to make good all damage or suffering
thereby inflicted.[5] The amount of torment, moreover, was to
be proportioned to the age, sex, and strength of the patient ;
women during pregnancy were never to be subjected to it ; and
in no case was it to be carried to such a point as to cause
permanent injury or death.[6]

[1] Legg. Capital. Carol. V. c. xxii. lxix.   [2] Ibid. c. xxviii.
[3] Ibid. c. xxiii. xxi.   [4] Ibid. c. xxxiii.–xliv.
[5] Ibid. c. xx. lxi.
[6] Ibid. c. lviii. lix.   Accusatus, si periculum sit, ne inter vel post tormenta
ob vulnera expiret, ea arte torquendus est, ne quid damni accipiat.

# CHAPTER VIII.

### FINAL SHAPE OF THE TORTURE SYSTEM.

CHARLES V. was too astute a ruler not to recognize the aid derivable from the doctrines of the Roman law in his scheme of restoring the preponderance of the Kaisership, and he lost no opportunity of engrafting them on the jurisprudence of Germany. In his Criminal Constitutions, however, he took care to embody largely the legislation of his predecessors and contemporaries, and though protests were uttered by many of the Teutonic princes, the code, adopted by the Diet of Ratisbon in 1532, became part and parcel of the common law of Germany.[1] A fair idea of the shape assumed, under these influences, by the criminal law in its relations with torture, can be obtained by examining some of the legal text-books which were current as manuals of practice from the sixteenth to the eighteenth century.[2] As most of the authors of these

---

[1] Heineccii Hist. Jur. Civ. Lib. II. §§ cv. sqq.—Meyer (Instit. Judiciaires, Liv. VI. chap. xi.) gives a very interesting sketch of the causes which led to the overthrow of the old system of jurisprudence throughout Germany. He attributes it to the influence of the emperors and the municipalities, each equally jealous of the authority of the feudal nobles, aided by the lawyers, now becoming a recognized profession. These latter of course favored a jurisprudence which required long and special training, thus conferring upon them as a class peculiar weight and influence.

[2] My principal authorities are :—

Rerum Criminalium Praxis, by Josse Damhouder, a lawyer and statesman of repute in Flanders, where he held a distinguished position under Charles V. and Philip II. His work was received as an authority throughout Europe for two centuries, having passed through numerous editions, from that of Louvain, in 1554, to that of Antwerp, in 1750. My edition is of Antwerp, 1601.

Tractatus de Quæstionibus seu Torturis Reorum, published in 1592 by

works appear to condemn the principle or to lament the necessity of torture, their instructions as to its employment may safely be assumed to represent the most humane and enlightened views current during the period.[1] It is easy to see from them, however, that though the provisions of the Caroline Constitutions were still mostly in force, yet the practice had greatly extended itself, and that the limitations prescribed for the protection of innocence and helplessness had become of little real effect.

Upon the theory of the Roman law, nobles and the learned professions had claimed immunity from torture, and the Roman law inspired too sincere a respect to permit a denial of the claim,[2] yet the ingenuity of lawyers reduced the privilege

Johann Zanger, of Wittenberg, a celebrated jurisconsult of the time, and frequently reprinted. My edition is that of 1730, with notes by the learned Baron Senckenberg, and there is a still later one, published at Frankfort in 1763.

Practica Criminalis, seu Processus Judiciarius ad usum et consuetudinem judiciorum in Germania hoc tempore frequentiorem, by Johann Emerich von Rosbach, published in 1645 at Frankfort on the Mayn.

Tractatio Juridica, de Usu et Abusu Torturæ, by Heinrich von Boden, a dissertation read at Halle in 1697, and reprinted by Senckenberg in 1730, in conjunction with the treatise of Zanger.

Scialojæ Praxis torquendi Reos, Neapoli, 1653.

Tractatus de Maleficiis, nempe D. Alberti de Gandino, D. Bonifacii de Vitalianis, D. Pauli Grillandi, D. Baldi de Periglis, D. Jacobi de Arena. Venetiis, 1560

[1] Cum nihil tam severum, tam crudele et inhumanum videatur quam hominem conditum ad imaginem Dei . . . tormentis lacerare et quasi excarnificare, etc.—Zangeri Tract. de Quæstion. cap. I. No. I.

Tormentis humanitatis et religionis, necnon jurisconsultorum argumenta repugnant.—Jo. Emerici a Rosbach. Process. Crimin. Tit. v. c. ix. No. I.

Saltem horrendus torturæ abusus ostendit, quo miseri, de facinore aliquo suspecti, fere infernalibus, et si fieri possit, plusquam diabolicis cruciatibus exponuntur, ut qui nullo legitimo probandi modo convinci poterant, atrocitate cruciatuum contra propriam salutem confiteri, seque ita destruere sive jure sive injuria, cogantur.—Henr. de Boden Tract. Præfat.

[2] Zangeri cap. I. Nos. 49-58.

to such narrow proportions that it was practically almost valueless.   For certain crimes, of course, such as *majestas*, adultery,
and incest, the authority of the Roman law admitted of no
exceptions, and to these were speedily added a number of
other offences, classed as *crimina excepta* or *nefanda*, which
were made to embrace almost all offences of a capital nature,
in which alone torture was as a rule allowable.   Thus, parri-
cide, uxoricide, fratricide, witchcraft, sorcery, counterfeiting,
theft, sacrilege, rape, arson, repeated homicide, etc., came to
be included in the exceptional cases, and the only privileges
extended in them to nobles were that they should not be subjected to "plebeian" tortures.[1]   As early as 1514, I find an
instance which shows how little advantage these prerogatives
afforded in practice.   A certain Dr. Bobenzan, a citizen of
good repute and syndic of Erfurt, who both by position and
profession belonged to the excepted class, when brought up
for sentence on a charge of conspiring to betray the city, and
warned that he could retract his confession, extracted under
torture, pathetically replied—"During my examination, I was
at one time stretched upon the rack for six hours, and at
another I was slowly burned for eight hours.   If I retract, I
shall be exposed to these torments again and again.   I had
rather die"—and he was duly hanged.[2]   In fact, all these

[1] Zangeri cap. I. Nos. 59–88.—Knipschild, in his voluminous " Tract.
de Nobilitate" (Campodun. 1693), while endeavoring to exalt to the utmost the privileges of the nobility, both of the sword and robe, is obliged
to admit their liability to torture for these crimes, and only urges that the
preliminary proof should be stronger than in the case of plebeians (Lib. II.
cap. iv. Nos. 108–120); though, in other accusations, a judge subjecting a
noble to torture should be put to death, and his attempt to commit such an
outrage could be resisted by force of arms (Ibid. No. 103).   He adds,
however, that no special privileges existed in France, Lombardy, Venice,
Italy, and Saxony (Ibid. Nos. 105–7).   Scialoja expressly says (Praxis
c. xiii. Nos. 40–49. 55) that in Naples no dignity, secular or ecclesiastical,
except that of judges, conferred immunity from torture; and all privileges
were set aside by a direct order from the sovereign.

[2] Erphurdianus Variloquus, ann. 1514 (Mencken. Script. Rer. German.
II. 527–8).

exemptions were rather theoretical than practical, and they were speedily set aside.[1]

In Catholic countries, of course, the clergy were specially favored, but the immunity claimed for them by the canon law was practically reduced to nearly the same as that accorded to nobles.[2] The torture inflicted on them, however, was lighter than in the case of laymen, and proof of a much more decided character was required to justify their being exposed to torment. As an illustration of this, von Rosbach remarks that if a layman is found in the house of a pretty woman, most authors consider the fact sufficient to justify torture on the charge of adultery, but that this is not the case with priests, who if they are caught embracing a woman are presumed to be merely blessing her.[3] They moreover had the privilege of being tortured only at the hands of clerical executioners, if such were to be had.[4] In Protestant territories respect for the cloth was manifested by degrading them prior to administering the rack or strappado.[5]

Some limitations were imposed as to age and strength. Children under fourteen could not be tortured, nor the aged whose vigor was unequal to the endurance, but the latter could be tied to the rack, and menaced to the last extremity ; and the elasticity of the rule is manifested in a case which attracted attention at Halle in the eighteenth century, in which a man more than eighty years of age was decided to be fit to bear the infliction, and only escaped by opportunely dying.[6] In fact, Grillandus argues that age confers no immunity from torture, but that a humane judge will inflict it only moderately,

---

[1] Grillandi de Quæst. et Tortura Q. vi.—Baldi de Periglis de Quæstionibus c. iii. § 4.—Alberti de Gandino de Quæstionibus §§ 7, 9, 36, 37.

[2] Damhouder. Rer. Crimin. Praxis cap. xxxvii. Nos. 23, 24. Cf. Passerini Regulare Tribunal Quæst. xv. Art. ix. No. 117.

[3] Emer. a Rosbach Process. Crimin. Tit. v. cap. xiv.

[4] Simancæ de Cathol. Instit. Tit. lxv. No. 50.

[5] Willenbergii Tract. de Excess. et Pœnis Cleric. 4to. Jenæ, 1740, p. 41.

[6] Braune Diss. de Tortura Valetudinar. p. 32.

except in atrocious crimes; as for children, though regular
torture could not be employed on them, the rod could be
legitimately used.[1]   Insanity was likewise a safeguard, and
much discussion was had as to whether the deaf, dumb, and
blind were liable or not.   Zanger decides in the affirmative
whenever, whether as principals or witnesses, good evidence
was to be expected from them;[2] and Scialoja points out that
though deaf-mutes as a rule are not to be tortured because
they cannot dictate a confession, yet if they can read and
write so as to understand the accusation and write out what
they have to say, they are fit subjects for the torturer.[3]   Pregnant women also were exempt until forty days after childbed,
even though they had become so in prison for the express
purpose of postponing the infliction.[4]   Some kinds of disease
likewise conferred exemption, and jurisconsults undertook with
their customary minuteness to define with precision this nosol-
ogy of torture, leading to discussions more prolonged than
profitable.   Gout, for instance, gave rise to doubt, and some
authors were found to affirm that they knew of cases in which
gouty patients had been cured by a brisk application of the implements of the *marter-kammer* or torture-chamber.[5]   Other
legists gravely disputed whether in the case of epileptics the
judge should bear in mind the aspects of the moon and the
equinoxes and solstices, at which times the paroxysms of the
disease were apt to be more violent.   Those who thus escaped
torture on account of disease presented a problem which the
jurists solved in their ordinary fashion by condemning them
to some other punishment than that provided for the crime of
which they had been accused but not convicted.[6]

In theory the accused could be tortured only once, but this,

---

[1] Grillandi de Quæstione et Tortura, Q. vi. §§ 4, 6, 9.—Baldi de Periglis
de Quæstionibus cap. i. § 4.

[2] Zangeri *op. cit.* cap. I. Nos. 34–48.

[3] Scialojæ c. xiii. No. 21.                              [4] Ibid. Nos. 24–30.

[5] Goetzii Dissert. de Tortura, Lipsiæ, 1742, pp. 46–8.

[6] Braune Diss. de Tortura Valetudinar. pp. 24, 43.

like all other restrictions in favor of humanity, amounted to but little. A repetition of torture could be justified on the ground that the first application had been light or insufficient; the production of fresh evidence authorized a second and even a third infliction; a failure to persevere in confession after torture rendered a repetition requisite; and even a variation in the confession required confirmation by the rack or strappado.[1] Many writers affirm that a second torture is requisite to purge away the defect of the infamy incurred by confession under the first, as well as to strengthen the evidence against accomplices.[2] In fact, some authorities go so far as to place it entirely at the discretion of the judge whether the accused shall be subjected or not to repeated torment without fresh evidence,[3] and Del Rio mentions a case occurring in Westphalia wherein a man accused of lycanthropy was tortured twenty times.[4] This practice of repeating torture we are told by many authorities was exceedingly common.[5]

Another positive rule was that torture could only be applied in accusations involving life or limb.[6] Thus, for instance, in provinces where usury was punishable only by confiscation, torture could not be used to prove it, but where it entailed also some corporal infliction, the accused could be subjected to the rack.[7] Yet when Bologna undertook to remove the abuses of her torture system she still allowed it in cases involving a pecuniary fine of a hundred lire, or over.[8] Whip-

[1] Zangeri cap. v. Nos. 73–83.

[2] Del Rio Magicarum Disquisit. Lib. v. Sect. iii. L.

[3] Damhouder. *op. cit.* cap. xxxviii. Nos. 3, 4.—Rosbach. Tit. v. cap. xv. No. 14.—Simancas, however, declares that only two applications of torture are allowable (De Cathol. Instit. Tit. LXV. Nos. 76, 81).

[4] Disquis. Magicar. Lib. v. sect. ix.

[5] Assessores tamen honoris et avidi et cupidi hoc non servant imo quotidie quæstiones repetunt absque novis indiciis.—Baldi de Periglis de Quæstionibus cap. i. § 6. So also Alberti de Gandino de Quæstionibus § 20, and Bonifacii de Vitalianis, Rubr. *Quæ Indicia* § 8.

[6] Zangeri Præfat. No. 31.            [7] Scialojæ *op. cit.* cap. i. No. 27.

[8] Statuta Criminalia Communis Bononiæ (Bononiæ, 1525, fol. 15 *a*).

ping being a corporal punishment, and yet a much lighter
infliction than torture, the legists were divided as to whether
a crime for which it was the only penalty was one involving
the liability of the accused to torture, but the weight of authority, as usual, leaned to the side of the free employment of
the rack.[1] All these fine-spun distinctions, however, were of
little moment, for Senckenberg assures us that he had known
torture to be resorted to in mercantile matters, where money
only was at stake.[2] Slaves could always be tortured in civil
suits when their testimony was required, and freemen when
there was suspicion of fraud;[3] and it was a general rule of
mercantile law that it could be employed in accusations of
fraudulent bankruptcy.[4] How easily, indeed, all these barriers were overleaped is seen in the rule that where the penalty was a fine, and the accused was too poor to pay it, he
could be tortured, the torture serving in lieu of punishment.
Thus, whether he was innocent or guilty, the judge was determined that he should not escape.[5] Another method in
constant use of evading the limitation in offences which by
statute did not involve torture was by depriving him of food
in prison, or stripping him of clothes in winter, the slow torment of starvation and cold not being classed legally as torture.[6]

Equally absolute was the maxim that torture could not be
employed unless there was positive proof that crime of some
sort had been committed, for its object was to ascertain the

[1] Goetzii Dissert. de Tortura, pp. 52–3.

[2] Zangeri Tract. Not. ad p. 903.

[3] Grillandi de Quæst. et Tortura Q. vii.

[4] Scialojæ op. cit. cap. i. No. 34.—Goetzii Dissert. de Tortura, p. 53.—
Grillandi, loc. cit.—Bernhard (Diss. Inaug. de Tort. cap. I. § iv.) states that
in these cases not only the principals but even the witnesses could be tortured if suspected of concealing the truth.

[5] Grillandi de Quæst. et Tortura, Q. v. § 6.

[6] Baldi de Periglis de Quæstionibus cap. iii. § 2.—Damhoud. cap. xxxviii.
No. 13.—Alberti de Gandino de Quæstionibus § 31.

criminal and not the crime;[1] yet von Rosbach remarks that
as soon as any one claimed to have lost anything by theft, the
judges of his day hastened to torture all suspect, without wait-
ing to determine whether or not the theft had really been
committed as assumed;[2] and von Boden declares that many
tribunals were in the habit of resorting to it in cases wherein
subsequent developments showed that the alleged crime had
really not taken place, a proceeding jocosely characterized
by a brother lawyer as putting the cart before the horse, and
bridling him by the tail.[3]  The history of torture is full of
cases illustrating its effectiveness when thus used.  Boyvin du
Villars relates that during the war in Piedmont, in 1559, he
released from the dungeons of the Marquis of Masserano an
unfortunate gentleman who had been secretly kept there for
eighteen years, in consequence of having attempted to serve
a process from the Duke of Savoy on the marquis.  His disappearance having naturally been attributed to foul play, his
kindred prosecuted an enemy of the family, who, under stress
of torture, duly confessed to having committed the murder,
and was accordingly executed in a town where Masserano
himself was residing.[4]  Godelmann relates that a monument
in a church in upper Germany, representing a man broken on
a wheel, commemorated a case in which two young journey-
men set out together to make the accustomed tour of the
country.  One of them returned alone, clad in the garments
of the other, and was suspected of having made way with him.
He was arrested, and in the absence of all other evidence was
promptly put to the torture, when he confessed the crime in
all its details and was executed on the wheel—soon after which
his companion returned.  Another case was that of a young

---

[1] Zangeri Præfat. No. 32.—Tortura enim datur non ad liquidandum factum
sed personam.—Damhouder. Rer. Crimin. Prax. cap. xxxv. No. 7.

[2] Process. Criminal. Tit. v. cap. ix. No. 17.

[3] De Usu et Ab. Tort. Th. ix.—Qui aliter procedit judex, equum cauda
frenat et post quadrigas caballum jungit.

[4] Boyvin du Villars, Mémoires, Liv. vii.

man near Bremen whose widowed mother lived in adultery
with a servant. The son quarrelled with the man, who fled
and took service with another employer at a considerable dis-
tance. His father, not knowing his departure, accused the
youth of murder, and torture speedily drew from the latter a
full confession of the crime, including his throwing the corpse
into the Weser. Not long after his execution the adulterous
serving-man reappeared and was duly put to death, as also
was his father, to make amends for the blunder of the law.[1]

A universal prescription existed that the torment should not
be so severe or so prolonged as to endanger life or limb or to
injure the patient permanently; but this, like all the other
precautions, was wholly nugatory. Senckenberg assures us
that he was personally cognizant of cases in which innocent
persons had been crippled for life by torture under false accusations;[2] and the meek Jesuit Del Rio, in his instructions
to inquisitors, quietly observes that the flesh should not be
wounded nor the bones broken, but that torture could scarce
be properly administered without more or less dislocation of
the joints.[3] We may comfort ourselves with the assurance of
Grillandus, that cases were rare in which permanent mutilation or death occurred under the hands of the torturer,[4] and
this admission lends point to the advice which Simancas gives
to judges, that they should warn the accused, when brought
into the torture-chamber, that if he is crippled or dies under
the torture he must hold himself accountable for it in not
spontaneously confessing the truth[5]—a warning which was
habitually given in the Spanish Inquisition before applying
the torture. Von Boden, moreover, very justly points out
the impossibility of establishing any rules or limitations of
practical utility, when the capacity of endurance varies so

[1] Godelmanni de Magis Lib. III. cap. x.
[2] Not. ad p. 907 Zangeri *op. cit.*
[3] Del Rio Magicar. Disquisit. Lib. v. sect. ix.
[4] Grillandi de Quæst. et Tortura, Q. vi. § 10.
[5] Simancæ de Cathol. Instit. Tit. LXV. No. 56.

greatly in different constitutions, and the executioners had so many devices for heightening or lessening, within the established bounds, the agony inflicted by the various modes of torture allowed by law. Indeed, he does not hesitate to exclaim that human ingenuity could not invent suffering more terrible than was constantly and legally employed, and that Satan himself would be unable to increase its refinements.[1] In this as in everything else the legists agreed that the discretion of the judge was the sole and final arbiter in deciding whether the accused was "competently" tortured—that is, whether the number and severity of the inflictions were sufficient to purge him of the adverse evidence.[2]

It is true that the old rules which subjected the judge to some responsibility were still nominally in force. When torture was ordered without a preliminary examination, or when it was excessive and caused permanent injury, the judge was held by some authorities to have acted through malice, and his office was no protection against reclamation for damages.[3] Zanger also quotes the Roman law as still in force, to the effect that if the accused dies under the torture, and the judge has been either bribed or led away by passion, his offence is capital, while if there had been insufficient preliminary evidence, he is punishable at discretion.[4] But, on the other hand, Baldo tells us that unless there is evidence of malice the presumption is in favor of the judge in whose hands a prisoner has died or been permanently crippled, for he is

---

[1] De Usu et Abusu Tort. Th. XIII.

It must not be supposed from this and the preceding extracts that von Boden was an opponent of torture on principle. Within certain bounds, he advocated its use, and he only deplored the excessive abuse of it by the tribunals of the day.

[2] Quando quis dicatur competenter tortus vel non, similiter quando quis dicatur purgasse indicia vel non, omnia ista demum relinquuntur arbitrio et discretioni honesti judicis, quoniam in his certa regula tradi non potest.— Grillandi de Quæst. et Tortura Q. vii. § 10.—Gf. Godelmanni de Magis Lib. III. cap. x. § 36.—Baldi de Periglis de Quæstionibus cap. i. § 5.

[3] Zangeri *op. cit.* cap. I. Nos. 42–44.    [4] Ibid. cap. III. Nos. 20–22.

assumed to have acted through zeal for justice,[1] and though there were some authorities who denied this, it seems to have been the general practical conclusion.[2]  The secrecy of criminal trials, moreover, offered an almost impenetrable shield to the judge, and the recital by Godelmann of the various kinds of evidence by which the prisoner could prove the fact that he had been subjected to torture shows how difficult it was to penetrate into the secrets of the tribunals.[3]  According to Damhouder, indeed, the judge could clear himself by his own declaration that he had acted in accordance with the law, and without fraud or malice.[4]  We are therefore quite prepared to believe the assertion of Senckenberg that the rules protecting the prisoner had become obsolete, and that he had seen not a few instances of their violation without there being any idea of holding the judge to accountability,[5] an assertion which is substantially confirmed by Goetz.[6]

Not the least of the evils of the system, indeed, was its inevitable influence upon the judge himself.  He was required by his office to be present during the infliction of torture, and to conduct the interrogatory personally.  Callousness to human suffering, whether natural or acquired, thus became a necessity, and the delicate conscientiousness which should be the moving principle of every Christian tribunal was well-nigh an impossibility.[7]  Nor was this all, for when even a conscientious judge

[1] Baldi de Periglis cap. iii. § 7.
[2] Bonifacii de Vitalianis, Rubr. *de Perseverentia* § 5.—Alberti de Gandino, De Quæstionibus § 35.
[3] Godelmanni l. c. § 54.          [4] Cap. xxxviii. No. 18.
[5] Zangeri cap. III. Nos. 20–22.      [6] Goetzii Dissert. de Tortura, p. 74.
[7] So thoroughly was this recognized, that in 1668 Racine represents a judge, desirous of ingratiating himself with a young girl, as offering to exhibit to her the spectacle of the question as an agreeable pastime.

"  DANDIN.  N'avez vous jamais vu donner la question?
    ISABELLE.  Non, et ne le verrai, que je crois de ma vie.
    DANDIN.  Venez, je vous en veux faire passer l'envie.
    ISABELLE.  Hé! Monsieur, peut-on voir souffrir les malhereux?
    DANDIN.  Bon! cela fait toujours passer une heure ou deux."
                                *Les Plaideurs*, Acte III. Sc. dernière.

had once taken upon himself the responsibility of ordering a
fellow-being to the torture, every motive would lead him to
desire the justification of the act by the extortion of a confession ;[1] and the very idea that he might be possibly held to
accountability, instead of being a safeguard for the prisoner
became a cause of subjecting him to additional agony. Indeed, the prudence of persevering in torture until a confession
was reached was at least recognized, if not advised, by jurists,
and in such a matter to suggest the idea was practically to
recommend it.[2]  Both the good and the evil impulses of the
judge were thus enlisted against the unfortunate being at his
mercy.  Human nature was not meant to face such tempta-
tions, and the fearful ingenuity which multiplied the endless
refinements of torture testifies how utterly humanity yielded
to the thirst of wringing conviction from the weaker party to
the unequal conflict, where he who should have been a pas-
sionless arbiter was made necessarily a combatant.  How
completely the prisoner thus became a quarry to be hunted
to the death is shown by the jocular remark of Farinacci, a
celebrated authority in criminal law, that the torture of sleeplessness, invented by Marsigli, was most excellent, for out of a
hundred martyrs exposed to it not two could endure it without becoming confessors as well.[3]  Few, when once engaged

[1] Fortescue, in his arguments against the use of torture, does not fail to
recognize that the acquittal of a tortured prisoner is the condemnation of the
judge—" qui judex eum pronuntiet innocentem, nonne eodem judicio judex
ille seipsum reum judicat omnis sævitiæ et pœnarum quibus innocentem
afflixit ?"—De Laud. Legg. Angl. cap. xxii.

[2] Occurrit hic cautela Bruni dicentis, si judex indebite torserit aliquem,
facit reum confiteri quod fuit legitime tortus, de qua confessione faciat nota-
rium rogatum.—Rosbach. Process. Crim. Tit. v. cap. xv. No. 6.

[3] Quoted by Nicolas, Diss. Mor. et Jurid. sur la Torture, p. 21.  This
mode of torture consisted in placing the accused between two jailers, who
pummelled him whenever he began to doze, and thus, with proper relays,
deprived him of sleep for forty hours.  Its inventor considered it humane,
as it endangered neither life nor limb, but the extremity of suffering to
which it reduced the prisoner is shown by its efficaciousness.

Marsigli received much credit for this ingenious invention.  Grillandus

in such a pursuit, could be expected to follow the example of
the Milanese judge, who resolved his doubts as to the efficacy
of torture in evidence by killing a favorite mule, and allowing
the accusation to fall upon one of his servants. The man of
course denied the offence, was duly tortured, confessed, and
persisted in his confession after torture. The judge, thus convinced by experiment of the fallacy of the system, resigned
the office whose duties he could no longer conscientiously discharge, and in his subsequent career rose to the cardinalate.
The mode in which these untoward results were usually treated
is illustrated in another somewhat similar case which was told
to Augustin Nicholas at Amsterdam in explanation of the fact
that the city was obliged to borrow a headsman from the
neighboring towns whenever the services of one were required
for an execution. It appears that a young man of Amsterdam,
returning home late at night from a revel, sank upon a door-
step in a drunken sleep. A thief emptied his pockets, secur-
ing, among other things, a dirk, with which, a few minutes

informs us that he experimented with it in a difficult case of two monks
" et profecto vidi ea quæ prius non credebam, quod illud affert maximum
tormentum et fastidium in corpore absque aliqua membrorum læsione."—
Grillandi de Quæstione et Tortura Art. ii.

I have purposely abstained from entering into the details of the various
forms of torture. They may be interesting to the antiquarian, but they
illustrate no principle, and little would be gained by describing these melancholy monuments of human error. Those who may be curious in such
matters will find ample material in Grupen Observat. Jur. Crim. de Ap-
plicat. Torment., 4to., Hanov. 1754; Zangeri *op. cit.* cap. IV. Nos. 9, 10;
Hieron. Magius de Equuleo cum Appendd. Amstelod. 1664, etc. According to Bernhardi, Johann Graefe enumerates no less than six hundred different instruments invented for the purpose. Damhouder (*op. cit.* cap.
xxxvii. Nos. 17–23) declares that torture can legally be inflicted only with
ropes, and then proceeds to describe a number of ingenious devices. One
of these, which he states to produce insufferable torment without risk, is
bathing the feet with brine and then setting a goat to lick the soles.

The strappado, or suspension by the arms behind the back with weights
to the feet, was the torture in most general use and most favored by legal
experts.—Grillandus, *loc. cit.*

later, he stabbed a man in a quarrel. Returning to the sleeper he slipped the bloody weapon back to its place. The young man awoke, but before he had taken many steps he was seized by the watch, who had just discovered the murder. Appearances were against him; he was tortured, confessed, persisted in confession after torture, and was duly hanged. Soon after the real criminal was condemned for another crime, and revealed the history of the previous one, whereupon the States-General of the United Provinces, using the ordinary logic of the criminal law, deprived the city of Amsterdam of its executioner, as a punishment for a result that was inevitable under the system.[1]

Slight as were the safeguards with which legislators endeavored to surround the employment of torture, they thus became almost nugatory in practice under a system which, in the endeavor to reduce doubts into certainties, ended by leaving everything to the discretion of the judge. It is instructive to see the parade of insisting upon the necessity of strong preliminary evidence,[2] and to read the elaborate details as to the exact kind and amount of testimony severally requisite in each description of crime, and then to find that common report was held sufficient to justify torture, or unexplained absence before accusation, prevarication under examination, and even silence; and it is significant of the readiness to resort to the question on the slenderest pretexts when we see judges solemnly warned that an evil countenance, though it may argue depravity in general, does not warrant the presumption of actual guilt in individual cases;[3] though pallor, under many circumstances,

[1] Augustin Nicholas, *op. cit.* pp. 169, 178.
[2] Even this, however, was not deemed necessary in cases of conspiracy and treason " qui fiunt secreto, propter probationis difficultatem devenitur ad torturam sine indiciis"—Emer. a Rosb. Tit. v. cap. x. No. 20.
[3] Fama frequens et vehemens facit indicium ad torturam (Zanger. c. II. No. 80. Cf. Alberti de Gandino de Quæst. § 39). Reus ante accusationem vel inquisitionem fugiens et citatus contumaciter absens, se suspectum reddit ut torqueri possit (Ibid. No. 91. Cf. Simancæ Cathol. Instit. Tit. LXV. Nos.

was considered to sanction the application of torture,[1] even as
a pot containing toads, found in the home of a suspected
witch, justified her being placed on the rack.[2]  In fact, witchcraft, poisoning, highway robbery, and other crimes difficult
of proof, were considered to justify the judge in proceeding to
torture on lighter indications than offences in which evidence
was more readily obtainable.[3]  Subtle lawyers thus exhausted
their ingenuity in discussing all possible varieties of indications, and there grew up a mass of confused rules, wherein,
on many points, each authority contradicted the other.  In a
system which thus waxed so complex, the discretion of the
judge at last became the only practical guide, and the legal
writers themselves acknowledge the worthlessness of the rules
so laboriously constructed when they admit that it is left for
his decision to determine whether the indications are sufficient
to warrant the infliction of torture.[4]  How absolute was this

28–30).  Inconstantia sermonis facit indicium ad torturam (Zanger. Nos.
96–99).  Ex taciturnitate oritur indicium ad torturam (Ibid. No. 103).
Physiognomia malam naturam arguit, non autem delictum (Ibid. No. 85).
How exceedingly lax was the application of these rules may be guessed
from a remark of Damhouder's, that although rumor was sufficient to justify
torture, yet a contrary rumor neutralized the first and rendered torture improper.—Damhouder. Rer. Crimin. Praxis cap. xxxv. Nos. 14, 15.

1 Deinde a pallore et similibus oritur indicium ad torturam secundum
Bartol. (Emer. a Rosbach Tit. v. c. vii. Nos. 28–31).  Whereupon von
Rosbach enters into a long dissertation as to the causes of paleness.

2 Godelmanni de Magis Lib. III. cap. x. § 29.

3 Scialojæ cap. iii. Nos. 5, 6.

4 Judicis arbitrio relinquitur an indicia sint sufficientia ad torturam (Zanger. cap. II. Nos. 16–20).  An indicia sufficiant ad torturam judicis arbitrio
relictum est. . . .  Indicia ad torturam sufficientia relinquuntur officio judicis
(Emer. a Rosbach Tit. v. c. ii. p. 529).  Damhouder, indeed, states that no
rules can be framed—" neque ea ullis innituntur regulis : sed universum id
negotium geritur penes arbitrium, discretionem ac conscientiam judicis."—
Rer. Crimin. Praxis cap. xxxvi. Nos. 1, 2.  Cf. Braune Dissert. de Tortura
Valetudin. Halæ Cattor. 1740.

So Grillandus (De Quæstione et Tortura Q. iii.)—" Quæ autem indicia

discretion, and how it was exercised, is manifest when Damhouder declares that in his day bloodthirsty judges were in
the habit of employing the severest torture without sufficient
proof or investigation, boasting that by its means they could
extract a confession of everything.[1]  This fact was no novelty,
for the practice had existed, we may say, since the first introduction of torture.    Ippolito dei Marsigli early in the
sixteenth century speaks of judges habitually torturing without
preliminary evidence, and goes so far as to assert, with all the
weight of his supreme authority, that a victim of such wrongs
if he killed his inhuman judge could not be held guilty of
homicide nor be punished with death for the slaying.[2]   It was
perhaps to avoid this responsibility that some of these zealous
law-despisers resorted to the most irregular means to procure
evidence.   Godelmann and von Rosbach both tell us that the
magistrates of their time, in the absence of all evidence, sometimes had recourse to sorcerers and to various forms of divina-
tion in order to obtain proof on which they could employ the
rack or strappado.   Boys whose shoes were newly greased with
lard were thought to have a special power of detecting witches,
and enthusiastic judges accordingly would sometimes station
them, after duly anointing their boots, at the church doors,
so that the luckless wretches could not get out without being
recognized.[3]

How shocking was the abuse made of this arbitrary power is

dicantur esse sufficientia ad torturam certa regula tradi non potest, sed hoc
relinquitur arbitrio et discretioni boni judicis."

And Albertus de Gandino (De Quæstionibus § 14)—"Nec de his possit
dari certa doctrina sed hoc committitur arbitrio judicantis."

[1] Sunt tamen nonnulli prætores et judices sanguine fraterno adeo inexsa-
turabiles ut illico quemvis malæ famæ virum, citra ulla certa argumenta aut
indicia, corripiant ad sævissimam torturam, inclementer dicentes, cruciatum
facile ab illis extorturum rerum omnium confessionem.—Damhouder. Rer.
Crimin. Praxis cap. xxxv. No. 13.

[2] Hipp. de Marsiliis Singularia, No. 455 (Venet. 1555).

[3] Godelmanni de Magis Lib. III. cap. v. § 26.—Emer. a Rosbach Tit. v.
c. x. No. 25.

well illustrated by a case which occurred in the Spanish colony
of New Granada about the year 1580. The judges of the royal
court of Santafé had rendered themselves odious by their
cruelty and covetousness, when one morning some pasquinades against them were found posted in the public plaza.
Diligent search failed to discover the author, but a victim
was found in the person of a young scrivener whose writing
was thought to bear some resemblance to that of the offensive
papers. He was at once seized, and though libel was not an
offence under the civil law which justified the application of
torture, he was ordered to the rack, when he solemnly warned
the judge deputed to inflict it that if he should die under it
he would summon his tormentor to answer in the presence of
God within three days. The judge was intimidated and refused to perform the office, but another was found of sterner
stuff, who duly performed his functions without extracting a
confession, and the accused was discharged. Then a man
who desired to revenge himself on an enemy asserted that the
writing of the latter was like that of the pasquinades. Juan
Rodriguez de los Puertos, the unfortunate thus designated,
was immediately arrested with all his family. An illegitimate
son was promptly tortured, and stated that his father had written the libels and ordered him to post them. Then Juan himself was ordered to the rack, but, while protesting his innocence, he begged rather to be put to death, as he was too old
to endure the torment. He was accordingly hanged, and his
son was scourged with two hundred lashes. All that was
needed to render manifest the hideous injustice of this proceeding was developed a few years later, when the judge who
was afraid to risk the appeal of the first victim was condemned
to death for an assassination, and on the scaffold confessed
that he himself had been the author of the libels against his
brother justices.[1]

1 Groot, Historia Eclesiastica y Civil de Nueva Granada, Bogotá, 1869,
T. I. pp. 114-5, 116-20. Cf. Scialojæ Praxis torquendi Reos, cap. i. No.
25.

Such a system tends of necessity to its own extension, and it is therefore not surprising to find that the aid of torture was increasingly invoked. The prisoner who refused to plead, whether there was any evidence against him or not, could be tortured until his obstinacy gave way.[1] Even witnesses were not spared, whether in civil suits or criminal prosecutions.[2] It was discretionary with the judge to inflict moderate torture on them when the truth could not otherwise be ascertained. Witnesses of low degree could always be tortured for the purpose of supplying the defect in their testimony arising from their condition of life. Some jurists, indeed, held that no witness of low or vile condition could be heard without torture, but others maintained that poverty alone was not sufficient to render it necessary. Witnesses who were infamous could not be admitted to testify without torture; those of good standing were tortured only when they prevaricated, or when they were apparently committing perjury;[3] but, as this was necessarily left with the judges to determine, the instructions for him to guide his decision by observing their appearance and manner show how completely the whole case was in his power, and how readily he could extort evidence to justify the torture of the prisoner, and then extract from the latter a confession by the same means. In prosecutions for treason, all witnesses, irrespective of their rank, were liable to torture,[4] so that when Pius IV., in 1560, was determined to ruin Cardinal Carlo Caraffa, no scruple was felt, during his trial, as to torturing his friends and retainers to obtain the evidence upon which he was executed.[5] There

[1] Rosbach Tit. v. cap. x. No. 2.

[2] Ibid. Tit. v. cap. xiv. No. 16.—Goetzii Dissert. de Tortura, p. 54.— Grillandi de Quæst. et Tortura, Q. vii.

[3] Scialojæ cap. xiv. Nos. 5–20.—Jo. Frid. Werner Dissert. de Tortura Testium, Erford. 1724, pp. 72 sqq.

[4] Passerini Regulare Tribunal, Quæst. xv. Art. ix. No. 115 (Colon. Agripp. 1665).

[5] Process. contr. Card. de Caraffa (Hoffman. Collect. Script. I. 632).

was a general rule that witnesses could not be tortured until
after the examination of the accused, because, if he confessed,
their evidence was superfluous ; but there were exceptions even
to this, for if the criminal was not within the power of the
court, witnesses could be tortured to obtain evidence against
him in his absence.[1]   Indeed, in the effort made early in the
sixteenth century to reform the abuse of torture in Bologna,
it was provided that if there were evidence to show that a
man was acquainted with a crime he could be tortured to
obtain evidence on which to base a prosecution, and this
before any proceedings had been commenced against the de-
linquent.[2]   Evidently there was no limit to the uses to which
torture could be put by a determined legislator.

An ingenious plan was also adopted by which, when two
witnesses gave testimony irreconcilable with each other, their
comparative credibility was tested by torturing both simulta-
neously in each other's presence.[3]   Evidence given under torture was esteemed the best kind, and yet with the perpetually
recurring inconsistency which marks this branch of criminal
law it was admitted that the spontaneous testimony of a man
of good character could outweigh that of a disreputable person under torment.[4]   Witnesses, however, could not be tortured more than three times ;[5] and it was a question mooted
between jurists whether their evidence thus given required,
like the confession of an accused person, to be subsequently
ratified by them.[6]   A reminiscence of Roman law, moreover,
is visible in the rule that no witness could be tortured against
his kindred to the seventh degree, nor against his near connec-
tions by marriage, his feudal superiors, or other similar persons.[7]

There doubtless was good reason underlying the Roman

---

1 Scialojæ c. xiv. No. 2.
2 Statuta Criminalia Communis Bononiæ (Bononiæ 1525, p. 15 *b*).
3 Damhouder, *op. cit.* cap. xlvii. No. 3.
4 Passerini, *loc cit.* Nos. 122-3.          5 Ibid. No. 118.
6 Simancæ de Cathol. Instit. Tit. LXV. No. 73.
7 Zangeri, *op. cit.* I. Nos. 8–25.

ruie, universally followed by modern legists, that, whenever several parties were on trial under the same accusation, the torturer should commence with the weakest and tenderest, for thus it was expected that a confession could soonest be extracted; but this eager determination to secure conviction gave rise to a refinement of cruelty in the prescription that if a husband and wife were arraigned together, the wife should be tortured first, and in the presence of her husband ; and if a father and son, the son before his father's face.[1]

Grillandus, who seems to have been an unusually humane judge, describes five degrees of torture, using as a standard the favorite strappado. The first is purely mental—stripping the prisoner and tying his hands behind him to the rope, but not hurting him. This can be used when there is no evidence, and he tells us he had found it very efficacious, especially with the timid and infirm. The other grades are indicated in accordance with the strength of the proof and the heinousness of the crime. The second is hoisting the accused and letting him hang for the space of an Ave or a Pater Noster, or even a Miserere, but not elevating him and letting him fall with a jerk. In the third grade this suspension is prolonged. In the fourth he is allowed to hang for a time varying from a quarter of an hour to an hour, according to the crime and the evidence, and he is jerked two or three times. In the fifth and severest form a weight is attached to his feet and he is repeatedly jerked. This Grillandus describes as terrible ; the whole body is torn, the limbs are ready to part from the trunk, and death itself is preferable. It should only, he says, be used in the gravest crimes, such as heresy or treason, but we have already seen that it was mild in comparison with many inflictions habitually employed.[2]

[1] Zangeri cap. IV. Nos. 25–30.—Damhouder, *op. cit.* cap. xxxvii. Nos. 15, 16.—Baldi de Periglis de Quæstionibus, cap. i. § 7.—Alberti de Gandino de Quæstionibus § 11.

[2] Grilland. de Quæstione et Tortura Q. iv. §§ 2–10. " Quod tunc corpus ipsius rei dilaniatur membraque et ossa quodammodo dissolvuntur et evelluntur a corpore."

Some facilities for defence were allowed to the accused, but in practice they were almost hopelessly slender. He was permitted to employ counsel, and if unable to do so, it was the duty of the judge to look up testimony for the defence.[1] After all the adverse testimony had been taken, and the prisoner had been interrogated, he could ask to see a copy of the proceedings, in order to frame a defence; but the request could be refused, in which case, the judge was bound to sift the evidence himself, and to investigate the probabilities of innocence or guilt. Von Rosbach states that judges were not in the habit of granting the request, though no authority justified them in the refusal;[2] and half a century later this is confirmed by Bernhardi, who gives as a reason that by withholding the proceedings from the accused they saved themselves trouble.[3] The right of the accused to see the evidence adduced against him was still an open question so recently as 1742, for Goetz deems it necessary to argue at some length to prove it.[4] The recognized tendency of such a system to result in an unfavorable conclusion is shown by Zanger's elaborate instructions on this point, and his warning that, however justifiable torture may seem, it ought not to be resorted to without at least looking at the evidence which may be attainable in favor of innocence;[5] while von Rosbach characterizes as the greatest fault of the tribunals of his day, their neglect to obtain and consider testimony for the accused as well as against him.[6] Indeed, when the public interest was deemed to require it, all safeguards were withdrawn from

[1] Zangeri, *op. cit.* cap. III. No. 3.

[2] Process. Criminal. Tit. V. cap. X. No. 7.

We have already seen (p. 514) that in France the accused was not allowed to see the evidence against him; and the same rule was in force in Flanders—"Toutes depositions de tesmoins en causes criminelles demeureront secrétes à l'égard de l'accusé."—Coutume d'Audenarde, Stile de la Procedure, Art. 10. (Le Grand, Coutumes de Flandre, Cambrai, 1719, p. 103).

[3] Diss. Inaug. cap. I. § xii.              [4] Goetzii, *op. cit.* p. 36.

[5] Zangeri, *op. cit.* cap. III. Nos. 1, 4, 5–43.

[6] Process. Crim. Tit. V. cap. xi. No. 6.

the prisoner, as when, in 1719 in Saxony, a mandate was issued declaring that in cases of thieves and robbers no defence or exceptions or delays were to be admitted.[1] In some special and extraordinary cases, the judge might allow the accused to be confronted with the accuser, but this was so contrary to the secrecy required by the inquisitorial system, that he was cautioned that it was a very unusual course, and one not lightly to be allowed, as it was odious, unnecessary, and not pertinent to the trial.[2]

Theoretically, there was a right of appeal against an order to inflict torture, but this, even when permitted, could usually avail the accused but little, for the *ex parte* testimony which had satisfied the lower judge could, of course, in most instances, be so presented to the higher court as to insure the affirmation of the order, and prisoners, in their helplessness, would doubtless feel that by the attempt to appeal they would probably only increase the severity of their inevitable sufferings.[3] Moreover, such appeals were ingeniously and effectually discouraged by subjecting the advocate of the prisoner to a fine or some extraordinary punishment if the appeal was pronounced to be frivolous;[4] and some authorities, among which was the great name of Carpzovius, denied that in the inquisitorial process there was any necessity of communicating to the accused the order to subject him to torture and then allow him time to appeal against it if so disposed.[5]

Slender as were these safeguards in principle, they were reduced in practice almost to a nullity. That the discretion lodged in the tribunals was habitually and frightfully abused is only too evident, when von Rosbach deems it necessary to reprove, as a common error of the judges of his time, the

---

[1] Goetzii, *op. cit.* p. 35.

[2] Zangeri cap. II. Nos. 49–50.—Cum enim confrontatio odiosa sit et species suggestionis, et remedium extraordinarium ad substantiam processus non pertinens, et propterea non necessaria.

[3] Zangeri, cap. IV. Nos. 1–6.    [4] Goetzii Dissert. de Tortura, p. 34.

[5] Braune Dissert. de Tortura Valetudin. p. 16.

idea that the use of torture was a matter altogether dependent upon their pleasure, "as though nature had created the bodies of prisoners for them to lacerate at will."[1] Thus it was an acknowledged rule that when guilt could be satisfactorily proved by witnesses, torture was not admissible;[2] yet Damhouder feels it necessary to condemn the practice of some judges, who, after conviction by sufficient evidence, were in the habit of torturing the convict, and boasted that they never pronounced sentence of death without having first extorted a confession.[3] Moreover, the practice was continued which we have seen habitual in the Châtelet of Paris in the fourteenth century, whereby, after a man had been duly convicted of a capital crime, he was tortured to extract confessions of any other offences of which he might be guilty;[4] and as late as 1764, Beccaria lifts his voice against it as a still existing abuse, which he well qualifies as senseless curiosity, impertinent in the wantonness of its cruelty.[5] Martin Bernhardi, writing in 1705, asserts that this torture after confession and conviction was also resorted to in order to prevent the convict from appealing from the sentence.[6] So, although a man who freely confessed a crime could not be tortured, according to the general principle of the law, still, if in his confession he ad-

---

[1] Process. Crimin. Tit. v. cap. ix. No. 10.    [2] Zangeri cap. i. No. 37.

[3] Rer. Crimin. Praxis cap. xxxviii. Nos. 6, 7.

[4] Boden de Usu et Abusu Torturæ Th. xii. Damhouder declares this practice to be unjustifiable, though not infrequent (Rer. Crimin. Praxis cap. xxxvii. No. 12).—Bonifazio de' Vitaliani speaks of it as a common but evil custom.—De Quæstionibus, Rubr. *Quæ indicia*, § 7.

[5] He represents the judge as addressing his victim "Tu sei il reo di un delitto, dunque è possibile che lo sii di cent' altri delitti: questo dubbio mi pesa, voglio accertarmene col mio criterio di verità : le leggi ti tormentano, perche sei reo, perche puoi esser reo, perche voglio che tu sii reo."—Dei Delitti e delle Pene, § xii.

[6] Martini Bernhardi Diss. Inaug. de Tortura cap. i. § 4. Scialoja, in 1653, assures us that this torture after confession to prevent appeals was no longer permitted in the Neapolitan courts, and that it was only allowed for the discovery of accomplices (Praxis torquendi Reos. c. i. Nos. 8-10).

duced mitigating circumstances, he could be tortured in order
to force him to withdraw them;[1] and, moreover, if he were
suspected of having accomplices and refused to name them,
he could be tortured as in the *question préalable* of the French
courts.[2]  Yet the accusation thus obtained was held to be of
so little value that it only warranted the arrest of the parties
incriminated, who could not legally be tortured without
further evidence.[3]  In the face of all this it seems like jesting
mockery to find these grim legists tenderly suggesting that the
prisoner should be tortured only in the morning lest his health
should suffer by subjecting him to the question after a full
meal.[4]

If the practice of the criminal courts had been devised with
the purpose of working injustice under the sacred name of law
it could scarce have been different.  Even the inalienable privilege of being heard in his defence was habitually refused to the
accused by many tribunals, which proceeded at once to torture
after hearing the adverse evidence, a refinement of cruelty and
injustice which called forth labored arguments by von Rosbach
and Simancas to prove its impropriety, thus showing it to be
widely practised.[5]  In the same way, the right to appeal from
an order to torture was evaded by judges, who sent the prisoner
to the rack without a preliminary formal order, thus depriving
him of the opportunity of appealing.[6]  Indeed, in time it was

[1] Scialojæ, *op. cit.* cap. i. No. 14.

[2] Damhouder, Rer. Crimin. Prax. cap. xxxv. No. 9, cap. xxxviii. No.
14.—Werner Dissert. de Tortura Testium, pp. 76 sqq.

[3] Damhoud. cap. xxxix. No. 6.

[4] Goetzii Dissert. de Tortura, p. 26.

[5] Emer. a Rosbach Process. Criminal. Tit. v. cap. x. Nos. 8–16.—Simancæ
Cath. Inst. LXV. 17.

[6] Bernhardi, *loc. cit.*  The difference between the practice and principles of the law is shown by the rules laid down in 1647 by Brunnemann,
coexisting with the above.  He directs that the proceedings are to be ex-
hibited to the accused or his friends, and then submitted to a college of
jurists who are to decide as to the necessity of torture, and he warns the
latter that they can have no graver question placed before them—" Et sane

admitted by many jurists that the judge at his pleasure could refuse to allow an appeal; and that in no case was he to wait more than ten days for the decision of the superior tribunal.[1]

The frequency with which torture was used is manifested in the low rate which was paid for its application. In the municipal accounts of Valenciennes, between 1538 and 1573, the legal fee paid to the executioner for each torturing of a prisoner is only two sous and a half, while he is allowed the same sum for the white gloves worn at an execution, and ten sous are given him for such light jobs as piercing the tongue.[2]

With all this hideous accumulation of cruelty which shrank from nothing in the effort to wring a confession from the wretched victim, that confession, when thus so dearly obtained, was estimated at its true worthlessness. It was insufficient for conviction unless confirmed by the accused in a subsequent examination beyond the confines of the torture-chamber, at an interval of from one to three days.[3] This confirmation was by no means universal, and the treatment of cases of retracted confession was the subject of much debate. Bodin, in 1579, complains that witches sometimes denied what they had confessed under torture, and that the puzzled judge was then obliged to release them.[4] Such a result, however, was so totally at variance with the determination to obtain a conviction which marks the criminal jurisprudence of the period that it was not likely to be submitted to with patience. Accordingly the general practice was that, if the confession was retracted, the accused was again tortured, when a second confession and retraction made an exceedingly awkward

nullam graviorem puto esse deliberationem in Collegiis Juridicis quam ubi de tortura infligenda agitur."—Brunneman. de Inquisitionis Processu cap. VIII. Memb. iv. No. 10; Memb. v. No. 1.

[1] Passerini Regulare Tribunal; Praxis, cap. viii. No. 170.

[2] Louïse, Sorcellerie et Justice Criminelle à Valenciennes (Valenciennes, 1861, pp. 121–125).

[3] Goetzii Diss. de Tortura, p. 71.

[4] Bodin de Magor. Dæmonom. (Basil. 1581, p. 325).

dilemma for the subtle jurisconsults. They agreed that he should not be allowed to escape after giving so much trouble. Some advocated the regular punishment of his crime, others demanded for him an extraordinary penalty; some, again, were in favor of incarcerating him;[1] others assumed that he should be tortured a third time, when a confession, followed as before by a recantation, released him from further torment, for the admirable reason that nature and justice alike abhorred infinity.[2] This was too metaphysical for some jurists, who referred the whole question to the discretion of the judge, with power to prolong the series of alternate confession and retraction indefinitely, acting doubtless on the theory that most prisoners were like the scamp spoken of by Ippolito dei Marsigli, who, after repeated tortures and revocations, when asked by the judge why he retracted his confession so often, replied that he would rather be tortured a thousand times in the arms than once in the neck, for he could easily find a doctor to set his arm but never one to set his neck.[3] The magistrates in some places were in the habit of imprisoning or banishing such persons, thus punishing them without conviction, and inflicting a penalty unsuited to the crime of which they were accused.[4] Others solved the knotty problem by judiciously advising that in the uncertainty of doubt as to his guilt, the prisoner should be soundly scourged and turned

[1] Zangeri cap. v. Nos. 79–81.

[2] Bernhardi Diss. Inaug. cap. I. § xi.

[3] Emer. a Rosbach, *op. cit.* Tit. v. cap. xviii. No. 13.—Godelmanni de Magis L. III. cap. x. § 52.—Gerstlacheri Comment. de Quæst. per Tormenta, p. 35.—Grillandi de Quæst. et Tortura Q. vii. § 11. So Beccaria (Delitt. e Pene, § XII.) —" Alcuni dottori ed alcune nazioni non permettono questa infame petizione di principio che per tre volte; altre nazioni ed altri dottori la lasciano ad arbitrio del giudice."

[4] This custom prevailed in Electoral Saxony until the abrogation of torture (Goetzii Diss. de Tort. p. 33), and was especially the case at Amsterdam. Meyer (Institutions Judiciaires, IV. 295) states that the registers there afford scarcely an instance of a prisoner discharged without conviction after enduring torture.

loose, after taking an oath not to bring an action for false imprisonment against his tormentors ;[1] but, according to some authorities, this kind of oath, or *urpheda* as it was called, was of no legal value.[2] Towards the end of the torture system, however, the more humane though not very logical doctrine prevailed in Germany that a retraction absolved the accused, unless new and different evidence was brought forward, and this had to be stronger and clearer than before, for the presumption of innocence was now with the accused, the torture having purged him of former suspicion.[3]

This necessity of repeating a confession after torture gave rise to another question which caused considerable difference of opinion among doctors, namely, whether witnesses who were tortured had to confirm their evidence subsequently, and whether they, in case of retraction or the presentation of fresh evidence, could be tortured repeatedly. As usual in doubts respecting torture, the weight of authority was in favor of its most liberal use.[4]

There were other curious inconsistencies in the system which manifest still more clearly the real estimate placed on confessions under torture. If the torture had been inflicted by an over-zealous judge without proper preliminary evidence, confession amounted legally to nothing, even though proofs were subsequently discovered.[5] If, on the other hand, absolute and incontrovertible proof of guilt were had, and the over-zealous judge tortured in surplusage without extracting a confession, there arose another of the knotty points to which the torture system inevitably tended and about which jurisconsults dif-

---

[1] Zanger. *loc. cit.*

[2] Bernhardi, cap. I. § xii.—Goetzii *op. cit.* p. 74.—Cf. Caroli V. Const. Crim. cap. xx. § I.—Goetz (p. 67) derives *urpheda* from *ur* before, and *fede* enmity.

[3] Goetzii Dissert. de Tortura, p. 31.

[4] Werner. Dissert. de Tortura, pp. 91-2.

[5] Zangeri cap. II. Nos. 9-10; cap. V. Nos. 19-28.—Damhouder. *op. cit.* cap. xxxvi. No. 36.—Baldi de Periglis de Quæstionibus cap. ii. § 9.

fered. Some held that he was to be absolved, because torture purged him of all the evidence against him; others argued that he was to be punished with the full penalty of his crime, because the torture was illegal and therefore null and void; others again took a middle course and decided that he was to be visited, not with the penalty of his crime, but with something else, at the discretion of his judge.[1] According to law, indeed, torture without confession was a full acquittal; but here, again, practice intervened to destroy what little humanity was admitted by jurists, and the accused under such circumstances was still held suspect, and was liable at any moment to be tried again for the same offence.[2] Indeed, at a comparatively early period after the introduction of torture, we are told that if the accused endured it without confession he was to be kept in prison to see whether new evidence might not turn up: if none came, then the judge was to assign him a reasonable delay for his defence; he was regularly tried, when if convicted he was punished; if not he was discharged.[3] If, again, a man and woman were tortured on an accusation of adultery committed with each other, and if one confessed while the other did not, both were acquitted according to some authorities, while others held that the one who confessed should receive some punishment different from that provided for the crime, while the accomplice was to be discharged on taking a purgatorial oath.[4] Nothing more contradictory and illogical can well be imagined, and, as if to crown the absurdity of the

[1] Zangeri cap. v. Nos. 1–18 —Goetzii Dissert. de Tortura, pp. 67–9.

[2] Damhouder. *op. cit.* cap. xl. No. 3.—Bigotry and superstition, especially, did not allow their victims to escape so easily. In accusations of sorcery, if appearances were against the prisoner—that is, if he were of evil repute, if he shed no tears during the torture, and if he recovered speedily after each application—he was not to be liberated because no confession could be wrung from him, but was to be kept for at least a year, "squaloribus carceris mancipandus et cruciandus, sæpissime etiam examinandus, præcipue sacratioribus diebus."—Rickii Defens. Aq. Probæ cap. i. No. 22.

[3] Alberti de Gandino de Quæstionibus § 21.

[4] Zangeri cap. v. No. 53–61.—Goetzii Dissert. de Tortura, p. 57.

whole, torture after conviction was allowed in order to prevent appeals ; and if the unfortunate, at the place of execution, chanced to assert his innocence, he was often hurried
from the scaffold to the rack in obedience to the theory that
the confession must remain unretracted ;[1] though, if the judge
had taken the precaution to have the prisoner's ratification of
his confession duly certified to by a notary and witnesses, this
trouble might be avoided, and the culprit be promptly executed in spite of his retraction.[2]  One can scarce repress a
grim smile at finding that this series of horrors had pious
defenders who urged that a merciful consideration for the
offender's soul required that he should be brought to confess
his iniquities in order to secure his eternal salvation.[3]  It was
a minor, yet none the less a flagrant injustice, that when a
man had endured the torture without confession, and was
therefore discharged as innocent, he or his heirs were obliged
to defray the whole expenses of his prosecution.[4]

The atrocity of this whole system of so-called criminal
justice is forcibly described by the honest indignation of
Augustin Nicolas, who, in his judicial capacity under Louis
XIV., had ample opportunities of observing its practical
working and results.  "The strappado, so common in Italy,
and which yet is forbidden under the Roman law . . . the
vigils of Spain, which oblige a man to support himself by
sheer muscular effort for seven hours, to avoid sitting on a
pointed iron, which pierces him with insufferable pain ; the
vigils of Florence, or of Marsiglio, which have been described
above ; our iron stools heated to redness, on which we place
poor half-witted women accused of witchcraft, exhausted by

---

[1] Boden, *op. cit.* Th. v. vi.

[2] Goetzii Dissert. de Tortura, p. 72.

[3] Boden, *op. cit.* Th. v. vi.

[4] Goetzii Dissert. de Tortura, p. 76.  Distinction was sometimes made
between crimes involving death or corporal punishment and those of lighter
grade, but Goetz states that in his time (1742) in Saxony the above was the
received practice.

frightful imprisonment, rotting from their dark and filthy dungeons, loaded with chains, fleshless, and half dead ; and we pretend that the human frame can resist these devilish practices, and that the confessions which our wretched victims make of everything that may be charged against them are true."[1] Under such a scheme of jurisprudence, it is easy to understand and appreciate the case of the unfortunate peasant, sentenced for witchcraft, who, in his dying confession to the priest, admitted that he was a sorcerer, and humbly welcomed death as the fitting retribution for the unpardonable crimes of which he had been found guilty, but pitifully inquired of the shuddering confessor whether one could not be a sorcerer without knowing it.[2]

If anything were wanting to show how completely the inquisitorial process turned all the chances against the accused, it is to be found in the quaint advice given by Damhouder. He counsels the prisoner, when required to plead, to prevent his judge from taking advantage of any adverse points that might occur, as, for instance, in a charge of homicide to assert his innocence, but to add that, if he were proved to have committed the crime, he then declares it to have been done in self-defence.[3]

We have seen above how great was the part of the Inquisition in introducing and moulding the whole system of torture on the ruins of the feudal law. Even so, in the reconstruction of European jurisprudence, during the sixteenth and seventeenth centuries, the ardor of the inquisitorial proceedings against witchcraft, and the panic on the subject which long pervaded Christendom, had a powerful influence in familiarizing the minds of men with the use of torture as a necessary instrument of justice, and in authorizing its employment to an extent which now is almost inconceivable.

---

[1] Dissert. Mor. et Jurid. sur la Torture, pp. 36-7.
[2] Ibid. p. 169.
[3] Damhoud. Rer. Criminal. Prax. cap. 34, § 7.

From a very early period, torture was recognized as indispensable in all trials for sorcery and magic. In 358, an edict of Constantius decreed that no dignity of birth or station should protect those accused of such offences from its application in the severest form.[1] How universal its employment thus became is evident from a canon of the council of Merida, in 666, declaring that priests, when sick, sometimes accused the slaves of their churches of bewitching them, and impiously tortured them against all ecclesiastical rules.[2] It was, therefore, natural that all such crimes should be regarded as peculiarly subjecting all suspected of them to the last extremity of torture, and its use in the trials of witches and sorcerers came to be regarded as indispensable.

The necessity which all men felt that these crimes should be extirpated with merciless severity, and the impalpable nature of the testimony on which the tribunals had mostly to depend, added to this traditional belief in the fitness of torture. Witchcraft was considered as peculiarly difficult of proof, and torture consequently became an unfailing resource to the puzzled tribunal, although every legal safeguard was refused to the wretched criminal, and the widest latitude of evidence was allowed. Bodin expressly declares that in so fearful a crime no rules of procedure are to be observed.[3] Sons were admitted to testify against their fathers, and young girls were regarded as the best of witnesses against their mothers; the disrepute of a witness was no bar to the reception of his testimony, and even children of irresponsible age

---

[1] Const. 7 Cod. IX. xviii.

[2] Concil. Emeritan. ann. 666 can. xv.

In the middle of the thirteenth century, the Emperor Theodore Lascaris invented a novel mode of torture in a case of this kind. When a noble lady of his court was accused of sorcery, he caused her to be inclosed naked in a sack with a number of cats. The suffering, though severe, failed to extort a confession.—Georg. Pachymeri Hist. Mich. Palæol. Lib. I. cap. xii.

[3] Bodini de Magorum Dæmonoman. Lib. IV. cap. 2.

were allowed to swear before they rightly knew the nature of
the oath on which hung the life of a parent. Boguet, who
presided over a tribunal in Franche Comté, in stating this
rule relates a most pathetic case of his own in which a man
named Guillaume Vuillermoz was convicted on the testimony
of his son, aged twelve, and the hardened nerves of the judge
were wrung at the despair of the unhappy prisoner on being
confronted with his child, who persisted in his story with a
callousness only to be explained by the will of God, who
stifled in him all natural affection in order to bring to condign
punishment this most hideous offence.[1] Louïse prints the
records of a trial in 1662, wherein Philippe Polus was condemned on the evidence of his daughter, a child in her ninth
year. There seems to have been no other proof against him,
and according to her own testimony the girl had been a
sorceress since her fourth year.[2] Even advocates and counsel
could be forced to give evidence against their clients.[3] Notwithstanding the ample resources thus afforded for conviction,
Jacob Rickius, who, as a magistrate during an epidemic of
witchcraft, at the close of the sixteenth century, had the
fullest practical experience on the subject, complains that no
reliance could be placed on legal witnesses to produce conviction ;[4] and Del Rio only expresses the general opinion
when he avers that torture is to be more readily resorted to in
witchcraft than in other crimes, in consequence of the extreme
difficulty of its proof.[5]

Even the wide-spread belief that Satan aided his worshippers

[1] Boguet, Discours des Sorciers, chap. lv. (Lyon, 1610).

[2] Louïse, La Sorcellerie et la Justice Criminelle à Valenciennes (Valenciennes, 1861, pp. 133-64).—For other similar instances see Bodin, *op.
cit.* Lib. IV. cap. 1, 2.

[3] Bodin. Lib. I. cap. 2.

[4] Per legales testes hujus rei ad convincendum fides certa haberi non
potest.—Rickii Defens. Aquæ Probæ cap. III. No. 117.

[5] Idque facilius in excepto et occulto difficilisque probationis crimine
nostro sortilegii admiserim quam in aliis.—Disquisit. Magicar. Lib. v. Sect.
iii. No. 8.

in their extremity by rendering them insensible to pain did
not serve to relax the efforts of the extirpators of witchcraft,
though they could hardly avoid the conclusion that they were
punishing only the innocent, and allowing the guilty to escape.
Boguet, indeed, seems to recognize this practical inconsistency,
and, though it is permissible to use torture even during church
festivals, he advises the judge not to have recourse to it because of its inutility.[1] How little his advice was heeded, and
how little the courts deemed themselves able to dispense with
torture, is shown in the charter of Hainault of 1619 where in
these cases the tribunal is authorized to employ it to ascertain
the truth of the charge, or to discover accomplices, or *for any
other purpose*.[2] In this dilemma, various means were adopted
to circumvent the arch enemy, of which the one most generally
resorted to was that of shaving the whole person carefully before
applying the torture,[3] a process which served as an excuse for
the most indecent outrages upon female prisoners. Yet notwithstanding all the precautions of the most experienced ex-
orcists, we find in the bloody farce of Urbain Grandier that
the fiercest torments left him in capital spirits and good humor.[4]
Damhouder relates at much length a curious case which
occurred under his own eyes while member of the council of

[1] Boguet, Instruction pour un juge en faict de Sorcelerie, art. xxxii.

[2] Soit pour ne trouver les délitz suffisament vérifiez, ou pour savoir tous
les complices, *ou autrement.*—Chart. nouv. du Haynau, chap. 125, art.
xxvi. (Louïse, p. 94).

[3] Nicolas, p. 145. The curious reader will find in Del Rio (Lib. v. Sect.
ix.) ample details as to the arts of the Evil One to sustain his followers
against the pious efforts of the Inquisition.

[4] " Q'après qu'on eut lavé ses jambes, qui avoient été déchirées par la
torture, et qu'on les eut présentées au feu pour y rapeller quelque peu
d'esprits et de vigueur, il ne cessa pas de s'entretenir avec ses Gardes, par
des discours peu sérieux et pleins de railleries; qu'il mangea avec apétit et
but avec plaisir trois ou quatre coups; et qu'il ne répandit aucuns larmes en
souffrant la question, ni après l'avoir souffert, lors même qu'on l'exorcisa de
l'exorcisme des Magiciens, et que l'Exorciste lui dit à plus de cinquante
reprises 'præcipio ut si sis innocens effundas lachrymas.' "—Hist. des
Diables de Loudon, pp. 157-8.

Bruges, when he assisted at the torture of a reputed witch who had exercised her power only in good works. During three examinations, she bore the severest torture without shrinking, sometimes sleeping and sometimes defiantly snapping her fingers at the judges. At length, during the process of shaving, a slip of parchment covered with cabalistic characters was found concealed in her person, and on its removal she was speedily brought to acknowledge her pact with the Evil One.[1] The tender-hearted Rickius was so convinced of this source of uncertainty that he was accustomed to administer the cold-water ordeal to all the miserable old women brought before him on such charges, but he is careful to inform us that this was only preparatory proof, to enable him with a safer conscience to torture those who were so ill-advised as to float instead of sinking.[2] Grillandus tells us that he had met with cases in which the insensibility to the severest tortures was so complete that only magic arts could explain it; the patient seemed to be supported in the air, or to be in a profound stupor, and he mentions some of the formulas which were employed for the purpose. In one case at Rome a notorious thief suspected of a large robbery came to him voluntarily and said he wanted to purge himself of the rumors against him. He was tortured repeatedly in various ways; when the operation began he muttered something and fell into a stupor in which he was absolutely insensible. After exhausting his ingenuity, Grillandus had to discharge him. In another case the formula " Quemadmodum lac beatæ," etc., produced the same effect.[3]

---

[1] Rerum Crimin. Praxis Cap. xxxvii. Nos. 21, 22.   Cf. Brunnemann. de Inquisit. Process. cap. viii. Memb. v. No. 70.

[2] Rickii *op. cit.* cap. i. No. 24.

[3] Grillandi de Quæstione et Tortura, Art. iii. §§ 12–16.   One of the conjurations is an allusion to the Crucifixion,

" Imparibus meritis tria pendent corpora ramis.
Dismas et Gestas, in medio est divina potestas.
Dismas damnatur, Gestas ad astra levatur."

From the time when the Cappadocians of old were said to harden their children with torture in order that they might profitably follow the profession of false witnesses, there existed so general a belief among experienced men that criminals of all kinds had secrets with which to deaden sensibility to torture that it is not improbable that the unfortunates occasionally were able to strengthen their endurance with some anæsthetic. Boguet complains that in modern times torture had become almost useless not only with sorcerers but with criminals in general, and Damhouder asserts that professional malēfactors were in the habit of torturing each other in order to be hardened when brought to justice, in consequence of which he advises the judge to inquire into the antecedents of prisoners, in order to proportion the severity of the torture to the necessities of the case.[1]

When the concentrated energies of these ingenious and determined law dispensers failed to extort by such means a confession from the wretched clowns and gossips thus placed at their mercy, they were even yet not wholly at fault. The primitive teachings of the Inquisition of the thirteenth century were not yet obsolete; they were instructed to treat the prisoner kindly, and to introduce into his dungeon some prepossessing agent who should make friends with him and induce him to confess what was wanted of him, promising to influence the judge to pardon, when at that moment the judge is to enter the cell and to promise grace, with the mental reservation that his grace should be shown to the community and not to the prisoner.[2] Or, still following the ancient traditions, spies were

Another "Quemadmodum lac beatæ gloriosæ Mariæ virginis fuit dulce et suave domino nostro Jesu Christo, ita hæc tortura sit dulcis et suavis brachiis et membris meis."

[1] Boguet, Instruction pour un juge, art. xxix.—Damhouderi Rer. Crim. Prax. cap. xxxviii. No. 19.

[2] Sprenger Mall. Maleficar. P. III. q. xvi. This was directly in contradiction to the precepts of the civil lawyers. Ippolito dei Marsigli says positively that a confession uttered in response to a promise of pardon cannot be used

to be confined with him, who should profess to be likewise sorcerers and thus lead him to incriminate himself, or else the unhappy wretch was to be told that his associate prisoners had borne testimony against him, in order to induce him to revenge himself by turning witness against them.[1] Boguet, indeed, does not consider it correct to mislead the accused with promises of pardon, and though it was generally approved by legists, he decides against it.[2] Simancas also considers such artifices to be illegal, and that a confession thus procured could be retracted.[3] Del Rio, on the other hand, while loftily condemning the outspoken trickery recommended by Sprenger and Bodin, proceeds to draw a careful distinction between *dolum bonum* and *dolum malum*. He forbids absolute lying, but advises equivocation and ambiguous promises, and then, if the prisoner is deceived, he has only himself to thank for it.[4] In fact, these men conceived that they were engaged in a direct and personal struggle with the Evil One, and that Satan could only be overcome with his own arts.

When the law thus pitilessly turned all the chances against the victim, it is easy to understand that few escaped. In the existing condition of popular frenzy on the subject, there was no one but could feel that he might at any moment be brought under accusation by personal enemies or by unfortunates compelled on the rack to declare the names of all whom they might have seen congregated at the witches' sabbat. We can thus readily comprehend the feelings of those who, living under such uncertainties, coolly and deliberately made up their minds in advance that, if chance should expose them to suspicion,

against the accused (Singularia, Venet. 1555, fol. 36 *b*). The Church, however, did not consider itself bound by the ordinary rules of law or morality. Marsigli in another passage (fol. 30 *a*) relates that Alexander III. once secretly promised a bishop that if he would publicly confess himself guilty of simony he should have a dispensation, and on the prelate's doing so, immediately deposed him.

[1] Bodin. Lib. IV. cap. I.      [2] Boguet, Instruction, art. xxvii.
[3] De Cathol. Instit. Tit. XIII. No. 12.
[4] Disquisit. Magicar. Lib. v. Sect. x.

they would at once admit everything that the inquisitors might desire of them, preferring a speedy death to one more lingering and scarcely less certain.[1] The evil fostered with such careful exaggeration grew to so great proportions that Father Tanner speaks of the multitude of witches who were daily convicted through torture;[2] and that this was no mere form of speech is evident when one judge, in a treatise on the subject, boasted of his zeal and experience in having dispatched within his single district nine hundred wretches in the space of fifteen years, and another trustworthy authority relates with pride that in the diocese of Como alone as many as a thousand had been burnt in a twelvemonth, while the annual average was over a hundred.[3]

Were it not for the steady patronage bestowed on the system by the Church, it would seem strange that torture should invade the quiet and holy retirement of the cloister. Its use, however, in monasteries was, if possible, even more arbitrary than in secular tribunals. Monks and nuns were exempt from the jurisdiction of the civil authorities, and were bound by vows of blind obedience to their superiors. The head of each convent thus was an autocrat, and when investigating the delinquencies of any of his flock he was subjected to no limitations. Not only could he order the accused to be tortured at will, but the witnesses, whether male or female, were liable to the same treatment, with the exception that in the case of nuns it was recommended that the tortures employed should not be indecent or too severe for the fragility of the sex. As elsewhere, it was customary to commence the torment with the weakest of the witnesses or criminals.[4]

---

[1] Father Tanner states that he had this from learned and experienced men.—Tanneri Tract. de Proc. adv. Veneficas, Quæst. II. Assert. iii. § 2.

[2] Ibid. *loc. cit.*        [3] Nicolas, p. 164.

[4] Chabot, Encyclopédie Monastique, p. 426 (Paris, 1827). For instances see Angeli Rumpheri Hist. Formbach. Lib. II. (Pez, I. III. 446).—A. Molinier in Vaissette, Ed. Privat, IX. 417.

## CHAPTER IX.

### ENGLAND AND THE NORTHERN RACES.

IN this long history of legalized cruelty and wrong the races of northern Europe are mostly exceptional. Yet it is somewhat remarkable that the first regular mediæval code in which tor⁻ ture is admitted as a means of investigation is the one of all others in which it would be least expected. The earliest extant law of Iceland, the Grágás, which dates from 1119, has one or two indications of its existence which are interesting as being purely autochthonic and in no sense derivable, as in the rest of Europe, from the Roman law. The character of the people, indeed, and of their institutions would seem to be peculiarly incompatible with the use of torture, for almost all cases were submitted to inquests or juries of the vicinage, and, when this was unsuitable, resort was had to the ordeal. The indigenous origin of the custom, however, is shown by the fact that while it was used in but few matters, the most prominent class subjected to it was that of pregnant women, who have elsewhere been spared by the common consent of even the most pitiless legislators. An unmarried woman with child, who refused to name her seducer, could be forced to do so by moderate torments which should not break or discolor the skin.[1] The object of this was to enable the family to obtain the fine from the seducer, and to save themselves from the expense of supporting the child. When the mother confessed, however, additional evidence was required to convict the putative father. When the inhabitants of a district, also, refused

[1] " Ita torquatur ut nec plagam referat nec color cutis livescat."—Grágás, Festathattr cap. xxxiii.

to deliver up a man claimed as an outlaw by another district, they were bound to torture him to ascertain the truth of the charge[1]—a provision doubtless explicable by the important part occupied by outlawry in all the schemes of Scandinavian legislation. These are the only instances in which it is permitted, while its occasional abuse is shown by a section providing punishment for its illegal employment.[2] Slaves, moreover, under the Icelandic, as under other codes, had no protection at law, and were at the mercy of their masters.[3] These few indications of the liability of freemen, however, disappear about the time when the rest of Europe was commencing to adopt the use of torture. In the *Jarnsida*, or code compiled for Iceland by Hako Hakonsen of Norway, in 1258, there is no allusion whatever to its use.

The Scandinavian nations, as a whole, did not admit torture into their systems of jurisprudence. The institution of the jury in various forms was common to all, and where proof upon open trial was deficient, they allowed, until a comparatively recent date, the accused to clear himself by sacramental purgation. Thus, in the Danish laws of Waldemar II., to which the date of 1240 is generally assigned, there is a species of permanent jury, *sandemend*, as well as a temporary one, *nefninge*, and torture seems to have formed no part of judicial proceedings.[4] This code was in force until 1683, when that of Christiern V. was promulgated. It is probable that the employment of torture may have crept in from Germany, without being regularly sanctioned, for we find Christiern forbidding its use except in cases of high treason, where the magnitude of the offence seems to him to justify the infraction of the general rule. He, however, encouraged one of its greatest abuses in permitting it on criminals condemned to death.[5]

---

[1] Grágás, Vigslothi cap. cxi.      [2] Ibid. Vigslothi cap. lxxxviii.

[3] Schlegel Comment. ad Grágás ₰ xxix.

[4] Legg. Cimbric. Woldemari Lib. II. cap. i. xl. (Ed. Ancher, Hafniæ, 1783).

[5] Christiani V. Jur. Danic. Lib. I. cap. xx. (Ed. Weghorst, Hafniæ, 1698). Senckenberg (Corp. Jur. German. T. I. Præf. p. lxxxvi.) gives the chapter

Among the kindred Frisians the tendency was the same. Their code of 1323 is a faithful transcript of the primitive Barbarian jurisprudence. It contains no allusions to torture, and as all crimes, except theft, were still compounded for with *wer-gilds*, it may reasonably be assumed that the extortion of confession was not recognized as a judicial expedient.[1]

So, in Sweden, the code of Raguald, compiled in 1441, and in force until 1614, during a period in which torture flourished in almost every European state, has no place for it. Trials are conducted before twelve *nempdarii*, or jurymen, and in doubtful cases the accused is directed to clear himself by oath or by conjurators. For atrocious crimes the punishments are severe, such as the wheel or the stake, but inflictions like these are reserved for the condemned.[2] Into these distant regions the Roman jurisprudence penetrated slowly, and the jury trial was an elastic institution which adapted itself to all cases.

To the same causes may be attributed the absence of torture from the Common Law of England. In common with the other Barbarian races, the Anglo-Saxons solved all doubtful questions by the ordeal and wager of law, and in the collection known as the laws of Henry I. a principle is laid down which is incompatible with the whole theory of torture, whether used to extract confession or evidence. A confession obtained by fear or fraud is pronounced invalid, and no one who has confessed his own crime is to be believed with respect to that of another.[3] Such a principle, combined with the gradual

heads of a code in Danish, the *Keyser Retenn*, furnished to him by Ancher, in which cap. iv. and v. contain directions as to the administration of torture. The code is a mixture of German, civil, and local law, and probably was in force in some of the Germanic provinces of Dènmark.

[1] Legg. Opstalbomicæ ann. 1323 (*ap.* Gärtner, Saxonum Leges Tres. Lipsiæ, 1730).

[2] Raguald. Ingermund. Leg. Suécor. Štockholmiæ, 1623.

[3] Ll. Henrici I. cap. v. § 16.

A curious disregard of this principle occurs in the Welsh laws, which provide that when a thief is at the gallows, with the certainty of being

growth of the trial by jury, doubtless preserved the law from
the contamination of inquisitorial procedure, though, as we
have seen, torture was extensively employed for purposes of
extortion by marauders and lawless nobles during periods of
civil commotion. Glanville makes no allusion to it, and
though Bracton shows a wide acquaintance with the revived
Roman jurisprudence, and makes extensive use of it in all
matters where it could be advantageously harmonized with
existing institutions, he is careful to abstain from introducing
torture into criminal procedure.[1] A clause in Magna Charta,
indeed, has been held by high authority to inhibit the employment of torture, but it has no direct allusion to the subject,
which was not a living question at the time, and was probably
not thought of by any of the parties to that transaction.[2]  In

hanged, his testimony as to his accomplices is to be received as sufficient
without requiring it to be sworn to on a relic—the inseparable condition of
all other evidence. By a singular inconsistency, however, the accomplice
thus convicted was not to be hanged, but to be sold as a slave.—Dimetian
Code, Bk. II. ch. v. § 9 (Owen I. 425).

[1] Many interesting details on the influence of the Roman law upon that
of England will be found in the learned work of Carl Güterbock, "Bracton and his Relation to the Roman Law," recently translated by Brinton
Coxe (Philadelphia, 1866). The subject is one which well deserves a
more thorough consideration than it is likely to receive at the hands of
English writers.

It is curious to observe that the *crimen læsæ majestatis* makes its appearance in Bracton (Lib. III. Tract. ii. cap. 3, § 1) about the middle of the
thirteenth century, earlier than in France, where, as we have seen, the
first allusion to it occurs in 1315. This was hardly to be expected, when
we consider the widely different influences exerted upon the jurisprudence
of the two countries by the Roman law.

[2] The passage which has been relied on by lawyers is chap. xxx.:
"Nullus liber homo capiatur, vel imprisonetur, aut dissaisiatur, aut utla-
getur, aut aliquo modo destruatur; nec super eum ibimus, nec super eum
mittemus, nisi per legale judicium parium suorum, vel per legem terræ."
If the law just above quoted from the collection of Henry I. could be
supposed to be still in force under John, then this might possibly be imagined to bear some reference to it; but it is evident that had torture been
an existing grievance, such as outlawry, seizure, and imprisonment, the barons

fact, the whole spirit of English law was irreconcilable with
the fundamental principles of the inquisitorial process. When
the accused was brought before court, he was, it is true, required to appear ungirdled, without boots, or cap, or cloak,
to show his humility, but it is expressly directed that he shall
not be chained, lest his fetters should embarrass his self-pos-
session in his defence, and he was not to be forced in any way
to state anything but of his own free will.[1] Men who could
frame legal maxims so honorable to their sense of justice and
so far in advance of the received notions of their age could
evidently have nothing in common with the principles which
placed the main reliance of the law on confession to be wrung
from the lips of an unfortunate wretch who was systematically
deprived of all support and assistance. To do so, in fact, is
classed with homicide, by a legal writer of the period;[2] but
that it was occasionally practised is shown by his giving a form
for the appeal of homicide against judges guilty of it.[3]

Under the common law, therefore, torture had properly no
existence in England, and in spite of occasional efforts on
the part of the Plantagenets[4] the character of the national

would have been careful to include it in their enumeration of restrictions.
Moreover, Magna Charta was specially directed to curtail the royal prerogative, and at a later period was not held by any one to interfere with that
prerogative whenever the king desired to test with the rack the endurance
of his loving subjects.

[1] Et come ascuns felons viendrount en Jugement respondre de lour fe-
lonie, volons que ils viegnent dechausses et descients sauns coiffe, et a teste
descouverte, en pure lour cote hors de fers et de chescun manere de liens,
issint que la peine ne lour toille nule manere de rason, selon par force ne
lour estouva mye respondre forsque lour fraunche volunte.—Britton, chap. v.

[2] Per volunté aussi se fait ceste pesché [homicide] si come per ceux qui
painent home tant que il est gehist pur avouer pesché mortelment.—Horne,
The Myrror of Justice, cap. I. sect. viii.—See also Fleta, Lib. I. cap. xxvi. § 5.

[3] Ou faussement judgea Raginald . . . . ou issint; tant luy penia pur
luy faire conoistre, approver il se conoist faussement aver pesché ou nient
ne pescha.—Horne, cap. II. sect. xv.

[4] Pike (Hist. of Crime in England I. 427) quotes a document of 1189
which seems indirectly to show that torture could be inflicted under an

institutions kept at bay the absorbing and centralizing influences of the Roman law.[1] Yet their wide acceptance in France, and their attractiveness to those who desired to wield absolute authority, gradually accustomed the crown and the crown lawyers to the idea that torture could be administered by order of the sovereign. Sir John Fortescue, who was Lord Chancellor under Henry VI., inveighs at great length against the French law for its cruel procedures, and with much satisfaction contrasts it with the English practice,[2] and yet he does not deny that torture was occasionally used in England. Indeed, his fervent arguments against the system, addressed to Prince Edward, indicate an anxiety to combat and resist the spread of civil law doctrines on the subject, which doubtless were favored by the influence of Margaret of Anjou. An instance of its application in 1468 has, in fact, been recorded, which resulted in the execution of Sir Thomas Coke, Lord Mayor of London;[3] and in 1485, Innocent VIII. remonstrated with Henry VII. respecting some proceedings against ecclesiastics who were scourged, tortured, and hanged.[4]

Under Henry VIII. and his children, the power of the crown was largely extended, and the doctrine became fashionable that, though under the law no one could be tortured for

order of the king. The expression is somewhat doubtful, and as torture had not yet established itself anywhere in Europe as a judicial procedure the document alleged can hardly be received as evidence of its legality.

[1] See Fortescue de Laud. Legg. Angliæ. cap. xxxiii.—The jealousy with which all attempted encroachments of the Roman law were repelled is manifested in a declaration of Parliament in 1388. "Que ce royalme d'Engleterre n'estait devant ces heures, ne à l'entent du roy nostre dit seignior et seigniors du parlement unque ne serra rulé ne governé par la ley civill."—Rot. Parl., 11 Ric. II. (Selden's Note to Fortescue, loc. cit.).

[2] De Laudibus Legum Angliæ, cap. xxii.

[3] See Jardine's "Reading on the Use of Torture in the Criminal Law of England," p. 7 (London, 1837), a condensed and sufficiently complete account of the subject under the Tudors and Stuarts.

[4] Partim tormentis subjecti, partim crudelissime laniati, et partim etiam furca suspensi fuerant.—Wilkins Concil. III. 617.

confession or evidence, yet outside and above the law the royal prerogative was supreme, and that a warrant from the King in Privy Council fully justified the use of the rack and the introduction of the secret inquisitorial process, with all its attendant cruelty and injustice.   It is difficult to conceive the subserviency which could reconcile men, bred in the open and manly justice of the common law, to a system so subversive of all the principles in which they had been trained. Yet the loftiest names of the profession were concerned in transactions which they knew to be in contravention of the laws of the land.

Sir Thomas Smith, one of the ornaments of the Elizabethan bar, condemned the practice as not only illegal, but illogical. "Torment or question, which is used by order of the civile law and custome of other countries,  . . . .  is not used in England.  . . .  The nature of Englishmen is to neglect death, to abide no torment; and therefore hee will confesse rather to have done anything, yea, to have killed his owne father, than to suffer torment." And yet, a few years later, we find the same Sir Thomas writing to Lord Burghley, in 1571, respecting two miserable wretches whom he was engaged in racking under a warrant from Queen Elizabeth.[1]

In like manner, Sir Edward Coke, in his Institutes, declares—"So, as there is no law to warrant tortures in this land, nor can they be justified by any prescription, being so lately brought in." Yet, in 1603, there is a warrant addressed to Coke and Fleming, as Attorney and Solicitor General, directing them to apply torture to a servant of Lord Hundsdon, who had been guilty of some idle speeches respecting King James, and the resultant confession is in Coke's handwriting, showing that he personally superintended the examination.[2]

---

[1] Jardine, *op. cit.* pp. 8–9, 24–5.   It is due to Sir Thomas to add that he earnestly begs Lord Burghley to release him from so uncongenial an employment.

[2] Ibid. pp. 8, 47.

Coke's great rival, Lord Bacon, was as subservient as his contemporaries. In 1619, while Chancellor, we find him writing to King James concerning a prisoner confined in the Tower on suspicion of treason—"If it may not be done otherwise, it is fit Peacock be put to torture. He deserveth it as well as Peacham did"—Peacham being an unfortunate parson in whose desk was found a MS. sermon, never preached, containing some unpalatable reflections on the royal prerogative, which the prerogative resented by putting him on the rack.[1]

As in other countries, so in England, when torture was once introduced, it rapidly broke the bounds which the prudence of the Roman lawgivers had established for it. Treason was a most elastic crime, as was shown in 1553 by its serving as an excuse for the torture of one Stonyng, a prisoner in the Marshalsea, because he had transcribed for the amusement of his fellow-captives a satirical description of Philip II., whose marriage with Queen Mary was then under contemplation.[2] But it was not only in cases of high treason that the royal prerogative was allowed to transgress the limits of the law. Matters of religion, indeed, in those times of perennial change, when dynasties depended on dogmas, might come under the comprehensive head of constructive treason, and be considered to justify the torture even of women, as in the instance of Ann Askew in 1546;[3] and of monks guilty of no other crime than the endeavor to preserve their monasteries by pretended miracles.[4] Under Elizabeth, engaged in a death-struggle with Rome, matters became even worse, and torture was habitually used on the unhappy Catholics who were thrown into the Tower. As the whole matter was with-

[1] Bacon's Works, Philadelphia, 1846, III. 126.
[2] Strype's Eccles. Memorials, III. 101.
[3] Burnet, Hist. Reform. Bk. III pp. 341–2.
[4] According to Nicander Nucius (Travels, Camden Soc. 1841, pp. 58, 62), the investigation of these deceptions with the severest tortures, βασάνοις ἀφορήτοις, was apparently the ordinary mode of procedure.

out the color of law, all legal limitations seem to have been disregarded. The Jesuit Campion was subjected to the rack no less than three times with extreme severity, and in the intervals was made to dispute with Protestant divines.[1] Having once thus secured its introduction in state trials for treason, the custom inevitably tended to spread to the sphere of the most ordinary criminal business. Suspicion of theft, murder, horse-stealing, embezzlement, and other similar offences was sufficient to consign the unfortunate accused to the tender mercies of the rack, the Scavenger's Daughter,[2] and the manacles, when the aggrieved person had influence enough to procure a royal warrant; nor were these proceedings confined to the secret dungeons of the Tower, for the records show that torture began to be habitually applied in the Bridewell. Jardine, however, states that this especially dangerous extension of the abuse appears to have ceased with the death of Elizabeth, and that no trace of the torture even of political prisoners can be found later than the year 1640.[3] The royal

[1] Diarium rerum gestarum in Turri Londinensi (Sanderi Schisma Anglicanum, *ad calcem*, Ingolstadt, 1586).

[2] Sir William Skevington, a lieutenant of the Tower, under Henry VIII., immortalized himself by reviving an old implement of torture, consisting of an iron hoop, in which the prisoner was bent, heels to hams and chest to knees, and was thus crushed together unmercifully. It obtained the nickname of Skevington's Daughter, corrupted in time to Scavenger's Daughter. Among other sufferers from its embraces was an unlucky Irishman, named Myagh, whose plaint, engraved on the walls of his dungeon, is still among the curiosities of the Tower :—

> " Thomas Miagh, which liethe here alone,
> That fayne wold from hens begon :
> By torture straunge mi truth was tryed,
> Yet of my libertie denied.
>             1581.   Thomas Myagh." (Jardine, *op. cit.* pp. 15, 30).

[3] Jardine, pp. 53, 57–8.

It is rather remarkable to find torture legalized at this period, even in qualified form of the *question définitive* in the Colony of Massachusetts. The Body of Liberties, enacted in 1641, declares :—

" 45. No man shall be forced by Torture to confesse any crime against

prerogative had begun to be too severely questioned to render such manifestations of it prudent, and the Great Rebellion finally settled the constitutional rights of the subject on too secure a basis for even the time-serving statesmen of the Restoration to venture on a renewal of the former practice. Yet how nearly, at one time, it had come to be engrafted on the law of the land is evident from its being sufficiently recognized as a legal procedure for persons of noble blood to claim immunity from it, and for the judges to admit that claim as a special privilege. In the Countess of Shrewsbury's case, the judges, among whom was Sir Edward Coke, declared that there was a "privilege which the law gives for the honor and reverence of the nobility, that their bodies are not subject to torture *in causa criminis læsæ majestatis*," and no instance is on record to disprove the assertion.[1]

In one class of offences, however, torture was frequently used to a later date, and without requiring the royal intervention. As on the Continent, sorcery and witchcraft were regarded as crimes of such peculiar atrocity, and the dread they excited was so universal and intense, that those accused of them were practically placed beyond the pale of the law, and no means were considered too severe to secure the conviction which in many cases could only be obtained by confession. We have seen that among the refinements of Italian torture, the deprivation of sleep for forty hours was considered by the most experienced authorities on the subject to be second to none in severity and effectiveness. It neither lacerated the flesh, dis-

himselfe nor any other, unless it be in some Capitall case where he is first fully convicted by cleare and suffitient evidence to be guilty, After which if the case be of that nature, That it is very apparent there be other conspiritours or confederates with him, Then he may be tortured, yet not with such Tortures as be Barbarous and inhumane."—Whitmore's Colonial Laws of Massachusetts, Boston, 1889 (N. Y. Nation, No. 1268, p. 318).

From this it would appear safe to conclude that this is a limitation on a pre-existing, more general use of torture.

[1] Jardine, p. 65.

located the joints, nor broke the bones, and yet few things
could be conceived as more likely to cloud the intellect, break
down the will, and reduce the prisoner into a frame of mind
in which he would be ready to admit anything that the questions of his examiners might suggest to him. In English
witch-trials, this method of torture was not infrequently resorted to, without the limitation of time to which it was
restricted by the more experienced jurists of Italy.[1]

Another form of torture used in Great Britain, which doubtless proved exceedingly efficacious, was the "pricking" adopted
to discover the insensible spot, which, according to popular belief, was one of the invariable signs of a witch. There were
even professional "prickers" who were called in as experts in
the witch-trials, and who thrust long pins into the body of the
accused until some result, either negative or positive, was obtained.[2] Thus at the prosecution of Janet Barker, in Edinburgh, in 1643, it is recorded that "she had the usual mark
on the left shoulder, which enabled one James Scober, a skilful
pricker of witches, to find her out by putting a large pin into
it, which she never felt."[3] One witch pricker, named Kin-
caid, used to strip his victims, bind them hand and foot, and
then thrust his pins into every part of their bodies, until, exhausted and rendered speechless by the torture, they failed to
scream, when he would triumphantly proclaim that he had

[1] Lecky, Hist. of Rationalism, Am. ed. I. 122.—In his very interesting
work, Mr. Lecky mentions a case, occurring under the Commonwealth, of
an aged clergyman named Lowes, who, after an irreproachable pastorate
of fifty years, fell under suspicion. "The unhappy old man was kept
awake for several successive nights, and persecuted 'till he was weary of
his life, and was scarcely sensible of what he said or did.' He was then
thrown into the water, condemned, and hung."—Ibid. p. 126.

[2] Cobbett's State Trials, VI. 686.—Although ostensibly not used to extort confession, this pricking was practically regarded as a torture. Thus
in 1677 the Privy Council of Scotland "found that they (*i. e.*, the inferior
magistracy) might not use any torture by pricking or by withholding them
from sleep" (*loc. cit.*).

[3] Spottiswoode Miscellany, Edinburgh, 1845, II. 67.

found the witch-mark. Another pricker confessed on the gallows that he had illegally caused the death of a hundred and twenty women whom he had thus pricked for witchcraft.[1]

In Scotland, torture, as a regular form of judicial investigation, was of late introduction. In the various codes collected by Skene, extending from an early period to the commencement of the fifteenth century, there is no allusion whatever to it. In the last of these codes, adopted under Robert III. by the Parliament of Scotland in 1400, the provisions respecting the wager of battle show that torture would have been superfluous as a means of supplementing deficient evidence.[2] The influence of the Roman law, however, though late in appearing, was eventually much more deeply felt in Scotland than in the sister kingdom, and consequently torture at length came to be regarded as an ordinary resource in doubtful cases. In the witch persecutions, especially, which in Scotland rivalled the worst excesses of the Inquisition of Italy and Spain, it was carried to a pitch of frightful cruelty which far transcended the limits assigned to it elsewhere. Thus the vigils, which we have seen consisted simply in keeping the accused awake for forty hours by the simplest modes, in Scotland were fearfully aggravated by a witch-bridle, a band of iron fastened around the face, with four diverging points thrust into the mouth. With this the accused was secured immovably to a wall, and cases are on record in which this insupportable torment was prolonged for five and even for nine days. In other cases an enormous weight of iron hoops and chains, amounting to twenty-five or thirty stone, would be accumulated on the body of the patient.[3] Indeed, it is difficult to believe that the accounts which have been preserved to us of these terrible scenes are not exaggerated. No cruelty is too great for the conscientious persecutor who believes that he is avenging his

---

[1] Rogers's Scotland, Social and Domestic, p. 266.
[2] Statut. Roberti III. cap. xvi. (Skene).
[3] Lecky, *op. cit.* I. 145-6.—Rogers, *op. cit.* pp. 267-30).

God, but the limitless capacity of human nature for inflicting is not complemented by a limitless capacity of endurance on the part of the victim; and well authenticated as the accounts of the Scottish witch-trials may be, they seem to transcend the possibility of human strength.[1] In another respect these witch-trials were marked with a peculiar atrocity. Elsewhere, as we have seen, confession was requisite for condemnation, thus affording some color of excuse for torture. In Scotland, however, the testimony of the pricker was sufficient, and torture thus became a wanton and cruel surplusage, rendered the less defensible in that the poor wretch who yielded to the torment and confessed was rewarded by being mercifully strangled before being burnt, while those who held out under torture were condemned and burnt alive.[2]

Torture thus maintained its place in the laws of Scotland as long as the kingdom preserved the right of self-legislation,

---

[1] I quote from Mr. Lecky (p. 147), who gives as his authority "Pitcairn's Criminal Trials of Scotland."

"But others and perhaps worse trials were in reserve. The three principal that were habitually applied were the penniwinkis, the boots, and the caschielawis. The first was a kind of thumbscrew; the second was a frame in which the leg was inserted, and in which it was broken by wedges driven in by a hammer; the third was also an iron frame for the leg, which was from time to time heated over a brazier. Fire matches were sometimes applied to the body of the victim. We read, in a contemporary legal register, of one man who was kept for forty-eight hours in 'vehement tortour' in the caschielawis; and of another who remained in the same frightful machine for eleven days and eleven nights, whose legs were broken daily for fourteen days in the boots, and who was so scourged that the whole skin was torn from his body." These cases occurred in 1596.

These horrors are almost equalled by those of another trial in which a Dr. Fian was accused of having caused the storms which endangered the voyage of James VI. from Denmark in 1590. James personally superintended the torturing of the unhappy wretch, and after exhausting all the torments known to the skill and experience of the executioners, he invented new ones. All were vain, however, and the victim was finally burnt without confessing his ill-deeds (Ibid. p. 123).

[2] Rogers, *op. cit.* p. 307.

though an attempt seems to have been made to repress it
during the temporary union with England under the Commonwealth.  In 1652, when the English Commissioners for
the administration of justice sat in Edinburgh, among other
criminals brought before them were two witches who had
confessed their guilt before the Kirk.  They were the remains of a party of six, four of whom had died under the
tortures employed to procure confession—such as hanging
by the thumbs tied behind the back, scourging, burning the
feet and head and putting lighted candles into their mouths,
clothing them in hair-cloth soaked in vinegar "to fetch off
the skin," &c.  Another woman was stripped naked, laid on
a cold stone with a hair-cloth over her, and thus kept for
twenty-eight days and nights, being fed on bread and water.
The diarist who records this adds that "The judges are resolved to inquire into the business, and have appointed the
sheriff, ministers, and tormentors to be found out, and to
have an account of the ground of this cruelty."[1]  What result their humane efforts obtained in this particular instance
I have not been able to ascertain, but the legal administration of torture was not abolished until after the Union, when,
in 1709, the United Parliament made haste, at its second session, to pass an act for "improving the Union," by which
it was done away with.[2]  Yet the spirit which had led to its

[1] Diurnal of Occurrences in Scotland (Spottiswoode Miscellany, II.
90–91).

[2] 7 Anne c. 21.—While thus legislating for the enlightenment of Scotland, the English majority took care to retain the equally barbarous practice of the *peine forte et dure*.  This was commenced in 1275 simply as a
"prisone forte et dure" (First Statute of Westminster, cap. xii.; Cf. Britton,
cap. xi.) for felons refusing to plead, and speedily developed into starvation
and nakedness (Fleta, Lib. I. cap. xxxii. § 33).  Horne (Myrror of Justice,
cap. I. § viii.; cap. II. § ix.) evidently regards as illegal "le horrible et
perillous lien," and treats as murder a death occasioned by it.  In spite of
this protest the process was rendered still more barbarous by piling weights
of iron on the poor wretch, and finally the device of a press was adopted
in which he was squeezed.  In this shape it lost its original justification of

abuse could not be repressed by Act of Parliament, and a case is on record, occurring in 1722, when a poor old woman in her dotage, condemned to be burnt as a witch, actually warmed her withered hands at the stake lighted for her destruction, and mumbled out her gladness at enjoying the unaccustomed warmth.[1]

---

## CHAPTER X.

### DECLINE OF THE TORTURE SYSTEM.

A SYSTEM of procedure which entailed results so deplorable as those which we have seen accompany it everywhere, could scarcely fail to arouse the opposition of thinking men who were not swayed by reverence for precedent or carried away by popular impulses. Accordingly, an occasional voice was raised in denunciation of the use of torture. Geiler von Kaisersberg, the most popular preacher of his time in Germany, who died in 1510, endeavored to procure its disuse, as well as to mitigate

wearing out his endurance and forcing him to plead either guilty or not guilty, and became a simple punishment of peculiar atrocity, for, after its commencement the prisoner was not allowed to plead, but was kept under the press until death, " donec oneris, frigoris atque famis cruciatu extinguitur" (Hale, Placit. Coron. c. xliii.). This relic of modern barbarism was not abolished until 1772, by 12 Geo. III. c. 20. The only case of its employment in America is said to have been that of Giles Cory, in 1692, during the witchcraft epidemic. Knowing the hopelessness of the trials, he refused to plead, and was duly pressed to death (Cobbett's State Trials, VI. 680).

When the *peine forte et dure* had become simply a punishment, it was sometimes replaced by a torture consisting of tying the thumbs together with whipcord until the endurance of the accused gave way and he consented to plead. This practice continued at least until so late as 1734. See an interesting essay by Prof. James B. Thayer, Harvard Law Review, Jan. 1892.

[1] Rogers, *op. cit.* p. 301.

the cruelties practised upon prisoners.[1] The Spaniard, Juan Luis Vives, one of the profoundest scholars of the sixteenth century, condemned it as useless and inhuman.[2] The sceptic of the period, Montaigne, was too cool and clear-headed not to appreciate the vicious principle on which it was based, and he did not hesitate to stamp it with his reprobation. "To tell the truth, it is a means full of uncertainty and danger; what would we not say, what would we not do to escape suffering so poignant? whence it happens that when a judge tortures a prisoner for the purpose of not putting an innocent man to death, he puts him to death both innocent and tortured. . . . . Are you not unjust when, to save him from being killed, you do worse than kill him?"[3] In 1624, the learned Johann Gräfe, in his *Tribunal Reformatum*, argued forcibly in favor of its abolition, having had, it is said, practical experience of its horrors during his persecution for Arminianism by the Calvinists of Holland, and his book attracted sufficient attention to be repeatedly reprinted.[4] Friedrich Keller, in 1657, at the University of Strassburg, presented a well-reasoned thesis urging its disuse, which was reprinted in 1688, although the title which he prefixed to it shows that he scarce dared to assume the responsibility for its unpopular doctrines.[5] When the French Ordonnance of 1670 was in preparation, various magistrates of the highest character and largest experience

[1] Herzog, Abriss der Gesammten Kirchengeschichte, II. 346.

[2] His arguments are quoted and controverted by Simancas, Bishop of Badajos, in his Cathol. Institut. Tit. LXV. No. 7, 8.

[3] Essais, Liv. II. chap. v.—This passage is little more than a plagiarism on St. Augustin, de Civ. Dei Lib. XIX. cap. vi.—Montaigne further illustrates his position by a story from Froissart (Liv. IV. ch. lviii.), who relates that an old woman complained to Bajazet that a soldier had foraged on her. The Turk summarily disposed of the soldier's denial by causing his stomach to be opened. He proved guilty—but what had he been found innocent?

[4] Bayle, Dict. Hist. s. v. *Grevius*.—Gerstlacheri Comment. de Quæst. per Torment. Francof. 1753, pp. 25–6.

[5] Frid. Kelleri Paradoxon de Tortura in Christ. Repub. non exercenda. Reimp. Jenæ, 1688.

gave it as their fixed opinion that torture was useless, that it rarely succeeded in eliciting the truth from the accused, and that it ought to be abolished.[1]  Towards the close of the century, various writers took up the question.  The best known of these was perhaps Augustin Nicolas, who has been frequently referred to above, and who argued with more zeal and learning than skill against the whole system, but especially against it as applied in cases of witchcraft.[2]  In 1692, von Boden, in a work alluded to in the preceding pages, inveighed against its abuses, while admitting its utility in many classes of crimes.  Bayle, not long after, in his Dictionary, condemned it in his usual indirect and suggestive manner.[3]  In 1705, at the University of Halle, Martin Bernhardi of Pomerania, a candidate for the doctorate, in his inaugural thesis, argued with much vigor in favor of abolishing it, and the dean of the faculty, Christian Thomas, acknowledged the validity of his reasoning, though expressing doubts as to the practicability of a sudden reform.  Bernhardi states that in his time it was no longer employed in Holland, and its disuse in Utrecht he attributes to a case in which a thief procured the execution, after due torture and confession of a shoemaker, against whom he had brought a false charge in revenge for the refusal of a pair of boots.[4]  His assertion, however, is too general, for it was not until the formation of

---

[1] Déclaration du 24 Août, 1780 (Isambert, XXVII. 374).

[2] Nicolas is careful to assert his entire belief in the existence of sorcery and his sincere desire for its punishment, and he is indignant at the popular feeling which stigmatized those who wished for a reform in procedure as " avocats des sorciers."

[3] Dict. Histor. s. v. *Grevius.*

[4] Bernhardi Diss. Inaug. cap. II. §§ iv. x.—Bernhardi ventured on the use of very decided language in denunciation of the system.—" Injustam, iniquam, fallacem, insignium malorum promotricem, et denique omni divini testimonii specie destitutam esse hanc violentam torturam et proinde ex foris Christianorum rejiciendam intrepide assero" (Ibid. cap. I. § I).

the Republic of the Netherlands, in 1798, that it was formally abolished.[1]

These efforts had little effect, but they manifest the progress of enlightenment, and doubtless paved the way for change, especially in the Prussian territories. Yet, in 1730, we find the learned Baron Senckenberg reproducing Zanger's treatise, not as an archæological curiosity, but as a practical text-book for the guidance of lawyers and judges. Meanwhile the propriety of the system continued to be a subject of discussion in the schools, with ample expenditure of learning on both sides.[2] In 1733, at Leipzig, Moritz August Engel read a thesis, which called forth much applause, in which he undertook to defend the use of torture against the dictum of Christian Thomas nearly thirty years before.[3] The argument employed is based on the theory of the criminal jurisprudence of the time, in which the guilt of the accused is taken for granted and the burden thrown upon him of proving himself innocent. Engel declares that in all well-ordered States torture is rightfully employed; those who are innocent and are the victims of suspicious circumstances have only themselves to blame for their imprudence, and must make allowance for the imperfections of human reason; and he airily disposes of the injustice of the system by declaring that the State need not care if an innocent man is occasionally tortured, for no human ordinance can be expected to be free from occasional drawbacks. Another disputant on the same side meets the argument that the differ-

[1] Meyer, Institutions Judiciaires, IV. 297. Even, then, however, the inquisitorial process was not abolished, and criminal procedure continued to be secret. For the rack and strappado were substituted prolonged imprisonment and other expedients to extort confession; and in 1803 direct torture was used in the case of Hendrik Janssen, executed in Amsterdam on the strength of a confession extracted from him with the aid of a bull's pizzle.

[2] An enumeration of the opponents of torture may be found in Gerstlacher's Comment. de Quæst. per Tormenta, pp. 24–30, and Werner's Dissert. de Tortura Testium, pp. 28–31.

[3] M. A. Engel de Tortura ex Foris Christ. non proscribenda. Lipsiæ, 1733.

ent sensibilities of individuals rendered torture uncertain, by boasting that in the Duchy of Zerbst the executioner had invented an instrument which would wring a confession out of the most hardened and robust.[1] It was shortly after this, however, that the process of reform began in earnest. Frederic the Great succeeded to the throne of Prussia May 31, 1740. Few of his projects of universal philanthropy and philosophical regeneration of human nature survived the hardening experiences of royal ambition, but while his power was yet in its first bloom he made haste to get rid of this relic of unreasoning cruelty. It was almost his earliest official act, for the cabinet order abolishing torture is dated June 3d.[2] Yet even Frederic could not absolutely shake off the traditional belief in its necessity when the safety of the State or of the head of the State was concerned. Treason and rebellion and some other atrocious crimes were excepted from the reform; and in 1752, at the instance of his high chancellor, Cocceji, by a special rescript, he ordered two citizens of Oschersleben to be tortured on suspicion of robbery.[3] With singular inconsistency, moreover, torture in a modified form was long permitted in Prussia, not precisely as a means of investigation, but as a sort of punishment for obdurate prisoners who would not confess, and as a means of marking them for subsequent recognition.[4] It is evident that the abrogation of torture did not carry with it the removal of the evils of the inquisitorial process.

When the royal philosopher of Europe thus halted in the reform, it is not singular that his example did not put an end to the controversy as to the abolition of torture elsewhere. German jurisprudence, in fact, was not provided with substi-

[1] Jo. Frid. Werner Dissert. de Tortura Testium, Erford. 1724. Reimpr. Lipsiæ, 1742.

[2] Carlyle, Hist. Friedrich II. Book XI. ch. i.

[3] I find this statement in an account by G. F. Günther (Lipsiæ, 1838) of the abolition of torture in Saxony.

[4] Günther, *op. cit.*

tutes, and legists trained in the inquisitorial process might well hesitate to abandon a system with which they were familiar in order to enter upon a region of untried experiment for which there was no provision in the institutions or the ancestral customs of the land. These natural doubts are well expressed by Gerstlacher, who, in 1753, published a temperate and argumentative defence of torture. He enumerates the substitutes which had been proposed by his opponents, and if he does them no injustice, the judges of the day might naturally feel indisposed to experiments so crude and illogical. It seems that the alternatives offered for the decision of cases in which the accused could not be convicted by external evidence reduced themselves to four—to dismiss him without a sentence either of acquittal or conviction, to make him take an oath of purgation, to give him an extraordinary (that is to say, a less) penalty than that provided for the crime, and, lastly, to imprison him or send him to the galleys or other hard labor, proportioned to the degree of the evidence against him, until he should confess.[1]

In Saxony, as early as 1714, an Electoral Rescript had restricted jurisdiction over torture to the magistrates of Leipzig, to whom all proceedings in criminal prosecutions had to be submitted for examination prior to their confirmation of the decision of the local tribunals to employ it.[2] This must have greatly reduced the amount of wrong and suffering caused by the system, and thus modified it continued to exist until, in the remodelling of the Saxon criminal law, between 1770 and 1783, the whole apparatus of torture was swept away. In Austria the *Constitutio Criminalis Theresiana*, issued in 1769 by Maria Theresa, still contains elaborate instructions as to the administration of torture, with careful descriptions and illustrations of the implements in use and the methods of em-

[1] Gerstlacheri Comment. de Quæst. per Tormenta, Francofurti, 1753, p. 56.

[2] Goetzii Dissert. de Tortura, Lipsiæ, 1742, p. 24.

ploying them ;[1] but the enlightenment of Joseph II., soon after
his accession in 1780, put an end to the barbarism, and in
Switzerland about the same time it was similarly disused.   In
Russia, the Empress Catherine, in 1762, removed it from the
jurisdiction of the inferior courts, where it had been greatly
abused ; in 1767, by a secret order, it was restricted to cases
in which the confession of the accused proved actually indispensable, and even in these it was only permitted under the
special command of governors of provinces.[2]   In the singularly enlightened instructions which she drew up for the framing
of a new code in 1767, the use of torture was earnestly argued
against in a manner which betrays the influence of Beccaria.[3]
Under these auspices it soon became almost obsolete, and it
was finally abolished in 1801.   Yet, in some of the States of
central Europe, the progress of enlightenment was wonder-
fully slow.   Torture continued to disgrace the jurisprudence
of Würtemberg and Bavaria until 1806 and 1807.   Though the
wars of Napoleon abolished it temporarily in other States, on
his fall in 1814 it was actually restored.   In 1819, however,
George IV. consented, at the request of his subjects, to dispense with it in Hanover ; while in Baden it continued to
exist until 1831.   Yet legists who had been trained in the
old school could not admit the soundness of modern ideas,
and in the greater part of Germany the theories which resulted in the use of torture continued to prevail.   The secret
inquisitorial process was retained and the principle that the
confession of the accused was requisite to his condemnation.
Torture of some kind is necessary to render the practical application of this system efficacious, and accordingly, though
the rack and strappado were abolished, their place was taken

[1] Constitutio Criminalis Theresiana, Wien, 1769.

[2] Du Boys, Droit Criminel des Peuples Modernes, I. 620.

[3] Instructions addressées par sa Majesté l'Impératrice de toutes les Russies
à la Commission établie pour travailler à l'exécution du projet d'un Nouveau
Code de Lois Art. x. §§ 82–87 (Pétersbourg 1769).—See also Grand Instructions of Catherine II., London, 1769, pp. 113–8.

by other modes in reality not less cruel.  When appearances
were against the prisoner, he was confined for an indefinite
period and subjected to all the hard usage to be expected from
officials provoked by his criminal obstinacy.  He was brought
up repeatedly before his judge and exposed to the most searching interrogatories and terrified with threats.  Legists, unwilling to abandon the powerful weapon which had placed every
accused person at their mercy, imagined a new justification for
its revival.  It was held that every criminal owed to society a
full and free confession.  His refusal to do this was a crime,
so that if his answers were unsatisfactory to the judge the latter
could punish him on the spot for contumacy.  As this punishment was usually administered with the scourge, it will be
seen that the abolition of torture was illusory, and that
the worst abuses to which it gave rise were carefully retained.[1]  Indeed, if we are to accept literally some letters of
M. A. Eubule-Evans in the London "Times" of 1872, the
*Untersuchungschaft* or inquisitorial process as employed in
Prussia to the present day lacks little of the worst abuses recorded by Sprenger and Bodin.  The accused while under
detention is subjected to both physical and moral torture, and
is carefully watched by spies.  In the prison of Bruchsal there
is a machine to which the prisoner is attached by leather thongs
passed around head, trunk, and limbs, and drawn so tight that
the arrested circulation forces the blood from mouth and ears;
or he is confined, perhaps for a week at a time, in a small cell
of which floor and sides are covered with sharp wooden wedges,
rivalling the fragments of potsherds which Prudentius considered the crowning effort of devilish ingenuity for the torture
of Christian martyrs.

Spain, as may readily be imagined, was in no haste to
reform the ancient system of procedure.  As late as 1796, in
the Vice-royalty of New Granada, when the spread of the

<hr/>

[1] Jardine, Use of Torture in England, p. 3.—Meyer, Institutions Judiciaires, T. I. p. xlvi.—T. II. p. 262.

ideas of the French Revolution began to infect society, some pasquinades appeared in Santafé displeasing to the government. Though the Viceroy Ezpeleta was regarded as a singularly enlightened man, he had a number of persons arrested on suspicion, one of whom was put to the torture to discover the author of the obnoxious epigrams. It is satisfactory to know that although several of the accused were convicted and sent to Spain to serve out long terms of punishment, on their arrival at Madrid they were all discharged and compensated.[1] After the revolution, the authorized use of torture was abolished, but as recently as 1879 its application, by various methods showing skill and experience in its use, on an American citizen falsely accused of theft, led to a correspondence between the governments of Venezuela and the United States, recorded in the journals of the time.

In the mother country the employment of torture, though becoming rarer as the eighteenth century neared its end, continued legal until the overthrow of the old monarchy, and it was not abolished until the Cortes of Cadiz in 1811 revolutionized all the institutions of the nation. In the reaction which followed the return of the Bourbons it was not reinstated, but moderated appliances known as *apremios*—which were sometimes as severe as the rack or the pulley—continued to be used, especially in political offences, by the arbitrary despotism of the Restoration.[2]

Even France had maintained a conservatism which may seem surprising in that centre of the philosophic speculation of the eighteenth century. Her leading writers had not hesitated to condemn the use of torture. In the *Esprit des Lois*, in 1748, Montesquieu stamped his reprobation on the system with a quiet significance which showed that he had on his side all the great thinkers of the age, and that he felt argument to be

[1] Groot, Hist. Ecles. y Civil de Nueva Granada II. 79-80.
[2] Toreno, Levantamiento, Guerra y Revolución de España, Paris, 1838, II. 371, 438.

mere surplusage.[1] Voltaire did not allow its absurdities and incongruities to escape. In 1765 he endeavored to arouse public opinion on the case of the Chevalier de la Barre, a youthful officer only twenty years of age, who was tortured and executed on an accusation of having recited a song insulting to Mary Magdalen and of having mutilated with his sword a wooden crucifix on the bridge of Abbeville.[2] He was more successful in attracting the attention of all Europe to the celebrated *affaire Calas* which, in 1761, had furnished a notable example of the useless cruelty of the system. In that year, at midnight of Oct. 13th, at Toulouse, the body of Marc-Antoine Calas was found strangled in the back shop of his father. The family were Protestants and the murdered man had given signs of conversion to Catholicism, in imitation of his younger brother. A minute investigation left scarcely a doubt that the murder had been committed by the father, from religious motives, and he was condemned to death. He appealed to the Parlement of Toulouse, which after a patient hearing sentenced him to the wheel, and to the *question ordinaire et extraordinaire*, to extract a confession. He underwent the extremity of torture and the hideous punishment of being broken alive without varying from his protestations of innocence. Though both trials appear to have been conducted with rigorous impartiality, the Protestantism of Europe saw in the affair the evidence of religious persecution, and a fearful outcry was raised. Voltaire, ever on the watch for means to promote toleration and freedom of thought, seized hold of it with tireless energy, and created so strong an agitation on the subject that in 1764 the supreme tribunal at Paris reversed the

[1] Tant d'habiles gens et tant de beaux génies ont écrit contre cette pratique que je n'ose parler après eux. J'allois dire qu'elle pourroit convenir dans les gouvernements despotiques; où tout qui inspire la crainte entre plus dans les ressorts du gouvernement: j'allois dire que les esclaves, chez les Grecs et chez les Romains——Mais j'entends la voix de la nature qui crie contre moi.—Liv. VI. ch. xvii.

[2] Desmaze, Pénalités Anciennes, Pièces Justicatives p. 423.

sentence, discharged the other members of the family, who
had been subjected to various punishments, and rehabilitated
the memory of Calas.[1] When Louis XVI., at the opening of
his reign, proposed to introduce many long-needed reforms,
Voltaire took advantage of the occasion to address to him in
1777 an earnest request to include among them the disuse of
torture ;[2] yet it was not until 1780 that the *question préparatoire* was abolished by a royal edict which, in a few weighty
lines, indicated that only the reverence for traditional usage
had preserved it so long.[3] This edict, however, was not
strictly obeyed, and cases of the use of torture still occasionally occurred, as that of Marie Tison at Rouen, in 1788,
accused of the murder of her husband, when thumb-screws
were applied to both thumbs and at the same time she was
hoisted in the strappado, in which she was allowed to hang
for an hour after the executioner had reported that both
shoulders were out of joint, all of which was insufficient to
extract a confession.[4] There evidently was occasion for
another ordonnance, which in that same year, 1788, was
promulgated in order to insure the observance of the previous one.[5] In fact, when the States-General was convened
in 1879, the *cahier des doléances* of Valenciennes contained
a prayer for the abolition of torture, showing that it had not
as yet been discontinued there.[6] The *question définitive* or
*préalable*, by which the prisoner after condemnation was
again tortured to discover his accomplices, still remained

[1] Mary Lafon, Histoire du Midi de la France, T. IV. pp. 325–355.—
The theory of the defence was that the murdered man had committed
suicide; but this is incompatible with the testimony, much of which is
given at length by Mary Lafon, a writer who cannot be accused of any
leanings against Protestantism.
[2] Chéruel, Dict. Hist. des Institutions de la France. P. II. p. 1220.
[3] Déclaration du 24 Août 1780 (Isambert, XXVII. 373).
[4] Desmaze, Pénalités Anciennes, pp. 176–77.
[5] Déclaration du 3 Mai 1788, art. 8. "Nôtre déclaration du 24 Août
sera exécutée" (Isambert, XXIX. 532).
[6] Louïse, Sorcellerie et Justice Criminelle à Valenciennes, p. 96.

until 1788, when it, too, was abolished, at least temporarily. It was pronounced uncertain, cruel to the convict and perplexing to the judge, and, above all, dangerous to the innocent whom the prisoner might name in the extremity of his agony to procure its cessation, and whom he would persist in accusing to preserve himself from its repetition. Yet, with strange inconsistency, the abolition of this cruel wrong was only provisional, and its restoration was threatened in a few years, if the tribunals should deem it necessary.[1] When those few short years came around they dawned on a new France, from which the old systems had been swept away as by the besom of destruction; and torture as an element of criminal jurisprudence was a thing of the past. By the decree of October 9th, 1789, it was abolished forever.

In Italy, Beccaria, in 1764, took occasion to devote a few pages of his treatise on crimes and punishments to the subject of torture, and its illogical cruelty could not well be exposed with more terseness and force.[2] It was probably due to the movement excited by this work that in 1786 torture was formally abolished in Tuscany. In this the enlightened Grandduke Leopold was in advance of his time, and the despots

---

[1] Isambert, XXIX. 529.—It is noteworthy, as a sign of the temper of the times, on the eve of the last convocation of the Notables, that this edict, which introduced various ameliorations in criminal procedure, and promised a more thorough reform, invites from the community at large suggestions on the subject, in order that the reform may embody the results of public opinion—"Nous élèverons ainsi au rang des lois les résultats de l'opinion publique." This was pure democratic republicanism in an irregular form.

The edict also indicates an intention to remove another of the blots on the criminal procedure of the age, in a vague promise to allow the prisoner the privilege of counsel.

[2] Dei Delitti e delle Pene, § XII.—The fundamental error in the prevalent system of criminal procedure was well exposed in Beccaria's remark that a mathematician would be better than a legist for the solution of the essential problem in criminal trials—"Data la forza dei muscoli e la sensibilità delle fibre di un innocente, trovare il grado di dolore che lo farà confessar reo di un dato delitto."

who ruled the divided fractions of the peninsula, although they might be willing to banish torture from ordinary criminal jurisprudence, had too well-grounded a distrust of the fidelity of their subjects to divest themselves of this resource in the suppression of political offences. Hardly had the Bourbons, after the overthrow of Napoleon, been reseated on the throne of the Two Sicilies when the restless dissatisfaction of the people seemed to justify the severest measures for the maintenance of so-called order. The troubles of 1820 led to arming the police with exceptional and summary jurisdiction, under which it deemed itself authorized to employ any methods requisite to detect and punish conspirators. This continued until the revolution of 1848 aggravated the fears of absolutism, and from its suppression until the expedition of Garibaldi the régime of the Neapolitan dominions was an organized Terror. Grave as we have seen were the abuses of torture when systematized in the detection of crime, they were outstripped by the licensed cruelty of the ex-galley slaves of the Neapolitan police, who were restrained by no codes or rules of practice, and were eager to demonstrate their zeal by the number of their victims. The terrible secrets of the dungeons of Naples and Palermo may never see the light, but enough is known to show that they rivalled those of Ezzelin da Romano. Police agents competed in inventing new and hideous modes of inflicting pain. Neither age nor sex was spared. In one case an old man and his daughter, five months gone in pregnancy, died under the lash. If a suspected man took alarm and fled, his mother or his wife and daughters would be tortured to discover his hiding-place. The evil records of the dark ages have nothing to show more brutal and inhuman than the application of torture in Naples and Sicily in the second half of the nineteenth century.[1]

That the mortal duel between autocracy and Nihilism in Russia should lead to the employment of torture in unravelling

[1] Carlo di la Varenne, La Tortura in Sicilia, 1860.

the desperate conspiracies of the malcontents is so natural that we may readily accept the current assertions of the fact. The conspirators are said frequently to carry poison in order, if arrested, to save themselves from endless torment and the risk of being forced to betray associates, and the friends of prisoners spare no effort to convey to them some deadly drug by means of which they may escape the infliction. Polish aspirations for liberty are repressed in the same manner, and in 1890 the journals recorded the case of Ladislas Guisbert, rendered insane by the prolonged administration of Marsigli's favorite torment of sleeplessness.

So long as human nature retains its imperfections the baffled impatience of the strong will be apt to wreak its vengeance on the weak and defenceless. As recently as 1867, in Texas, the Jefferson "Times" records a case in which, under the auspices of the military authorities, torture was applied to two negroes suspected of purloining a considerable amount of money which had been lost by a revenue collector. More recently still, in September, 1868, the London journals report fearful barbarities perpetrated by the Postmaster-General of Roumania to trace the authors of a mail robbery. A woman was hung to a beam with hot eggs under the armpits; others were burned with grease and petroleum, while others again were tied by the hair to horses' tails and dragged through thorn bushes. It must be added that the offending officials were promptly dismissed and committed for trial. A still more recent case is one which has been the subject of legislative discussion in Switzerland, where it appears that in the Canton of Zug, under order of court, a man suspected of theft was put on bread and water from Oct. 26th to Nov. 10th, 1869, to extort confession, and when this failed he was subjected to thumb-screws and beaten with rods.

In casting a retrospective glance over this long history of cruelty and injustice, it is saddening to observe that Christian communities, where the truths of the Gospel were received with unquestioning veneration, systematized the administration of torture with a cold-blooded ferocity unknown to the legislation of the heathen nations whence they derived it.  The careful restrictions and safeguards, with which the Roman jurisprudence sought to protect the interests of the accused, contrast strangely with the reckless disregard of every principle of justice which sullies the criminal procedure of Europe from the thirteenth to the nineteenth century.  From this no race or religion has been exempt.  What the Calvinist suffered in Flanders, he inflicted in Holland; what the Catholic enforced in Italy, he endured in England; nor did either of them deem that he was forfeiting his share in the Divine Evangel of peace on earth and goodwill to men.

The mysteries of the human conscience and of human motives are well-nigh inscrutable, and it may seem shocking to assert that these centuries of unmitigated wrong are indirectly traceable to that religion of which the second great commandment was that man should love his neighbor as himself.  Yet so it was.  The first commandment, to love God with all our heart, when perverted by superstition, gave a strange direction to the teachings of Christ.  For ages, the assumptions of an infallible Church had led men to believe that the interpreter was superior to Scripture.  Every expounder of the holy text felt in his inmost heart that he alone, with his fellows, worshipped God as God desired to be worshipped, and that every ritual but his own was an insult to the Divine nature.  Outside of his own communion there was no escape from eternal perdition, and the fervor of religious conviction thus made persecution a duty to God and man.  This led the Inquisition, as we have seen, to perfect a system of which the iniquity was complete.  Thus commended, that system became part and parcel of secular law, and when the Reformation arose the habits of thought which ages had consolidated were universal.  The boldest Reformers who shook off the yoke of Rome, as soon as they had attained power, had as little scruple as Rome itself in rendering obligatory their interpretation of divine truth, and in applying to secular as well as to religious affairs the cruel maxims in which they had been educated.

Yet, in the general enlightenment which caused and accompanied the Reformation, there passed away gradually the passions which had created the rigid institutions of the Middle Ages. Those institutions had fulfilled their mission, and the savage tribes that had broken down the worn-out civilization of Rome were at last becoming fitted for a higher civilization than the world had yet seen, wherein the precepts of the Gospel might at length find practical expression and realization. For the first time in the history of man the universal love and charity which lie at the foundation of Christianity are recognized as the elements on which human society should be based. Weak and erring as we are, and still far distant from the ideal of the Saviour, yet are we approaching it, even if our steps are painful and hesitating. In the slow evolution of the centuries, it is only by comparing distant periods that we can mark our progress; but progress nevertheless exists, and future generations, perhaps, may be able to emancipate themselves wholly from the cruel and arbitrary domination of superstition and force.

# APPENDIX.

# JUDICIAL TORTURE:
# DOCUMENTS AND
# COMMENTARY.

The torture of slaves and strangers in the Greek and Roman worlds may have had its origins in the denial of the privilege of legal personality to members of these two categories of humans. Possibly the broad proprietary powers of the head of the Roman household, elsewhere so conspicuous in Roman law, may also have influenced this aspect of unfree status.[1] The most explicit statement of the Roman law of torture is to be found in the *Digest*, Book 48, Title 18, the first several sections of which consist of extracts from the second- and third-century jurist Ulpian's lost treatise on the office of the Proconsul. The *Digest*, the great synthesis of earlier imperial jurisprudence, is part of Justinian's *Corpus Iuris Civilis*, published in 534.

I. From *The Civil Law*, trans. S. P. Scott (Cincinnati, 1932; rep. New York, 1973), Vol. V, pp. 98–106.

## TITLE XVIII.

### CONCERNING TORTURE.

1. *Ulpianus, On the Duties of Proconsul, Book VIII.*

It is customary for torture to be applied for the purpose of detecting crime. Let us see when, and to what extent, this should be done. A beginning ought not to be made by the actual infliction of the question, and the Divine Augustus decided that confidence should not unreservedly be placed in torture.

(1) This is also contained in a letter of the Divine Hadrian addressed to Sennius Sabinus. The terms of the Rescript are as

follows: "Slaves are to be subjected to torture only when the accused is suspected, and proof is so far obtained by other evidence that the confession of the slaves alone seems to be lacking."

(2) The Divine Hadrian also stated the same thing in a Rescript to Claudius Quartinus, and in this Rescript he decided that a beginning should be made with the person who was most suspected, and from whom the judge believed that the truth could most easily be ascertained.

(3) Those whom the accuser produces from his own house should not be tortured, for it is not easy to believe that a substitution has been made for one whom both parents consider their dear daughter; as is stated in a Rescript of the Divine Brothers addressed to Lucius Tiberianus.

(4) They also stated in a Rescript to Cornelius Proculus, that confidence should not be reposed in the torture of a single slave, but that the case should be investigated after the evidence has been given.

(5) The Divine Antoninus and the Divine Hadrian stated in a Rescript to Sennius Sabinus that where it was alleged that slaves, in company with their master, had carried away gold and silver, they should not be interrogated against their master, and not even anything which they may have said when not under torture will prejudice him.

(6) The Divine Brothers stated in a Rescript addressed to Lelianus Longinus that torture should not be applied to a slave belonging to the heirs, to obtain information with reference to the estate, even though it was suspected that the heir had obtained the ownership of the property by means of a fictitious sale.

(7) It has frequently been stated in Rescripts that a slave belonging to a municipality can be tortured when citizens are accused, because he is not their slave, but the slave of the community. The same thing should be stated with reference to the slaves of other corporations, for a slave is not considered to belong to several masters, but to the corporate body.

(8) When a slave is serving me in good faith, even though I do not have the ownership of him, it may be said that he can not be tortured to obtain evidence against me.

The same rule applies to a freeman who is serving in good faith as a slave.

(9) It has also been established that a freedman cannot be tortured in a case where his patron is accused of a capital crime.

(10) Our Emperor, together with his Divine Father, stated in a Rescript that one brother could not be put to the question on account of another; and added as the reason that he should not be tortured to obtain evidence to implicate one against whom he could not be compelled to testify, if he was unwilling to do so.

(11) The Divine Trajan stated in a Rescript to Servius Quartus that the slave of a husband could be tortured to obtain evidence to convict his wife.

(12) He also stated in a Rescript to Mummius Lollianus that the slaves of a person who had been convicted could be tortured to obtain evidence against him, because they had ceased to be his.

(13) When a slave has been manumitted to prevent him from being put to torture, the Divine Pius stated in a Rescript that he could be tortured, provided this was not done to obtain evidence against his master.

(14) But where a slave belonged to another at the time when the investigation was begun, but afterwards became the property of the defendant, the Divine Brothers stated in a Rescript that he could, nevertheless, be tortured in the case in which his master was involved.

(15) If anyone should allege that a slave has been purchased at a sale which was void, he cannot be tortured before it has been established that the sale was not valid. This our Emperor, with his Divine Father, stated in a Rescript.

(16) Severus also stated in a Rescript to Spicius Antigonus: "As the torture of slaves should not be inflicted against their masters, and, if this has been done, as it cannot be used to influence the decision of the judge about to render it, still less should the statements of slaves against their masters be admitted."

(17) The Divine Severus stated in a Rescript, that the confessions of accused persons should not be considered as proofs

of crime, if no other evidence is offered to influence the sense of duty of the judge who is to decide the case.

(18) When anyone is ready to deposit the price of a slave, in order that he may be tortured to give evidence against his master, our Emperor, with his Divine Father, did not permit this to be done.

(19) Where slaves are tortured as accomplices in a crime, and they confess something in court which involves their master, the Emperor Trajan stated in a Rescript that the judge should render his decision as circumstances demand.

It is shown by this Rescript that masters can be implicated by the confessions of their slaves, but more recent constitutions indicate that it is no longer in force.

(20) When tributes, which no one doubts are the sinews of the republic, are concerned, consideration of the danger which menaces with capital punishment a slave who is the accomplice of a fraud should cause his statements to be rejected.

(21) The magistrate in charge of the torture ought not directly to put the interrogation whether Lucius Titius committed the homicide, but he should ask in general terms who did it; for the other way rather seems to suggest an answer than to ask for one. This the Divine Trajan stated in a Rescript.

(22) The Divine Hadrian stated the following in a Rescript addressed to Calpurnius Celerianus: "Agricola, the slave of Pompeius Valens, may be interrogated concerning himself; but if, while undergoing torture, he should say anything more, it will be considered as proof against the defendant, and not the fault of him who asked the question."

(23) It was declared by the Imperial Constitutions that while confidence should not always be reposed in torture, it ought not to be rejected as absolutely unworthy of it, as the evidence obtained is weak and dangerous, and inimical to the truth; for most persons, either through their power of endurance, or through the severity of the torment, so despise suffering that the truth can in no way be extorted from them. Others are so little able to suffer that they prefer to lie rather than to endure the question, and hence it happens that they make con-

fessions of different kinds, and they not only implicate themselves, but others as well.

(24) Moreover, faith should not be placed in evidence obtained by the torture of enemies, because they lie very readily; still, under the pretext of enmity, its employment should not be rejected.

(25) After the case has been duly investigated, it can be decided whether confidence is to be placed in torture, or not.

(26) When anyone has betrayed robbers, it is stated by certain rescripts that no confidence should be placed in those who betrayed them. In others, however, which are more specific, it is provided that the evidence should not be entirely rejected, as is usual in similar cases; but, after proper consideration, it should be determined whether it is entitled to credit or not. For the majority of such persons, who fear that those who have been arrested may mention them, are accustomed to betray the latter for the purpose of themselves obtaining immunity, because accused persons who denounce those who have betrayed them are not readily believed; nor should immunity indiscriminately be granted to them as a reward for betrayals of this kind; nor should their allegations be believed, when they say that they have been accused by the others for having given them up, for this week proof based on mendacity or calumny ought not to be considered against them.

(27) If anyone voluntarily confesses a crime, faith should not always be reposed in him; for sometimes one makes a confession through fear or for some other reason. An Epistle of the Divine Brothers addressed to Voconius Saxa declares that a man who had made a confession against himself, and whose innocence was established, must be discharged after his conviction.

The terms of the Epistle are as follows: "It is in compliance with the dictates of prudence and humanity, my dear Saxa, that, where a slave was suspected of having falsely confessed himself guilty of homicide, through fear of being restored to his master, you condemned him, still persevering in his false statement, with the intention of subjecting to torture his alleged accomplices, whom he had also accused falsely, in order that you might render his statements with reference to himself more certain.

"Nor was your judicious intention in vain, as it was established by the torture that the persons referred to were not his accomplices, but that he had accused himself falsely. You can then set aside the judgment, and order him to be officially sold, under the condition that he never shall be returned to the power of his master, who, having received the price, will certainly be very willing to be rid of such a slave."

The Rescript indicates that, when a slave is condemned, if he should subsequently be discharged from liability, he will belong to the person whose property he was before his conviction. The Governor of the province, however, cannot restore anyone whom he has condemned to his original condition, as he cannot even revoke a decision in which money is involved. What then should be done? He should have recourse to the Emperor when anyone who at first appeared to be guilty, afterwards has his innocence established.          .

2. *Ulpianus, On the Edict, Book XXXIX.*

Slaves forming part of an estate cannot be put to the torture to obtain evidence against their masters, as long as it is uncertain to whom the property belongs.

3. *The Same, On the Edict, Book LVI.*

It was established by a Constitution of Our Emperor and the Divine Severus that a slave belonging to several owners cannot be subjected to torture against any of them.

4. *The Same, Disputations, Book III.*

In a case of incest (according to the opinion of Papinianus, which is also set forth in a Rescript), slaves are not liable to torture, because the Julian Law relating to Adultery does not apply.

5. *Marcianus, Institutes, Book II.*

Where anyone debauches a widow or a woman married to another, with whom he could not legally have contracted matrimony, he should be departed to an island, as the crime is a double one; incest, because, contrary to Divine Law, he has violated a woman related to him, and has added adultery or fornication to this offence. Finally, in a case of this kind, slaves can be tortured for the purpose of obtaining evidence against their masters.

6. *Papinianus, On Adultery, Book II.*

When a father or a husband brings an accusation of adultery, and a demand is made that the slaves of the party accused be put to the question, if an acquittal should result, after the case has been argued, and the witnesses produced, an estimate must be made of the value of the slaves who have died; but if a conviction should be obtained, the surviving slaves shall be confiscated.

(1) When the case is one involving a forged will, the slaves belonging to the estate can be tortured.

7. *Ulpianus, On Adultery, Book III.*

The judges must determine the measure of torture, and therefore it should be inflicted in such a way that the slave may be preserved either for his acquittal, or his punishment.

8. *Paulus, On Adultery, Book II.*

The Edict of the Divine Augustus, which he published during the Consulate of Vivius Avitus and Lucius Apronianus, is as follows: "I do not think that torture should be inflicted in every instance, and upon every person; but when capital and atrocious crimes cannot be detected and proved except by means of the torture of slaves, I hold that it is most effective for ascertaining the truth, and should be employed."

(1) The slave who is to be free under a condition may be subjected to torture, because he is the slave of the heir, but he will still retain his hope of freedom.

9. *Marcianus, On Public Prosecutions, Book II.*

The Divine Pius stated in a Rescript that torture could be inflicted upon slaves in cases where money was involved, if the truth could not otherwise be ascertained, which is also provided by other rescripts. This, however, is true to the extent that this expedient should not be resorted to in a pecuniary case, but only where the truth cannot be ascertained unless by the employment of torture is it lawful to make use of it, as the Divine Severus stated in a Rescript. Hence it is permitted to put the slaves of others to the question if the circumstances justify it.

(1) In cases in which torture should not be inflicted upon slaves to obtain evidence against their masters they cannot even be interrogated, and still less can the statements of slaves against their masters be admitted.

(2) Torture should not be inflicted upon one who is deported to an island, as the Divine Pius stated in a Rescript.

(3) Nor should it be inflicted in a pecuniary case, upon a slave who is to be free under a condition, unless the condition fails to be fulfilled.

10. *Arcadius, Charisius, On Witnesses.*

Torture should not be inflicted upon a minor under fourteen years of age, as the Divine Pius stated in a Rescript addressed to Caecilius Jubentinus.

(1) All persons, however, without exception, shall be tortured in a case of high treason which has reference to princes, if their testimony is necessary, and circumstances demand it.

(2) It may be asked whether torture cannot be inflicted upon slaves belonging to the *castrense peculium* of a son in order to obtain evidence against his father. For it has been established that a father's slave should not be tortured to obtain evidence against his son. I think that it may be properly held that the slaves of a son should not be tortured to obtain evidence against his father.

(3) Torture should not be applied to the extent that the accuser demands, but as reason and moderation may dictate.

(4) The accuser should not begin proceedings with evidence derived from the house of the defendant, when he calls as witnesses the freedmen or the slaves of the person whom he accuses.

(5) Frequently, also, in searching for the truth, even the tone of the voice itself, and the diligence of a keen examination afford assistance. For matters available for the discovery of truth emerge into the light from the language of the witness, and the composure or trepidation he displays, as well as from the reputation which each one enjoys in his own community.

(6) In questions where freedom is involved, it is not neces-

sary to seek for the truth by the torture of those whose status is in dispute.

11. *Paulus, On the Duties of Proconsul, Book II.*

Even if a slave should be returned under a condition of the sale, he shall not be tortured to obtain evidence against his master.

12. *Ulpianus, On the Edict, Book LIV.*

When anyone, to avoid being tortured, alleges that he is free, the Divine Hadrian stated in a Rescript that he should not be put to the question before the case brought to decide his freedom has been tried.

13. *Modestinus, Rules, Book V.*

It is established that a slave can be tortured after he has been appraised, or the required stipulation has been entered into.

14. *The Same Rules, Book VIII.*

A slave who is to be free under a condition, and who has been convicted of crime, will be entitled to the privilege of expecting his liberty, so that on account of the uncertainty of his status he will be punished as a freeman, and not as a slave.

15. *Callistratus, Judicial Inquiries, Book V.*

It is not necessary to inflict torture in the case of a freeman, where his testimony is not vacillating.

(1) In the case of a minor under fourteen years of age, the Divine Pius stated in a Rescript to Maecilius that torture should not be inflicted to obtain evidence against another, especially as the accusation was by no means established by other evidence, since it did not result that the minor should be believed, even without the application of torture; for he says that age, which appears to protect persons against the harshness of torture, renders them also more suspected of falsehood.

(2) He who has given security to another claiming a slave should be considered as the master; and therefore such slaves cannot be put to torture to obtain evidence against him. The Divine Pius stated the following in a Rescript: "You must prove your case by other testimony, for torture should not be

inflicted upon slaves, when the possessor of an estate has given security to a claimant, and in the meantime, is considered as the master."

16. *Modestinus, On Punishments, Book III.*

The Divine Brothers stated in a Rescript that torture could be repeated.

(1) The Divine Pius stated in a Rescript that one who has made a confession implicating himself, shall not be tortured to obtain evidence against others.

17. *Papinianus, Opinions, Book XVI.*

Again, when a stranger brings an accusation, it has been established that slaves can be tortured to obtain evidence against their masters; a rule which the Divine Marcus, and afterwards the Emperor Maximus, followed in rendering their decisions.

(1) Slaves are not tortured against their master where a charge of fornication is made.

(2) In a case of fraudulent birth, if a person whom the other children assert is not their brother claims the estate, torture shall be applied to slaves belonging to the estate, for the reason that it is not employed against the other children as masters, but in order to determine the succession of the deceased owner. This agrees with what the Divine Hadrian stated in a Rescript, for when a man was accused of having murdered his partner, the Emperor decreed that a slave owned in common could be put to the question, because this appeared to be done in behalf of his master who had been killed.

(3) I gave it as my opinion that where a slave has been sentenced to the mines, he should not be tortured to obtain evidence against the person who had been his master, and that it made no difference if he had confessed that he had been the perpetrator of the crime.

18. *Paulus, Sentences, Book V.*

Where several persons are accused of the same offence, they should be heard in such a way as to begin with the one who is the most timid, or appears to be of tender age.

(1) An accused person who is overwhelmed with conclusive evidence can be tortured a second time; especially if he has hardened his mind and body against the torments.

(2) In a case in which nothing has been proved against the defendant, torture should not be applied without due consideration; but the accuser should be urged to confirm and substantiate what he has alleged.

(3) Witnesses should not be tortured for the purpose of convicting them of falsehood, or to ascertain the truth; unless they are alleged to have been present when the deed was committed.

(4) When a judge cannot otherwise obtain reliable information concerning a family, he can torture the slaves belonging to the estate.

(5) No confidence should be placed in a slave who voluntarily makes charges against his master, for the safety of masters must not be left to the discretion of their slaves.

(6) A slave cannot be interrogated to obtain evidence against his master, by whom he has been sold, and whom for some time he served as a slave, in remembrance of his former ownership.

(7) A slave should not be interrogated, even if his master offers to have him put to the torture.

(8) It is clear that every time an inquiry is made whether slaves should be interrogated to obtain evidence against their masters, it must first be ascertained that the latter are entitled to their ownership.

(9) A governor who is to take cognizance of a criminal accusation must publicly appoint a day when he will hear the prisoners, for those who are to be defended should not be oppressed by the sudden accusation of crime; although, if at any time the defendant requests it, he should not be refused permission to defend himself, and on this account, the day of the hearing, whether it has been designated or not, may be postponed.

(10) Prisoners can not only be heard and convicted in court, but also elsewhere.

19. *Tryphoninus, Disputations, Book IV.*

He who is entitled to freedom under the terms of a trust

cannot be tortured as a slave, unless he is accused by others who already have been subjected to torture.

20. *Paulus, Decisions, Book III.*

A husband, as the heir of his wife, brought suit against Surus for money which he alleged the deceased had deposited with him during his absence, and, in proof of it, he produced a single witness, the son of his freedman. He demanded before the Agent of the Treasury that a certain female slave should be put to torture. Surus denied that he had received the money, and stated that the testimony of one man should not be admitted; and that it was not customary to begin proceedings with torture, even though the female slave belonged to another. The Agent of the Treasury caused the female slave to be tortured. The Emperor decided, on appeal, that torture had been unlawfully inflicted, and that the testimony of one witness should not be believed, and therefore that the appeal had been properly taken.

21. *The Same, On the Punishments of Civilians.*

The Divine Hadrian stated in a Rescript that no one should be condemned because he was liable to be subjected to torture.

22. *The Same, Sentences, Book I.*

Those who have been arrested without having any accusers, can not be tortured, unless well-grounded suspicion is attached to them.

•        •        •

The juristic expertise of the jurists whose opinions contributed so extensively to the rational character of Roman law carried far more weight in late antiquity than the philosophical and rhetorical opinions for and against torture. Among the most intense opponents of torture are a number of early Christian writers, particularly Tertullian.[2] The following extract from St. Augustine's *City of God*, however, does not condemn torture outright or the judge who imposes it, but rather reflects Augustine's acute sensitivity to the contradictions between the individual conscience and the demands of public office.

II. From St. Augustine, *The City of God*, trans. Marcus Dods (New York, 1950), Book XIX, Chapter 6, pp. 681-83.

What shall I say of these judgments which men pronounce on men, and which are necessary in communities, whatever outward peace they enjoy? Melancholy and lamentable judgments they are, since the judges are men who cannot discern the consciences of those at their bar, and are therefore frequently compelled to put innocent witnesses to the torture to ascertain the truth regarding the crimes of other men. What shall I say of torture applied to the accused himself? He is tortured to discover whether he is guilty, so that, though innocent, he suffers most undoubted punishment for crime that is still doubtful, not because it is proved that he committed it, but because it is not ascertained that he did not commit it. Thus the ignorance of the judge frequently involves an innocent person in suffering. And what is still more unendurable—a thing, indeed, to be bewailed, and, if that were possible, watered with fountains of tears—is this, that when the judge puts the accused to the question, that he may not unwittingly put an innocent man to death, the result of this lamentable ignorance is that this very person, whom he tortured that he might not condemn him if innocent, is condemned to death both tortured and innocent. For if he has chosen, in obedience to the philosophical instructions to the wise man, to quit this life rather than endure any longer such tortures, he declares that he has committed the crime which in fact he has not committed. And when he has been condemned and put to death, the judge is still in ignorance whether he has put to death an innocent or a guilty person, though he put the accused to the torture for the very purpose of saving himself from condemning the innocent; and consequently he has both tortured an innocent man to discover his innocence, and has put him to death without discovering it. If such darkness shrouds social life, will a wise judge take his seat on the bench or no? Beyond question he will. For human society, which he thinks it a wickedness to abandon, constrains him and compels him to this duty. And he thinks it no wickedness that innocent witnesses are tortured regarding the crimes of which other men are accused; or that the accused are put to the torture, so that they are often overcome with anguish, and though innocent, make false confessions regarding themselves, and are punished; or that, though they be not condemned to die, they often die during, or in consequence of, the torture; or that sometimes the accusers, who perhaps have been prompted by a desire to benefit society by bringing criminals to justice, are themselves condemned through the ignorance of the judge, because they are unable to prove the truth of their accusations though they are true, and because the witnesses lie, and the accused endures the torture without being moved to confession. These numerous and important evils he does not consider sins; for the wise judge does these things, not with any intention of doing harm, but because his ignorance compels him, and because human society claims him as a judge. But though we therefore acquit the judge of malice, we must none the less condemn human life as miserable. And if he is compelled to torture and punish the innocent because his office and his ignorance constrain him, is he a happy as well as a guiltless man? Surely it were proof of more profound considerateness and finer feeling were he to recognise the misery of these necessities, and shrink from his own implication in that misery; and had he any piety about him, he would cry to God, "From my necessities deliver Thou me."

•        •        •

Among those Germanic kingdoms that retained traces of Roman law in their judicial procedure, that of Visigothic Spain contained particularly numerous references to torture.[3] The mid-seventh-century *Forum Judicum* was the result of a century and a half of Visigothic lawmaking and law-declaring. It not only embodied much late Roman law, but also exerted considerable influence upon subsequent medieval Castilian law codes such as the *Siete Partidas* of Alfonso X in 1265 and upon the Spanish laws of the New World; hence, it still exists as part of the laws of several of the states in the southern and southwestern United States.[4]

III. From *The Visigothic Code,* trans. S. P. Scott (Boston, 1910), (A) Book II, Title III, IV, p. 49; (B) Book VI, Title I, II-IV, pp. 194-99.

## A.

## FLAVIUS CHINTASVINTUS, KING.

**IV. Torture shall, in no Case, be inflicted upon Persons of Noble Birth who are acting as Representatives of Others; and, In what way a Freeman of the Lower Class, or a Slave, may be subjected to Torture.**

No person of noble rank shall, under any circumstances, be put to the torture by authority of a commission given to another. It is, however, hereby permitted that any freeborn person of low rank who is poor, and has already been convicted of crime, may be tortured under such a commission; but only when the principal gives authority in writing to do this, signed by him, and attested by three witnesses, which shall be entrusted for delivery, to a freeman, and not to a slave. And if he should cause the torture to be inflicted upon an innocent person, the aforesaid principal is hereby admonished, that he has incurred the penalty of the law which is found in the sixth book, first title, second chapter; wherein it is stated for what things freeborn persons are to be put to the question. It is lawful for other criminal causes to be prosecuted under commission; and, as has been said above, tortures may be applied to a freeman by the representative of another who is also free. And it is granted by the law to a freeman or a slave, to subject a slave to torture, with this provision, to wit: that if either torture or injury should be inflicted upon an innocent person, the principal shall be compelled to give complete satisfaction, under the instructions of the judge. Nor is he to be discharged who received the commission, until either the principal may be produced in court, or shall make amends according to law. And whoever desires to inflict the torture, having received authority to do so under a commission,, shall be compelled by the judge to give bond.

## B.

## THE GLORIOUS FLAVIUS CHINTASVINTUS, KING.

### II. For what Offences, and in what Manner, Freeborn Persons shall be put to the Torture.

If moderation is displayed in the treatment of crimes, the wickedness of criminals can never be restrained. Therefore, if anyone should, in behalf of the king or the people, bring an accusation of homicide or adultery against a person equal to him in rank, or in palatine dignity, he who thus seeks the blood of another shall first have an opportunity to prove what he alleges. And if he cannot prove it in the presence of the king, or those appointed by the royal authority, an accusation shall be drawn up in writing, and signed by three witnesses; and the accused person may then be put to the question.

If the latter, after undergoing the torture, should prove to be innocent, the accuser shall at once be delivered up to him as a slave, to be disposed of at his will, except that he shall not be deprived of life. But if he should be willing to make a compromise with his accuser, he may accept from the latter as large a sum as may compensate him for the sufferings he has endured. The judge shall take the precaution to compel the accuser to specifically describe the alleged offence, in writing; and after he has done so, and presented it privately to the judge, the torture shall proceed; and if the confession of him who is subjected to the torture should correspond with the terms of the accusation, his guilt shall be considered to be established. But if the accusation should allege one thing, and the confession of the person tortured the opposite, the accuser must undergo the penalty hereinbefore provided; because persons often accuse themselves of crime while being tortured. But if the accuser, before he has secretly given the written accusation to the judge as aforesaid, should, either in his own proper person, or by anyone else, inform the party of what he is accused, then it shall not be lawful for the judge to subject the latter to torture, because the alleged offence has become publicly known. This rule shall also apply to all other freeborn persons. But if the accusation should not be that of a capital crime, but merely of theft, or of some minor breach of the law, nobles, or persons of superior rank, such as the officials of our palace, shall, upon such an accusation, under no circumstances, be put to the question; and if proof of the alleged offence is wanting, he who is accused must declare his innocence under oath.

All persons of inferior rank, and freeborn persons, when accused of theft, homicide, or any other crime, shall not be tortured upon such an accusation, unless the property involved is worth more than fifty *solidi*. But if the property is of less value than fifty *solidi*, and the accused is convicted upon legal testimony, he shall be compelled to make restitution, as prescribed by other laws; or if he should not be convicted, after purging himself by oath he shall receive the satisfaction granted by the law for those who have suffered from an improper demand for torture.

We hereby especially provide that a lowborn person shall not presume to accuse a noble or one of higher rank than himself; but if such a person should accuse another of crime, and proof of the same should be wanting, the person accused shall at once purge himself of all guilt by oath, and swear that he never took, nor has in his possession, the property on account of which he was prosecuted; and oath having been made, as aforesaid, he who brought the false accusation shall undergo the penalty for the same, as prescribed by a former law. But whether the person subjected to the torture is a noble, one of inferior rank, or a freeman, he must be tortured in the presence of the judge, or of certain respectable men appointed by him; and in such a way as not to lose his life, or the use of any of his limbs; and because the torture must be applied for the space of three days, if, as the result of accident, or through the malice of the judge, or the treachery of anyone else, he who is subjected to it should die; or if the judge, having been corrupted by the bribes of the adversary of the accused, should not prohibit the infliction of such torments as are liable to produce death; the judge himself shall be delivered up to the nearest relatives of the accused person, that, on account of his injustice, he may undergo at their hands the same sufferings which he unlawfully inflicted upon the accused.

If, however, he should declare himself under oath to be innocent, and witnesses who were present should swear that death did not result from any malice, treachery, or corruption of which he was guilty, but only as a result of the torture itself; for the reason that the said judge did not use his discretion to prevent excessive cruelty, he shall be compelled to pay fifty *solidi* to the heirs of the deceased; and if he should not have sufficient property to pay said sum, he shall be delivered up as a slave to the nearest heirs of the former. The accuser shall be surrendered to the nearest relatives of the deceased, and shall suffer the penalty of death, which he suffered who perished through his accusation.

## ANCIENT LAW.

### III. For what Offences, and in what manner, Slaves, of Either Sex, shall be put to the Torture, on account of the Crimes of their Masters.

No slave, of either sex, shall be tortured in order to obtain evidence of crime against either his or her master or mistress, unless for adultery; or for some offence against the Crown, or against their country; or for counterfeiting, homicide, or witchcraft. And if slaves tortured for such reasons should be proved to be cognizant of the crimes of their masters, and to have concealed them, they shall be punished along with their masters in such way as the king may direct. But if they should voluntarily confess the truth before being put to the question, it will be sufficient if they undergo the torture in order to confirm their testimony, and they shall not suffer the penalty of death. But any slave of either sex, who, after being put to the torture for a capital crime, should also implicate his or her master, and the commission of said crime can be proved by competent evidence, they shall be subject to the same punishment as their master.

## FLAVIUS CHINTASVINTUS, KING.

### IV. For what Offences, and in what manner, a Slave, or a Freedman, shall be Tortured.

Where a slave is accused of any crime, the accuser must,

before the torture is inflicted, bind himself to give to the
master in his stead, another slave of equal value, if the innocence of the slave should be established. But if the accused
slave should be found innocent, and should die, or be disabled
from the effects of the torture, the accuser must at once give to
the master two other slaves, each equal in value to the one
killed or disabled. The one who was injured shall be free, and
remain under the protection of his master; and the judge who
neglected to use moderation in the infliction of torture, and
thus violated the law, shall give to the master another slave
equal in value to the one who perished by torture.

In order that all doubt may be removed concerning the value
of slaves in dispute, no statement of artificial or fraudulent
value of the same shall be accepted; but information of their
age and usefulness shall be obtained by personal examination
of the slaves themselves; and if he who was disabled was
skilled in any trade, and he who injured him when he was
innocent possesses no slave proficient in the same trade, he
shall be forced to give to the master a slave skilled in some
other trade; but if he should not have such a skilled artisan,
and he whose slave was injured by the torture should not be
willing to accept another in his stead, then the accuser shall
pay to the master the value of the slave that was injured,
according to a reasonable estimate made by the judge, or by
men of respectability and established character. It must, however, be observed, that no one shall presume to subject any
freeborn person or slave to torture, unless he shall make oath
in the presence of a judge, or his representative, the master of
the slave or his agent being also present, that through no arti-
fice, fraud, or malice, he is inflicting torture upon an innocent
person. And if, after having been put to the question he should
die, and his accuser should not have the means to make the
reparation required by law, he himself shall be reduced to slavery, for the reason that he was the cause of the death of an
innocent man. And if anyone, through treachery, should
attempt to subject the slave of another to torture, and the
master of said slave should prove that he was innocent of
crime, the accuser shall be compelled to give to the master of
the accused slave another of equal value, and to reimburse said

master for any reasonable expense that he has incurred in defence of his slave, until, in the opinion of the judge, full satisfaction has been rendered by the unjust accuser to the master of the innocent slave.

In case a slave is found guilty of a minor offence, the master, if he chooses to do so, shall have a right to compound the same; but every thief shall be scourged according to the degree of his guilt. Where a master is not willing to give satisfaction for graver offences, he must immediately surrender the slave to justice. Any freeborn person who desires to subject a respectable freedman to the torture, in the case of a capital crime, or of offences of less gravity, shall not be permitted to do so, unless the value of the property involved in the accusation amounts to at least two hundred and fifty *solidi*. But if said freeborn person should be of inferior rank, and a boar, he may be tortured, if the value of the property amounts to a hundred *solidi*.

Where he who is put to the question should, through want of proper care, be disabled, then the judge who did not exercise moderation in the infliction of torture, shall pay two hundred *solidi* to him who suffered by his negligence; and he who caused him to be tortured unjustly, shall be compelled to pay him three hundred *solidi*; and if he should die while undergoing torture, the judge, as well as the accuser, shall each pay to the nearest relatives of the deceased the sums of money aforesaid. And, in like manner, in the case of freedmen of still lower rank, should anyone of them undergo mutilation or death, through want of caution on the part of those employing the torture, half of the sum hereinbefore mentioned as applying to respectable freedmen shall be paid to him who was tortured, should he be still living, or, if he is dead, to his heirs.

•     •     •

Not until the thirteenth century did judicial torture reappear in the law codes of European societies. First applied to notorious criminals in the urban constitutions of northern Italy, it was soon joined to the *crimen laesae majestatis*, treason, and later, by analogy between treason and heresy, to heresy itself, thereby entering the tribunals of the Inquisition.[5] Once the question was raised in ecclesiastical courts, however, it encountered formidable obstacles in the views of traditional ecclesiastical jurisprudence. The most widely used collection of ecclesiastical law, the *Decretum* of Gratian, which appeared around 1140, had stated flatly that "confession in such cases ought not to be extorted, but rather offered voluntarily. It is the worst possible act to judge on the basis of mere suspicion or an extorted confession."[6] As we have seen above, however, the consciousness of the threat constituted by heresy and the formation of a particular tribunal to try cases of heresy, the Inquisition, opened the door for a modification of traditional Romano-canonical procedures, and the development of a doctrine of notoriety, *infamia*, admitted evidence from hitherto unacceptable witnesses and at the same time made the requirement of a confession particularly important. The need for a confession, dependent partly upon the history of inquisitorial procedure and partly upon the character of the crime of heresy, was perhaps the greatest incentive for the introduction of torture, particularly because of the underlying doctrine of penitence and the Church's responsibility for the salvation of even the heretic and its duty to keep Christian society free of contamination.

The introduction of torture into the procedure of the Inquisition was first authorized by Pope Innocent IV in the decretal *Ad extirpanda* of 1252. Even this remarkable document, however, did not permit the Inquisitors themselves to apply torture, because the twelfth-century attack upon early procedures, particularly the ordeal, had laid down that the clergy could not shed blood, a doctrine that was enunciated with great force and widespread influence at the Fourth Lateran Council of 1215.[7] Inquisitors, even after *Ad extirpanda*, could not apply torture themselves without becoming canonically irregular. Not until the next pontificate, that of Alexander IV, did Inquisitors obtain the authority to absolve one another from canonical irregularities incurred by their work. The following documents are the decretals *Ad extirpanda* of Innocent IV (1252) and *Ut negotium* of Alexander IV (1256), the two most important documents in the history of judicial torture in ecclesiastical courts. The first text begins with the introduction of Francesco Peña, a sixteenth-century commentator.

IV. From the *Directorium Inquisitorum F. Nicolai Eymerici . . . Cum Commenatiis Francisci Pegnae* (Rome, 1587), pp. 592-93.

Originally, when the Inquisition was first constituted, it seems that it was not permitted to the Inquisitors to torture offenders under the danger (as I believe) of incurring irregularity, and so torture was used against heretics or those suspected of heresy by lay judges; however, in the constitution of Innocent IV beginning *Ad extirpanda,* it is written:

In addition, the official or Rector should obtain from all heretics he has captured a confession by torture without injuring the body or causing the danger of death, for they are indeed thieves and murderers of souls and apostates from the sacraments of God and of the Christian faith. They should confess to their own errors and accuse other heretics whom they know, as well as their accomplices, fellow-believers, receivers and defenders, just as rogues and thieves of worldly goods are made to accuse their accomplices and confess the evils which they have committed.

V. From Henry Charles Lea, *A History of the Inquisition of the Middle Ages,* Vol. I (New York, 1888), Appendix, Doc. XII, p. 575: Bull of Alexander IV Authorizing Inquisitors to Absolve Each Other.

In order to expedite the work of faith that you carry out, we authorize you by this permission that if you incur in any cases the sentence of excommunication or irregularity, whether it should occur from human weakness or if you should incur it later on because you are not able to have recourse to your superiors at the moment, you may absolve each other of these things according to the proper form of the Church and by this authority you are enabled to dispense each other, just as this power has been conceded to your superiors by apostolic authority.

•      •      •

From the criminal courts of towns and the association of treason and heresy, to the ecclesiastical courts, torture entered the various criminal laws of Europe, and it remained a part of most of these until the eighteenth and nineteenth centuries.

Even in such kingdoms as England, in which torture and the inquisitorial process never took root, the fifteenth and sixteenth centuries witnessed an appearance of torture in political cases, usually outside the areas of competence of the common law. The handbooks for Inquisitors of the fourteenth through the seventeenth centuries refined the procedural aspects of torture, although the actual role of these guides in the day-to-day activities of the Inquisitorial courts is not clear.[8] In addition, however, torture appeared in secular courts long before these possessed even the dubious advantages of rational guidebooks, and the procedures involving torture became markedly worse, administered by incompetents and thugs who lacked even the theoretical supervisory powers of the Inquisitors.[9] Thus, when witchcraft became a widespread offense cognizible in secular as well as ecclesiastical courts, a new area for the activities of torturers opened up, and, with heresy and treason, witchcraft investigations probably contained the most frequent and the most brutal uses of torture during the sixteenth, seventeenth, and early eighteenth centuries.

To be sure, the protests of the Italian jurists of the thirteenth and fourteenth centuries extended to the outrages of Inquisitorial procedure as well as to the practice of the secular courts, but protests were few and generally ineffectual until the sixteenth and seventeenth centuries. And it should be remembered that along with the literature of protest there grew up a detailed, learned, and widely accepted literature on criminal procedure in which torture was widely condoned. It is from this literature, both for and against torture, that the most detailed information can be obtained.[10]

Among the most widely read descriptions of criminal procedure, an important and generally neglected literary genre of the sixteenth century, was the *Tractatus ad Defensam Inquisitorum, Carceratorum, Reorum et Condemnatorum super Quocunque Crimine*, written in 1612 and published several years later by Sebastian Guazzini, a well-known and respected Italian judge.

VI. From Sebastian Guazzini, *Tractatus ad Defensam . . .*, translated and condensed by James C. Welling, *The Law of*

*Torture: A Study in the Evolution of Law* (Washington, 1892), pp. 6–15. In the edition published at Geneva in 1664, these passages may be found on pp. 71–130, *Defensio* XXX. *Circa Torturam pro habenda veritate.*

"What is called Torture is distress of body devised for extracting truth. The mode of administering torture by the use of the rope was invented by the Civil Law, and this torment of the rope, sometimes called the queen of torment, was justly invented by the Civil Law, as a mode of discovering truth, for the sake of the public welfare, to the end that crimes might not remain unpunished. It is called a species of evidence substituted to supply the lack of witnesses.

"But let judges be on their guard against resorting to torture with facility, as it is an expedient which may prove fragile and perilous, and may play false to truth; because some persons have such an incapacity for the endurance of pain that they are more willing to lie than to suffer torments. Others again are so obstinate that they are more willing to suffer any torments whatsoever than to confess the truth.

"Having been invented only as a subsidiary form of evidence where truth cannot be otherwise discovered in the ordinary way, *i.e.,* by witnesses, the authorities say that this rule holds good in every case whatsoever, in which resort is had, either by law or usage, to the institute of torture. It is always a subsidiary remedy, to be invoked only when truth cannot be discovered in any other way."

"Torture cannot be repeated more than three times on the same subject, and then only for justifying reasons and with respect had to the persons and the crimes involved.

"Confession of guilt made under torture works no damage to the party confessing until the confession has been reaffirmed without torture. Under this head the lawyer has the firmest rule for his guidance, and the rule has been established, as the text-writers say, because the remedy of torture 'is fallacious, fragile, and perilous' for reasons already given; and this ratification should be made outside of the place of torment, at the bar of public justice, and in presence of the witnesses required by law. It should also be made at a sufficient interval after the torture to protect it from the suspicion of being made under the surviving stress of the torture which has extorted the confession. But in practice this rule is very elastic, and the interval, according to the discretion of courts or judges, may vary from three days to four or five hours.

"Torture legally administered in a legal case and sustained with constancy has for its effect to work the legal absolution of the party accused.

"More than this, if, after a person has confessed his guilt, has been convicted, and has been condemned, the judge shall proceed to torture him for ulterior information concerning his accomplices, suborners, or abettors without first premising and protesting that the torture *does not relate to the matters confessed and of which the culprit has been convicted,* or without first premising and protesting that the torture is inflicted *without prejudice to his condemnation,* in such cases the torture, if sustained, will work not only his expurgation from the presumptions, but also from the proofs on which he has been convicted. But where such a precautionary reservation has been made the judge may proceed to torture a confessed or convicted culprit for the discovery of accessories before or after the fact.

"Torture, in cases where it is applicable, works the rehabilitation of competent witnesses who are affected with a single defect, but will not deliver from a multiplicity of defects. It cannot be used to purge the defect of perjury, of personal enmity, etc.

"A judge who unduly tortures an accused party from malice, hatred, enmity, or for reward, is guilty of a capital offence if the patient dies under torture. Some writers hold that the victim of unjust torture may slay the judge who ordered it, and may do so without being subject to the ordinary penalty of homicide, especially when this vengeance is taken by the victim immediately on being dismissed from torture.

"The text-writers hold that prisoners who make or take remedies to harden the body against torture should be punished, since such remedies are altogether prohibited; and, as such, the text-writers are likely to characterize all incantations and malefic arts, if they induce taciturnity or insensibility to bodily torture. If anybody desires to know how accused parties make use of such-like incantations and remedies, let him consult Paul. Grill., *De quæst. et tort., quæst.* 4, *numer.* 11. If anybody desires to know the remedies which the judge should use against the remedies of the accused, let him consult Grill., *ibid., numer.* 16. The authorities lay down many other antidotes against these diabolic incantations, but Cavalcanus thinks, for his part, that there is no remedy more appropriate than the upright mind of the judge himself, when he directs it solely to the end of attaining the way of truth and justice, and not to the end of clutching after vainglory or striving for the sake of gain. Hence the judge should pray God to be propitious to him in the way of truth and justice.

"If a prisoner about to be tortured shall use the words of the Holy Evangely or Prophets, even though the words should induce taciturnity or silence, he may not deserve for this reason to be punished in this world or in the secular forum. Such, at least, is the opinion of certain commentators."

"Even when these legitimate presumptions exist, the judge, before he proceeds to torture, must file a decree or an interlocutory plea stating his purpose to resort to torture, and alleging the grounds on which this plea is based. After a decree of torture shall have been allowed, an appeal may be taken from it by the counsel of the accused, and, pending this appeal, at least in most jurisdictions (that of the French Parliament and of other courts in Dauphiny being exceptions), the judge cannot renew any proceedings in the way of torture. If, in spite of the appeal, a judge shall have proceeded to torture and extorted a confession, such a confession shall be wholly null. It is not competent for the government prosecutor or for the plaintiff to take an appeal from a decree disallowing torture. Wary judges, it is true, when they wish to torture and do not want to have their hands tied, are accustomed to pass the decree of torture secretly, and do not interpose it until it is too late for the accused to take an appeal. But this surprise action on the part of judges may be countermined by wary attorneys, who are wont to obtain in advance an inhibition [from the superior court] against the menace of torture; and, the instant that the judge shows a disposition to proceed to torture, they present the inhibition to him, and thus compel him to stay his hand and to consign the case to the court above. A frivolous and false appeal can be rejected at once, and it resides in the discretion of the judge to decide when an appeal is manifestly frivolous and false. In such case he can administer torture without usurpation; but if any doubt remain, whether of fact or law, he must wholly desist from torture, or he will expose himself to punishment and peril.

"If the decree of torture shall be overruled [by the court of appeals], there are regulations which prescribe who shall hear the principal matter involved in the case—*an judex a quo vel judex ad quem.*

"Torture can be administered only in cases which involve a heavy penalty such as banishment, death, or severe bodily punishment of some kind. In nowise should a resort to torture be allowed in actions at law sounding in money damages alone. In an action, for instance, arising from contract, express or implied, torture is not to be thought of, even though the truth cannot otherwise be attained, because in civil suits the laws afford other remedies, for if the plaintiff makes complete proof of his declaration judgment is given; if a half-complete proof is made, the supplementary oath is administered to him; if a proof less than half complete is made, then the oath of purgation is granted to the defendant; if the plaintiff makes no proof at all, the defendant is acquitted.

"Sometimes, however, or at least in the judgment of some authorities, it may be competent to torture vile persons in actions where only a money penalty is involved, it being presumed that such persons will make more account of money, 'the second blood of men,' than of their physical comfort; but in all such cases the torture inflicted must be moderate or even light."

"1. The first principal requisite is that the truth of the facts cannot be otherwise elicited, and that the torture, as declared in the decree allowing it, is employed only as a subsidiary remedy and for the reasons already assigned by the judge in his interlocutory plea.

"2. The second principal requisite is that the *corpus delicti* be manifest before resort is had to torture.

"3. The third principal requisite is that legitimate presumptions of fact held sufficient to justify torture shall precede its administration, it being abhorrent both to the canon and the civil laws that the judge should begin his inquest with torture. These presumptions should be so accusatory, according to some authorities, as to leave nothing wanting except the confession alone of the culprit—that is, in their character as accusatory indications they should be, so to say, clearer than light; and let judges beware lest, in virtue of any discretion conceded to them, either by law or by man, they push on to torture without the legitimate presumptions precedent, because this discretion of theirs should be regulated by the rules of the common law. Some authorities hold that a judge who has the faculty of proceeding with the Royal Arm [that is, by Prerogative Right] can resort to torture, in cases of difficult proof, because of the bad character of the accused; because of the atrocity of the crime alleged; because of a widespread public rumor, or such like probable indication; yet even in such cases there should be certain concurrent and precedent indications.

"The Prince [that is, in the Italian diction of the time, the Government] cannot order that anybody should be tortured without legitimate indications, nor can a judge be held to obey him, as, by so obeying, the judge is subject to public impeachment [*tenetur in syndicatu*].

"Just as little can a judge lawfully terrorize an accused party without legitimate presumptions precedent. Yea, many hold that, in default of legitimate indications precedent, an accused party cannot be tortured even with his own consent.

"If the prosecutor shall say, 'I have no presumptions of fact and no proofs against the accused, but I wish to stand with him in torture, and in this way prove the crime imputed to him,' such a prosecutor shall not be heard, and the accused shall not be tortured on this plea.

"And let the judge make sure that the indications are not only sufficient for torture, but that they are such as can be lawfully received; and this rule holds good even where the judge has the faculty of proceeding summarily in the administration of torture.

"Nor let the [ordinary] judge suppose that without the legitimate indications precedent he can proceed to torture because of the gravity of the crime, for the rule that in atrocious crimes 'it may be lawful to exceed the laws' is a rule which holds good only after the accused has been found guilty, and cannot be pleaded in regard to the mode of procedure. The logic of the rule would seem to be that the greater the crime is, so much the more vehement should be the presumptions of fact which ought to precede torture; and, without these legitimate presumptions of fact, the judge must be on his guard against resorting to torture under the pretext that the crime is hard to prove. Just as little can a judge use torture to extract truth, under pretext that on account of torture inflicted for certain crimes even without legitimate presumptions of fact, a great public scandal may be allayed.

"All the indications which may suffice for inflicting torture cannot be enumerated, nor can any certain or determinate doctrine on the subject be propounded; but the whole matter is committed to the discretion of the prudent judge, having regard to the nature of the facts, of the crime, of the person involved, and of other circumstances and characteristics deduced from the process. This discretion, however, must not be based on any indication at the pleasure of the judge, but only on certain concurrent circumstances and characteristics implicit in each case. The judge's discretion is a regulated discretion, because regulated by rules of common law, and does not spring out of the judge's mere brain. The faculty of torturing accused parties is so far restricted and limited to terms of law that, in my opinion, not even the Royal Bailiffs [*Trunculatores*] sent to try highway robbers should presume that God has created human bodies to be agonized and lacerated at the torturer's free will. Yet true it is that if the judge has the Royal Arm he may torture on the strength of indications which hold good under natural, divine, or canon laws.

"Thus far the whole question has moved in presumptions of *fact* resulting from the inquest. It is otherwise where presump-

tions of *law* are concerned, and where any indication shall
have been *proved*, whether by confession made out of court or
by the testimony of a single witness, because in such cases it
will not reside in the discretion of the judge to decide whether
the indication is sufficient for torture or not. He will be bound
to torture the accused without demur. If anybody is curious to
see certain particular indications which are sufficient for torture, let him consult Campeg. *de testib. reg.*, 395; Menoch. *de
præsumpt.*, lib. 9, *quæst.* 89, where the latter heaps up forty-
three indications for torture, while Cavalcanus discusses indications that may be used before an ordinary judge and indications that may be used before a judge of the Royal Arm.

"Question has been raised whether one indication will suffice
for torture or whether several indications should be required.
The distinction to be observed is that one may suffice provided
it is proximate to the crime [that is, very close to the crime in
its accusatory significance]. Where the indications are remote
in their bearing, several are required. The common rule is, in
both the canon and the civil laws, that at least two indications
should be required for torture, and that one remote indication
is not enough to justify torture. If, however, there shall be several remote indications, which are proved by single witnesses,
the accused can be tortured on the strength of them. If there
should be at least three indications, proved by single witnesses,
they will suffice for torture, though the indications may not be
very cogent, especially where the witnesses are men of known
probity and of high authority.

"4. The fourth requisite for torture is that the issue at law
with the accused shall be fully and legally joined, except where
the judge has the power of proceeding summarily.

"5. The fifth requisite is that the interlocutory plea for torture shall have been filed and duly allowed after the suit has
been made public, and after the matter has been discussed with
the counsel of the accused; though, as before implied, such a
decree of torture is not required where the judge has the faculty of proceeding summarily. Maur. Burg. lays down in such
cases a form for the summary procedure to torture, and enumerates eight special prerogatives which a judge has in virtue
of such faculty of summary procedure. In passing a decree of

torture the judge should collect and, as it were, condense into a brief compass all the several indications scattered through the process in its several parts, by way of exhorting the accused to make a clean breast of it, inasmuch as, in the face of so many indications, he cannot persist in a denial. In this way accused parties may place themselves in the clemency of the Prince, and will do a service to their lawyers, who will clearly discern wherein the difficulty of a case may lie.

"6. The sixth requisite is that a copy of the indications and of the whole process must be furnished to the accused, and that the process itself must be published. Where the accused is found *in flagranti delicto*, no copy, either of the indications or of the process, need be furnished, as, for instance, in the celebrated case of the noblemen who were caught with their ladders at the windows of a certain noble lady [in the act of abduction]. In a crime like that, the rule is not to observe rule.

"7. The seventh requisite is that inspection be made of the person of the accused, to ascertain whether he is privileged or not, because a privileged person cannot be tortured even with legitimate presumptions precedent.

"8. The eighth requisite is that if the accused shall ask that the accuser make oath to the good faith of the charge, no torture shall be inflicted until such oath shall have been made.

"9. The ninth requisite is that the accuser, in the presence of the judge, shall demand the torture of the accused, and shall swear that he has no further proofs; but this rule has fallen into desuetude in the whole of Italy.

"10. The tenth requisite is that the accused shall not have eaten for nine or ten hours before torture, that the process of digestion may have been completed before the torture begins. If accident happen and suffering ensue to the accused from a failure to observe this rule, the judge will be liable to public impeachment.

"11. The eleventh requirement is that if the accused be under the age of twenty-five years the judge shall appoint a curator to watch for his safety under torture. In such cases, a confession made without a curator is null and void. Of late years, however, an exception of nullity, when based on this ground, has been so reduced as to extend only to minors under the age of fourteen years; but it will always be competent for counsel to insist, in such cases, that special usage shall not prevail against common law.

"12. The twelfth requisite is that the judge must have plenary power for the administration of torture. A *Locumtenens Potestatis* [an acting judge] or a simple assessor on the bench has not the power of torture.

"13. The thirteenth requisite is that indications of the government prosecutor, if sufficient for torture, shall not have been quashed by the counter-indications of the accused.

"14. The fourteenth requisite is that when several persons are to be tortured they shall not all be tortured alike, but some more severely and others more mildly, according to the quality of the persons and the presumptions lying against them, having regard to their age, their physical constitution, their mental habits, and their social status.

"15. The fifteenth requisite is that the accused must not be disabled in any of his members, for in that case, as for instance, if he has an issue of blood, has a wound in the breast, is troubled with shortness of breath, has hernia, or is suffering from venereal disease, he cannot be tortured.

"16. The sixteenth requisite is, as before stated, that torture cannot be employed to make manifest the *corpus delicti* (since this must appear *aliunde*), but only for the purpose of discovering the authors and accomplices of the crime. It also ought to be inflicted [as before implied] only in cases in which a confession can and ought to sound in felony (*possit et debeat sonare in delictum*), since torture should not be inflicted uselessly.

"17. The seventeeth requisite is that before accused parties can be tortured their counsel should be inquired of and duly heard on the question whether the accused can be tortured or not. The rule that counsel should be inquired of holds good especially in the Kingdom of Naples, though little observed in practice; but counsel ought to be heard if they wish to be heard.

"After counsel have been duly heard for a client they are not permitted, by usage, to be present at the act of torture, though, of right, it should be said otherwise; and, of right, the govern-

ment prosecutor should not be present at the infliction of torture, though, by custom, it is sometimes allowed. Baiardus
says that for the sake of suppressing the vain exclamations of
the government, he always wished the presence of the government prosecutor or of some substitute for the said prosecutor
—a rule which I have always observed for the sake of avoiding
the vain acclamations of the aforesaid attorney for the government.

"18. The eighteenth requisite is that in inflicting torture on a
clergyman degradation from office shall precede the infliction,
though this rule is poorly observed in practice.

"19. The nineteenth requisite is that an accused party shall
not be tortured on a Feast Day celebrated in honor of God,
except in grave cases. Judges who fear God observe this rule,
says Julius Clarus, but judges otherwise minded do not pay
much respect to it.

"A culprit pardoned by the Prince can be tortured as to any
contingent remainder of suspected guilt not covered by the
pardon. For instance, a pardoned culprit may be tortured in
order to remove the stain of his guilt, so that his testimony
under torture may be held valid against his accomplices. But a
full pardon works exemption from torture.

"Where a party confesses the act, but denies criminal intent,
as in case of homicide alleged to have been committed in self-
defence, it is a moot point whether such a mixed confession
should be received at all, or whether it should be received by
the government as a confession of guilt unless the accused can
establish the absence of criminal intent. In case of such mixed
confession it would be safer not to torture, for torture sustained in such a case would work the acquittal of the accused.

"A culprit, confessing a crime, cannot be tortured to procure
the confession of other crimes, in the absence of competent
presumptions to that effect. The contrary usage prevails, however, in the whole of Italy. But such torture is subject to the
following qualifications: It must be moderate; it cannot be
applied to clergymen; it is applicable only to notorious criminals, and it is abolished in the States of the Church.

"Whether benefit of clergy works immunity from torture or
not, is a disputed question among the authorities. Some hold

that a clergyman can be tortured, but not so severely as a layman, and not by a lay judge, nor by a lay minister even at the mandate of a bishop. A clergyman should not be admitted to canonical purgation when he is weighed down with presumptions that justify torture.

"A deaf-mute from birth cannot be tortured, though opinion and practice are at variance on this point. A pregnant woman and a woman giving suck to her children cannot be tortured.

"Torture must be suspended so soon as the victim falls into a faint under its effects, and unless the judge, in the act of such suspension, is careful to reserve a right of renewing torture, the right lapses. The notary is bound to make a minute of all proceedings in torture, with its effect on the subject, and the measures taken to recover him from a faint. The prisoner's counsel, in such moments, must watch for his rights and protect him from the renewal of the torture, if the judge, in his alarm at the fainting spell, forgets to reserve the right of renewing the torture. [Guazzini confesses that he had several times fallen into negligence under this head when he first began to practice the duties of his office.]

"Bishops and others in high civil dignity are exempt from torture even under strong presumptions of guilt. Noblemen, town councillors, doctors, lawyers, have a general immunity from torture, though the practice varies under these heads. Privilege from torture works a perfectly valid defence against all confessions extorted under its illegal infliction, except in cases of high treason. When several persons are to be tortured at the same time the general rule is that the judge should begin with the more timid, with the weaker, with the meaner [in social rank], with the younger, with the one who stands more nearly related to the charge, and with men before women, though some authorities hold that it is better to begin with women, because women are less afraid of torture than men, and will longer persist in a negative. In such cases the judge may proceed at his discretion.

"In administering torture it is competent for the judge, according to some authorities, to begin with the culprit who, from the name he bears, is known to belong to a family of criminals, and, as examples of such bad names, may be cited the names of Forabosco, Sgaramella, Saltalamachia, Mardolino, Spazzacroce, Pizzaguerra, Falameschia, Mazzasette, etc. Some hold that it is proper to begin with the man who has a bad physiognomy, provided he labors under other presumptions.

"Where father and son rest under the same charge and the same presumptions, it may be proper to begin with the son rather than the father, that the father, being more tortured in the person of his son than in his own proper person, may be the sooner urged to confession. [But Guazzini says he had never seen this rule observed, and had not observed it himself when once, in Perugia, he had a father and a son before him *in pari delicto*.] The preponderant weight of opinion would seem to be that the judge should begin with the person to whom the strongest suspicions of guilt attach.

"Let judges beware of aspiring after a vainglory in the infliction of torture, and let them strive only to attain truth through legitimate channels, conducting themselves with moderation and considering the physical condition, temperament, age, social status, etc., etc., of the accused. Torture must be administered only with the usual and established instruments. The accused is to be so tortured that his life may be safe, whether with a view to his innocence [in case his innocence shall be demonstrated by his constancy] or with a view to his punishment [in case he shall confess his guilt].

"The judge must not administer torture by his own hands, but by the intervention of satellites and bailiffs."

•     •     •

As a number of scholars have observed, the meticulous subtleties of such lawyers as Guazzini, with their restrictions, shadings of the weight of different kinds of evidence, technical considerations, and detailed insistence upon legal minutiae may well have contributed to the ultimate rejection of judicial torture by creating conditions too difficult for any court or judge to observe. Such an argument, of course, would have to be traced carefully through many volumes such as Guazzini's through the work of such seventeenth-century jurists as Bene-

dict Carpzov.[11] Far better known, however, and certainly
influential in their own right, are those denunciations that
reflect an outraged humanity rather than juridical
pedantry. The most famous indictment of judicial torture came
from the pen of Cesare Beccaria, the eighteenth-century Italian
thinker whose essay *On Crimes and Punishments* became the
foremost treatise on penal reform produced by the Enlightenment, an enormously influential work whose circulation and
impact contributed to penal reform over most of Europe.[12]

VII. From Cesare Beccaria, *On Crimes and Punishments*,
translated, with an introduction, by Henry Paolucci (New
York, 1963), Ch. XII, pp. 30–36. Paolucci's Introduction provides a good survey of Beccaria's life and thought. The notes
in the following selection are those of the translator.

## TORTURE.[24]

A cruelty consecrated by the practice of most nations is torture of the accused during his trial, either to make him confess
the crime or to clear up contradictory statements, or to discover accomplices, or to purge him of infamy in some metaphysical and incomprehensible way, or, finally, to discover
other crimes of which he might be guilty but of which he is
not accused.

No man can be called *guilty* before a judge has sentenced
him, nor can society deprive him of public protection before it
has been decided that he has in fact violated the conditions
under which such protection was accorded him. What right is
it, then, if not simply that of might, which empowers a judge
to inflict punishment on a citizen while doubt still remains as
to his guilt or innocence? Here is the dilemma, which is noth-

[24] [The historical references and juridical citations of this celebrated
chapter were supplied by Pietro Verri, who had, at the time this work was
being written, already compiled his notes for the posthumously published
*Osservazioni sulla tortura* (1804). Alessandro Manzoni, Beccaria's grand-
son, subjecting many of the citations to a very rigorous examination in his
*Storia della Colonna Infame*, Chapter Two, has demonstrated that they
are, for the most part, misrepresented in the accounts given by Verri and
echoed by Beccaria. See Introduction, p. xxii.]

ing new: the fact of the crime is either certain or uncertain: if certain, all that is due is the punishment established by the laws, and tortures are useless because the criminal's confession is useless; if uncertain, then one must not torture the innocent, for such, according to the laws, is a man whose crimes are not yet proved.

What is the political intent of punishments? To instill fear in other men. But what justification can we find, then, for the secret and private tortures which the tyranny of custom practices on the guilty and the innocent? It is important, indeed, to let no known crime pass unpunished, but it is useless to reveal the author of a crime that lies deeply buried in darkness. A wrong already committed, and for which there is no remedy, ought to be punished by political society only because it might otherwise excite false hopes of impunity in others. If it be true that a greater number of men, whether because of fear or virtue, respect the laws than break them, then the risk of torturing an innocent person should be considered greater when, other things being equal, the probability is greater that a man has rather respected the laws than despised them.

But I say more: it tends to confound all relations to require that a man be at the same time accuser and accused, that pain be made the crucible of truth, as if its criterion lay in the muscles and sinews of a miserable wretch.

The law that authorizes torture is a law that says: "Men, resist pain; and if nature has created in you an inextinguishable self-love, if it has granted you an inalienable right of self-defense, I create in you an altogether contrary sentiment: a heroic hatred of yourselves; and I command you to accuse yourselves, to speak the truth even while muscles are being lacerated and bones disjointed."

This infamous crucible of truth is a still-standing memorial of the ancient and barbarous legislation of a time when trials by fire and by boiling water, as well as the uncertain outcomes of duels, were called "judgments of God,"[25] as if the links of

[25] [Beccaria, following Verri, is quite mistaken in asserting that torture is of the same juridical order as "trials by fire or boiling water." On the contrary, when men trust the competence of gods or of a jury of their fellow men, to determine guilt or innocence, the confession which torture

the eternal chain, which is in the bosom of the First Cause, must at every moment be disordered and broken by frivolous human arrangements. The only difference between torture and trials by fire and boiling water is that the outcome seems to depend, in the first, on the will of the accused, and in the second, on a purely physical and extrinsic fact; but this difference is only apparent, not real. One is as much free to tell the truth in the midst of convulsions and torments, as one was free then to impede without fraud the effects of fire and boiling water. Every act of our will is invariably proportioned to the force of the sensory impression which is its source; and the sensory capacity of every man is limited. Thus the impression of pain may become so great that, filling the entire sensory capacity of the tortured person, it leaves him free only to choose what for the moment is the shortest way of escape from pain. The response of the accused is then as inevitable as the impressions of fire and water. The sensitive innocent man will then confess himself guilty when he believes that, by so doing, he can put an end to his torment. Every difference between guilt and innocence disappears by virtue of the very means one pretends to be using to discover it. [Torture] is an infallible means indeed—for absolving robust scoundrels and for condemning innocent persons who happen to be weak. Such are the fatal defects of this so-called criterion of truth, a criterion fit for a cannibal, which the Romans, who were barbarous themselves on many counts, reserved only for slaves, the victim of a fierce and overly praised virtue.[26]

is meant to extract from the accused becomes superfluous. It is only when men lose their trust in gods or in human jurors that the law must search for a witness of greater authority. Historically it is possible to demonstrate that torture of the accused has sometimes been introduced simply as a desperate abuse of the rationalistic desire to secure that "consent of the governed" which alone "justifies" governmental power, even when the power to be exercised is that of criminal punishment. For a brief summary of the relations between appeals to God, proofs by oaths, proofs by ordeals, judicial combats, indictments by jury, trial by jury, and torture, in the development of Anglo-American legal procedures, see *The Collected Papers of Frederic William Maitland*, ed. H. A. L. Fisher (Cambridge, 1911), II, 445–65.]

[26] [It has been noted that Roman jurists, as well as Roman philoso-

Of two men, equally innocent or equally guilty, the strong and courageous will be acquitted, the weak and timid condemned, by virtue of this rigorous rational argument: "I, the judge, was supposed to find you guilty of such and such a crime; you, the strong, have been able to resist the pain, and I therefore absolve you; you, the weak, have yielded, and I therefore condemn you. I am aware that a confession wrenched forth by torments ought to be of no weight whatsoever, but I'll torment you again if you don't confirm what you have confessed."

The effect of torture, therefore, is a matter of temperament and calculation that varies with each man according to his strength and sensibility, so that, with this method, a mathematician could more readily than a judge resolve this problem: given the muscular force and nervous sensibility of an innocent person, find the degree of pain that will make him confess himself guilty of a given crime.

The examination of an accused person is undertaken to ascertain the truth. But if this truth is difficult to discover in the air, gesture, and countenance of a man at ease, much more difficult will its discovery be when the convulsions of pain have distorted all the signs by which truth reveals itself in spite of themselves in the countenances of the majority of men. Every violent action confounds and dissolves those little differences in objects by means of which one may occasionally distinguish the true from the false.

A strange consequence that necessarily follows from the use of torture is that the innocent person is placed in a condition worse than that of the guilty, for if both are tortured, the circumstances are all against the former. Either he confesses the crime and is condemned, or he is declared innocent and has suffered a punishment he did not deserve. The guilty man, on the contrary, finds himself in a favorable situation; that is, if, as a consequence of having firmly resisted the torture, he is

phers, including Cicero, Seneca, Quintilian, and Ulpian, had written eloquently against the abuse and often even against the use of torture in juridical proceedings. Verri cites a number of their views in his *Osservazioni*, but minimizes their significance. Cf. St. Augustine, *The City of God*, XIX, 6.]

absolved as innocent, he will have escaped a greater punishment by enduring a lesser one. Thus the innocent cannot but lose, whereas the guilty may gain.

The truth is felt, finally though confusedly, by those very persons who shrink from it in practice. The confession made under torture is of no avail if it be not confirmed with an oath after the torture has stopped, but if the accused does not then confirm the crime, he is again tortured. Some jurists, and some nations, allow this infamous begging of principles to be repeated no more than three times; other nations, and other jurists, leave it to the discretion of the judge.

It would be superfluous to intensify the light, here, by citing the innumerable examples of innocent persons who have confessed themselves criminals because of the agonies of torture; there is no nation, there is no age that does not have its own to cite; but neither will men change nor will they deduce the necessary consequences. Every man who has ever extended his thought even a little beyond the mere necessities of life has at least sometimes felt an urge to run toward Nature, who, with secret and indistinct voices, calls him to her; custom, that tyrant of minds, drives him back and frightens him.

Torture is alleged to be useful, also, as applied to suspected criminals, when they contradict themselves under examination; as if fear of punishment, the uncertainty of the sentence, the pomp and majesty of the judge, the almost universal ignorance of both the wicked and the innocent, were not apt enough to plunge the innocent man who is afraid, as well as the guilty who is seeking to conceal, into contradiction; as if contradictions, which are common enough in men when they are at ease, are not likely to be multiplied in the perturbations of a mind altogether absorbed in the thought of saving itself from imminent peril.

Torture is applied to discover whether the criminal is guilty of crimes other than those of which he is accused; it amounts to this sort of reasoning: "You are guilty of one crime, therefore it is possible that you are guilty also of a hundred others; this doubt weighs on me, and I want to convince myself one way or another by using my criterion of truth: the laws torture you because you are guilty, because you may be guilty, because I insist that you be guilty."

Torture is applied to an accused person to discover his accomplices in the crime. But if it is demonstrated that torture is not an opportune means for discovering the truth, how can it serve to reveal the accomplices, which is one of the truths to be discovered? As if a man who accuses himself would not more readily accuse others. Is it right to torment men for the crime of another? Will not the accomplices be disclosed from the examination of witnesses, from the examination of the accused, from the proofs and from the material fact of the crime—in sum, from all of the very means that should serve to convict the accused of having committed the crime? Accomplices usually fly as soon as their companion is taken; the uncertainty of their lot of itself condemns them to exile, and frees the nation from the danger of further offenses, while the punishment of the criminal who is taken achieves its sole purpose, which is to deter other men, by fear, from committing a similar crime.

Another ridiculous pretext for torture is purgation from infamy; which is to say, a man judged infamous by the laws must confirm his deposition with the dislocation of his bones. This abuse should not be tolerated in the eighteenth century. It is believed that pain, which is a sensation, can purge infamy, which is a purely moral relationship. Is torture perhaps a crucible, and infamy, perhaps, a mixed impure substance? But infamy is a sentiment subject neither to the laws nor to reason, but to common opinion. Torture itself brings real infamy to its victims. Thus, by this method, infamy is to be removed by adding to it.

It is not difficult to trace the origin of this ridiculous law, because the very absurdities that are adopted by an entire nation have always some relation to other common ideas that it respects. The usage seems to have derived from religious and spiritual ideas, which exert a great influence on the thoughts of men, nations, and ages. An infallible dogma assures us that the stains contracted through our human frailty, which have not merited the eternal anger of the Grand Being, must be purged by an incomprehensible fire. Now infamy is a civil stain, and as suffering and fire remove spiritual and incorporeal stains, why should not spasms of torture remove the civil stain, which is infamy? I believe that the confession of the criminal which is exacted as essential for condemnation in certain tribunals has a similar origin, for in the mysterious tribunal of penance the confession of sins is an essential part of the sacrament. Thus do men abuse the surest lights of Revelation, and as these are the only ones that subsist in times of ignorance, docile humanity turns to them on all occasions and makes of them the most absurd and far-fetched applications.

These truths were known to the Roman legislators, among whom one does not encounter the use of torture, except with slaves, who were denied any personality. They are adopted by England, a nation whose glorious attainments in literature, whose superiority in commerce and in wealth, and consequently in power, and whose examples of virtue and of courage, leave no doubt as to the goodness of her laws. Torture has been abolished in Sweden: abolished by one of the wisest monarchs of Europe,[27] who, having brought philosophy to the throne, a legislator that befriends subjects, has rendered them equal and free in dependence on the laws; this is the sole equality and liberty that reasonable men can desire in the present state of things. Torture is not deemed necessary in the laws that regulate armies, though these are, for the most part, made up of the dregs of nations, which would seem to have more use for it than any other class. How strong a thing, indeed, it must seem to anyone who fails to consider how great is the tyranny of usage that the laws of peace should have to learn a more humane method of judgment from spirits hardened to slaughter and bloodshed!

[27] [The punctuation suggests that Beccaria is writing of the king responsible for the abolition of torture in Sweden referred to in the first part of the sentence. However, Gustavus III (1746–1792), an enlightened monarch to whom Beccaria's words might well apply, did not attain the throne until 1771, seven years after Beccaria's treatise was published. The reference is perhaps to Frederick II of Prussia (1712–1786).]

# NOTES TO APPENDIX.

1. For Greek law, see A. R. W. Harrison, *The Law of Athens: Procedure*, Vol. II (Oxford, 1971), pp. 147–50. For Roman Law, see Introduction, above, n. 4.

2. For Tertullian, see the *Liber Apologeticum*, ed. J. Mayor and A. Souter (Cambridge, 1917), and for St. Augustine, see Herbert A. Deane, *The Social and Political Ideas of St. Augustine*, (New York, 1963), pp. 134–37; 301–303.

3. Other Germanic law codes in English translation are Katherine Fischer Drew, trans., *The Burgundian Code* (Philadelphia, 1972) and K. F. Drew, trans., *The Lombard Laws*, (Philadelphia, 1973).

4. For the general development, see E. N. Van Kleffens, *Hispanic Law until the End of the Middle Ages* (Edinburgh, 1968).

5. On the early history of treason, see Floyd Seyward Lear, *Treason in Roman and Germanic Law* (Austin, Tex., 1965). For the Middle Ages, see the works cited above in the notes to the Introduction, n. 11.

6. *Decretum Gratiani*, C.5 q.5 c.4.

7. See the works cited in the notes to Henry C. Lea, *The Ordeal* (Philadelphia, 1973).

8. Besides the work of Eymeric, cited above, see Bernard Gui, *Manuel de l'Inquisiteur*, ed. and trans. G. Mollat, 2 vols. (Paris, 1926–27).

9. On the much-discussed question of the character of late medieval magistrates, see the bibliography and the discussion in L. Th. Maes, "L'humanité de la magistrature du déclin du Moyen-Age," *Tijdschrift voor Rechtsgeschiedenis* 19 (1951), pp. 158–93.

10. Much of this material is discussed in Lea, *Materials toward a History of Witchcraft*, ed. Arthur Howland (Philadelphia, 1939), Vol. II.

11. For Carpzov, see Lea, *Materials*, Vol. II, pp. 813–50.

12. For some examples, see, besides Paolucci's Introduction, J. W. Bosch, "Beccaria et Voltaire chez Goswin de Fierlant et quelques autres juristes belges et néerlandais," *Tijdschrift voor Rechtsgeschiedenis* 29 (1921), 1–21.